'The great mass of people will more easily fall victim to a big lie than to a small one.'
Adolf Hitler (*Mein Kampf*, 1925)

'The truth, nothing but the truth and, as near as possible, the whole truth.'
Sir John Reith (British Ministry of Information, 1940)

Propaganda

The British Library

David Welch

Power and Persuasion

First published in 2013 by **The British Library**
96 Euston Road
London NW1 2DB

On the occasion of the British Library exhibition
Propaganda: Power and Persuasion
17 May–17 September 2013

Copyright © in text **David Welch** 2013
Copyright © in images **The British Library Board**
and other named copyright holders

British Library Cataloguing-in-Publication Data
A catalogue record for this book
is available from The British Library

ISBN 978 0 7123 5700 5

Project managed & edited by **Mark Hawkins-Dady**
Designed & typeset by **Ken Wilson | point 918**
Printed in Italy by **Printer Trento S.r.l.**

Contents

For Anne

I would like to thank my colleagues in the School of
History at Kent University, especially Professors Mark
Connelly and Ulf Schmidt and Dr Philip Boobbyer
for their help with textual analysis and translation.
These thanks also go to Professor Richard Sakwa. For
the translated text appearing on page 156 I am grateful
to 'The *Roman des Franceis* of Andrew de Coutances:
Text, Translation and Significance' in *Normandy and Its
Neighbours, 900–1250*: *Essays for David Bates* (edited by
D. Crouch and K. Thompson, 2011). I would also like
to thank my two Ph.D students Jan Barker and James
Farley for providing propaganda artefacts from their
own collections. Thanks also to Dr Jude England and
Ian Cooke at the British Library. Working with them on
the exhibition 'Propaganda: Power and Persuasion' has
been a joy—even though we did not always agree on what
should be included and what should be omitted ('Tufty
Fluffytail' being a case in point!). Finally, as always,
I would like to thank my wife Anne, for all she has done
to make this work possible. Only she knows the full extent
of my debt and gratitude. I would like to dedicate this
volume to her.

DAVID WELCH

'A much maligned and misunderstood word'

A brief history of propaganda

1

PROPAGANDA IS THOUSANDS OF YEARS OLD. But it came of age in the 20th century, when the development of mass media (and later multimedia communications) offered a fertile ground for its dissemination, and the century's global conflicts provided the impetus needed for its growth. In many societies, as electorates and audiences became more sophisticated they also began to question the nature and uses of propaganda, both in the past and in contemporary society.

Investigating the long history of propaganda necessarily invites consideration of what the word itself means. In truth, it has become a portmanteau word, which can be interpreted in a variety of ways, so 'propaganda' has never been a static term, especially at a time of rapidly changing methods of spreading messages. Nevertheless, there are some basic descriptions that can be applied. If we exclude purely religious and commercial propaganda (advertising), it is a distinct political activity and it is one that can be distinguished from related phenomena such as information and education. The distinction lies in the purpose of the instigator. Put simply, propaganda is the dissemination of ideas intended to convince people to think and act in a particular way and for a particular persuasive purpose.

Although propaganda can be unconscious, it is most often the conscious, deliberate attempt to employ the techniques of persuasion for specific goals. More precisely, it can be defined as the deliberate attempt to influence the public opinions of an audience, through the transmission of ideas and values, for a specific persuasive purpose that has been consciously thought out and designed to serve the self-interest of the propagandist, either directly or indirectly. Whereas 'information' presents its audience with a straightforward statement of facts, propaganda packages those facts in order to evoke a certain response. And whereas education, at least in the liberal tradition, teaches people *how* to think and how to make up their own minds, propaganda normally tries to tell people *what* to think. Information and education are concerned to broaden the audience's perspectives and to open their minds, but propaganda strives to narrow and preferably close them. The core distinction lies in the *purpose*.

That definition, though, still encompasses a broad range of possible categories of propaganda, added to which is the question of propaganda's reputation. 'Propaganda is a much maligned and often misunderstood word. The layman uses it to mean something inferior or even despicable. The word propaganda always has a bitter after-taste.' It is singularly appropriate that these words should have been spoken in March 1933 by Joseph Goebbels, immediately after his appointment as Minister for Popular Enlightenment and Propaganda in Adolf Hitler's first government. Arguably, in this role *he* did more than most to ensure and perpetuate this bitter 'after-taste'. 'But,' Goebbels continued:

> … if you examine propaganda's most secret causes, you will come to different conclusions: then there will be no more doubting that the propagandist must be the man with the greatest knowledge of souls. I cannot convince a single person of the necessity of something unless I get to

1 **Cartoon by the Polish artist Andrzej Krauze. The gulf between 'Reality' and 'Propaganda' threatens to grow so wide as to swallow the figure (based on Poland's General Jaruzelski) trying to bridge it. It reflects our everyday assumptions that anything defined as 'propaganda' must, inevitably, be departing from a truthful reflection of events. In reality, propaganda can be more subtle, more various, richer—and it *can* be true!**

know the soul of that person, unless I understand how to pluck the string in the harp of his soul that must be made to sound.

It is supremely ironic that it was the Nazi regime's architect of propaganda who should set himself the mission of rescuing the word from negative misconceptions.

Propaganda was not, of course, invented by Goebbels, although it is largely as a result of Nazi propaganda that the term has come to have such pejorative associations. In the minds of most, the word continues to imply something sinister, at the very least dubious—synonyms frequently include 'lies', 'deceit' and 'brainwashing'. In recent years unfavourable comparisons have been made with the practices of 'spin-doctors' and the manner in which they (allegedly) control the images of politicians and public figures, reducing the political agenda to simplistic soundbites; and the public have become wary of what are sometimes regarded as corporate euphemisms for propaganda in the form of 'public relations' and 'communications'. A widely held belief is that propaganda is akin to

1

a cancer on the body politic, manipulating our thoughts, and something that should be avoided at all costs.

Is this really the case, and should we fight shy of the word? It is the contention here that such assumptions should be challenged and that propaganda is not necessarily—and was often not, historically—a practice motivated by evil intent.

■ Propaganda as persuasion

The Ancient Greeks regarded the art of persuading as a form of rhetoric and recognised that logic and reason were necessary components for communicating ideas successfully. Three of Plato's dialogues—the *Gorgias,* the *Phaedrus* and the *Menexenus*—deal with the question of rhetoric, while Aristotle's *Rhetoric,* as the name suggests, went into even greater detail about its role as a form of persuasion.

Throughout history, those who govern have attempted to influence the way in which the governed viewed the world. In 4th-century BC Greece, historians and philosophers were the first people to describe the use of propaganda in the service of the state. Architecture and sculpture provided evidence of a growing sophistication in the art of persuasion: statues of gods and men became larger and more realistic as politicians attempted to project themselves and their achievements before the people, while Athens provides the clearest example of the use of architecture to promote the glory of a city. The growth of Greek democracy, notably in Athens in the 5th century BC, had been accompanied by a process of humanising the pantheon of gods, in an attempt to explain the universe in terms of the relationship between the state and the individual citizen. In his discussion with his master Socrates at the time of the Peloponnesian War, Plato worried that this humanising process might undermine the 'propagandist' role that hitherto the gods had played in influencing human behaviour, and he called upon a degree of censorship—especially of the epic poems being written at the time, which depicted a grim picture of the afterlife. In *The Republic,* while advocating that rulers should at least adopt the appearance of truthfulness, Plato recognised that they might, at times, need to employ censorship (and deception) in the greater interest of implementing democracy.

Plato's pupil Aristotle pursued this line of thought in his *Rhetoric,* in which he laid down certain guidelines for orators who, he argued, should base their persuasion on truth. In so doing, Aristotle set out one of the basic axioms of successful propaganda in a modern democratic state. It was, however, Xenophon, a pupil of Socrates, who undertook the first detailed study of propaganda and morale in warfare. Writing in his *Anabasis,* at the beginning of the 4th century BC, he affirmed: 'I am sure that neither numbers nor strength bring victory in war, but whichever army goes into battle stronger in soul, their enemies generally cannot withstand them.'

Perhaps the greatest early exponent of successful propaganda was Alexander the Great, who came to power as King of Macedon in 336 BC. His reputation as a military commander is undisputed, but his skill as a propagandist is less

Propaganda is not simply what the other side does, while one's own side concentrates on 'information' or 'publicity'

2

2 The two sides of a silver coin issued in the late 4th or early 3rd century BC, under the reign of Lysimachus, formerly one of Alexander the Great's generals and by this time ruler of Thrace and parts of Asia Minor. One side portrays Alexander wearing the ram's horn of the Egyptian god Ammon; the other portrays the goddess Athena and text that reads 'Of King Lysimachus'. So strong was Alexander's image that the successor rulers who divided up his empire were eager to associate themselves with his memory.

commented upon. Following his victory over the Persian Empire in the years to follow, Alexander is credited with demanding his own deification as the son of Zeus. Accordingly, coins were produced in which Alexander's face replaced that of Herakles (Hercules), the traditional son of Zeus. This act of political propaganda was supplemented by the naming of conquered cities after him—a legacy that lasts to this day, most notably in Egypt's Alexandria—and by employing artists and crafts-men to depict him, and his deeds, in bronze statues and paintings.

Alexander appreciated an important point about propaganda: that it was a substitute for his *actual* presence, so that his image—on coins, statues, buildings, pottery and art in general— were present throughout his empire. He was effectively cultivating what we would call the 'cult of personality'—a perennial practice of rulers, but one that has become such a major feature of political leadership in the modern era.

Clearly, propaganda can be traced back deep into history. The pyramids of Egypt provide a form of visual eulogy; they are some of the oldest monumental structures designed to symbolise the power and magnificence of individual rulers

and dynasties. Around the late 6th century BC, the Chinese general Sun Tzu was writing *The Art of War*, and he knew all about the power of persuasion, the 'munitions of the mind': 'For to win one hundred victories in one hundred battles is not the acme of skill. To subdue the enemy without fighting is the acme of skill.'

As such varied purposes suggest, if propaganda is to be a useful concept it first has to be divested of its solely pejorative connotations. Propaganda is not simply what the other side does, while one's own side concentrates on 'information' or 'publicity'. Ironically, it has been the modern dictatorships that have tended to take a more open view of the term, as reflected in the unashamed Nazi 'Ministry of Popular Enlightenment and Propaganda', while the Soviet Union had its 'Propaganda Committee of the Communist Party'. By contrast, the British resorted to their 'Ministry of Information' and the Americans to an 'Office of War Information'. And the Allies in both the First and Second world wars preyed on the negative connotations of the word, describing the enemy's opinion-forming activity as 'propaganda', while claiming that it was only they themselves who disseminated the truth.

■ The history of a word

The origin of the actual *word* 'propaganda' can be traced back to the Reformation, when the spiritual and ecclesiastical unity of Christian Europe was shattered and the medieval Roman Church lost its hold on Northern countries. During the ensuing political and religious struggles, the Roman Catholic Church of the Counter-Reformation found itself faced with the problem of how to maintain and strengthen its position. In the late 16th century, a Commission of Cardinals was set up by Pope Gregory XIII, charged with spreading Catholicism and regulating ecclesiastical affairs in 'heathen' lands. A generation later in 1622, when the Thirty Years War was ravaging much of Europe, Pope Gregory XV made the Commission permanent as the *Sacra Congregatio de Propaganda Fide* (Sacred Congregation for the Propagation of the Faith). It was charged with the management of foreign missions and financed by a 'ring tax' assessed on each newly appointed cardinal. Finally, in 1627 Pope Urban VII established the *Collegium Urbanum*, or College of Propaganda, to serve as a

i *Collegio de Propaganda Fide ampliato da N.° S. Papa Alesandro Settimo.*
2 *Chiesa dell'Adoratione de Magi in detto Collegio fatta da N. Sig.*
COLLEGIO DE PROPAGANDA FIDE.
Per Gio Iacomo Rossi in Roma alla Pace - 16 P. del S.P.
3 *Chiesa di S. Andrea delle Fratte.*
4 *Cuppola, e Campanile di detta Chiesa.*
9
Gio. Batta Falda diet f.

3

3 The baroque *Collegio de Propaganda Fide* ('College of the Propagation of the Faith') in Rome's Piazza di Spagna, designed in the mid-17th century by architects Gian Lorenzo Bernini and Francesco Borromini. It was built to be the headquarters of the Church's *Sacra Congregatio de Propaganda Fide*, the organisation founded by Pope Gregory XV to help spread the Church's teachings. (Engraving commissioned by Antonio Barberini.)

4 'The Donkey-Pope of Rome', a woodcut (1523) by Lucas Cranach. In this example of allegorical Lutheran propaganda, the Pope is depicted as a combination of a donkey and a mythological gryphon (or 'griffin', an eagle merged with a lion). The Devil can seen emerging from the donkey's rump. Crude in style and rude in intent, such illustrations were intended to embellish a number of broadsides launched against the papacy by Martin Luther.

5 An engraving of Oliver Cromwell created by his supporters towards the end of his rule as Lord Protector in the 1650s. It provides images and ideas intended to show his virtues. The pillars represent spiritual and temporal (political and military) strength. The whole is imbued with a strong religious and Puritan tone, as exemplified in the images of Mount Zion and Noah's Ark. Other pictorial elements emphasise peace, justice and prosperity, particularly those at the foot of the picture.

6 A highly effective piece of political propaganda (1649, but published in a book at the time of Charles II's restoration, 1660), which attacks Cromwell for dismantling the regime of Charles I. Cromwell is shown ordering republican soldiers to chop down the royal oak, the symbol of the monarchy; the royal crown, sceptre and coat of arms can be seen in the tree. Hanging off the branches are *Eikon Basilike*, a book supposedly containing the thoughts of Charles I before his execution, along with the Bible, Magna Carta, 'Statutes' and 'Reports'. Cromwell is standing on a ball described as a 'slippery place' and, in a blow against Cromwell's supposed piety, is at the entrance to Hell.

training ground for a new generation of Catholic propagandists and to educate young priests who were to undertake such missions.

The first propagandist institute was therefore simply a body charged with improving the dissemination of religious dogma. But the word 'propaganda' soon came to be applied to any organisation set up for the purpose of spreading a doctrine. Subsequently it was applied to the doctrine itself, and lastly to the methods employed in undertaking its dissemination.

Between the 17th and 20th centuries, we hear comparatively little about 'propaganda' as a term.

It had but a limited use and, though ill-flavoured, was largely unfamiliar. Its practice, however, by those in authority continued apace, as witnessed, for example, in the metaphors of power propagated by France's 'Sun King', Louis XIV. During the English Civil Wars (1642–51) and the breakdown of the censorship and licensing system established under the Tudors and early Stuarts, propaganda by pamphlet and newsletter became a regular accessory to military action, Oliver Cromwell's Parliamentarian army being concerned nearly as much with the spread of radical religious and political doctrines as with victory in the field.

6

7 Woodcut from the *Massachusetts Almanac* of 1772, recording the Boston Massacre (5 March 1770), in which British Army soldiers killed five civilian men and injured six others. Referred to in the accompanying text as 'MURDER', the massacre is considered one of the most important events that turned colonial sentiment against King George III and British Parliamentary authority.

8 Anonymous revolutionary caricature depicting an unequivocally scatological response given to the 'Brunswick Manifesto' (1792) proclaimed by the Duke of Brunswick, commander of Prussian and Austrian forces, which threatened to burn Paris to the ground should the French royal family be harmed. A figure representing Fame (an angel with trumpet) flies overhead holding a sign that makes the political allegiance clear: 'République Française'.

7

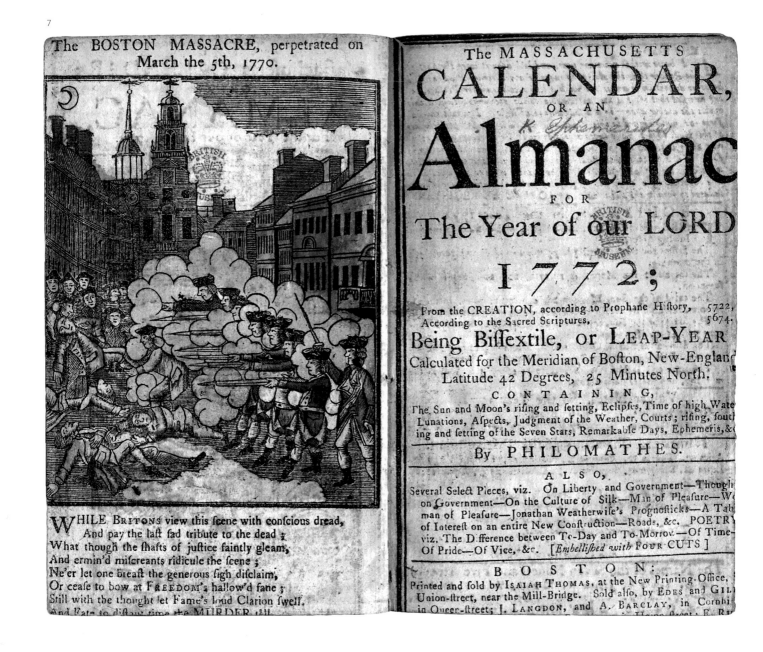

The BOSTON MASSACRE, perpetrated on March the 5th, 1770.

WHILE BRITONS view this scene with conscious dread,
    And pay the last sad tribute to the dead ;
What though the shafts of justice faintly gleam,
And ermin'd miscreants ridicule the scene ;
Ne'er let one breast the generous sigh disclaim,
Or cease to bow at FREEDOM's hallow'd fane ;
Still with the thought let Fame's loud Clarion swell,
And Fate to distant time the MURDER tell.

The MASSACHUSETTS CALENDAR, OR AN Almanac FOR The Year of our LORD 1772;

From the CREATION, according to Prophane History, 5722,
According to the Sacred Scriptures, 5674.

Being Bissextile, or LEAP-YEAR Calculated for the Meridian of Boston, New-England, Latitude 42 Degrees, 25 Minutes North.

CONTAINING,

The Sun and Moon's rising and setting, Eclipses, Time of high Water, Lunations, Aspects, Judgment of the Weather, Courts; rising, southing and setting of the Seven Stars, Remarkable Days, Ephemeris, &c.

By PHILOMATHES.

ALSO,

Several Select Pieces, viz. On Liberty and Government—Thoughts on Government—On the Culture of Silk—Man of Pleasure—Woman of Pleasure—Jonathan Weatherwise's Prognosticks—A Table of Interest on an entire New Construction—Roads, &c. POETRY, viz. The Difference between To-Day and To-Morrow—Of Time—Of Pride—Of Vice, &c. [*Embellished with* FOUR CUTS]

BOSTON:

Printed and sold by ISAIAH THOMAS, at the New Printing-Office, Union-street, near the Mill-Bridge. Sold also, by EDES and GILL in Queen-street; J. LANGDON, and A. BARCLAY, in Cornhill.

Cas du Manifeste du Duc de Brunswick.

8

The employment of propaganda increased steadily throughout the 18th and 19th centuries, particularly at times of ideological struggle, as in the American Revolutionary War (War of Independence; 1775–83) and the French Revolutionary Wars (1792–1802). American revolutionary propagandists are among the most eloquent in history, their efforts on behalf of the Rights of Man striking a chord that resonates to this day. Prominent among them was the English radical Tom Paine, who had become a convert to American independence and in 1776 wrote a 50-page propaganda pamphlet entitled *Common Sense*. Within weeks it became America's first bestseller, with 100,000 copies sold. Referring to King George III as the 'Royale Brute', Paine wrote ringingly: 'the authority of Great Britain over this continent is a form of government which sooner or later must have an end ... Everything that is right or reasonable pleads for separation, "TIS TIME TO PART".' In 1791 he published *Rights of Man*, in which he argued that popular political revolution was permissible when a government did not safeguard its people, their natural rights and their national interests. He was defending the ideals that underpinned French revolutionary fervour,

as a rebuttal to Edmund Burke's attack on them in *Reflections on the Revolution in France* (1790)—and Paine was subsequently tried in England, *in absentia*, for his efforts.

As old monarchical propaganda in France was replaced by new republican imagery, the revolutionaries distributed broadsheets among French (and foreign) troops urging them to join the revolution and offering them rewards for desertion ('Brave soldiers, mingle with your brothers, receive their embraces. You are no longer satellites of the despot, the jailors of your brothers.') Inspired by revolutionary propaganda, the French rapidly became a nation-in-arms. As the ordinary citizens became soldiers of the new *Patrie*, war became the business of the people—and the French were able to secure victory over an invading Austro-Prussian army at Valmy in 1792.

This mobilisation of French society to support, and indeed export, a revolution was the nearest thing to 'total war' prior to the 20th century—and it suggests a major propaganda success. But it was under Napoleon Bonaparte that France became the first truly modern propaganda state, and Napoleon must rank as one of the most able self-propagandists in history. His control over French thought affected all aspects of national life. He claimed that 'three hostile newspapers are more to be feared than a thousand bayonets' and, in 1801, he accordingly closed down 64 out of 73 French newspapers. At his imperial coronation in 1804, in Notre Dame cathedral amid great pomp and ceremony, *he* took the imperial crown from Pope Pius VII and placed it on his own head, a gesture symbolising that this self-made emperor owed allegiance to no-one. In 1810—and by this time there were only four newspapers left in France—he established the *Direction Générale de l'Imprimerie et de la Librairie* to control all French cultural activity, while artists, architects and writers were mobilised to serve the glorification of his empire.

From the end of the Napoleonic Wars to the outbreak of the First World War in 1914, Europe witnessed many changes. They included a range of smaller revolutionary and independence struggles, the unification of a powerful new Prussian-led Germany (which defeated and humiliated France

in 1870), and the emergence of simmering tensions in the Balkans as the weakening Ottoman Empire retreated to the edges of Europe. But there were no great wars of revolution on a French or American scale. Nevertheless, the new and burgeoning visual language of political cartoons and satirical prints continued to feature prominently in propaganda campaigns, including those associated with the regional conflicts. It is evident that the production of propaganda was becoming ever more associated with periods of stress and turmoil, in which violent controversy about doctrine (political or otherwise) accompanied the use of force.

Industrialisation, too, played its part now in the growth of propaganda. In the most advanced societies, large and growing print circulations during the late 18th and 19th centuries, together with improving literacy, created new audiences for messages of all kinds. As consumer societies developed, so did a demand for greater political and economic rights—fertile territory for propaganda.

9

10 **Napoleon Bonaparte as he wished to be depicted**—exuding power as emperor, in robes of state in front of his throne (painted by M. Borly for the municipality of Montpellier, *c*.1813). His head is crowned with two branches of gold laurel, while in his right hand he holds the sceptre of Charlemagne. Napoleon also used medallions as tools to promote his desired image: by the time of his death, he had commissioned more of them than kings Louis XV and Louis XVI combined.

9 **Napoleon as he did not wish to be depicted,** in a satirical etching (1809) about French frustrations in Spain. He is shown as Don Quixote from Cervantes' epic, seated on his horse Rocinante (the pro-French Prime Minister Godoy), attempting to console Sancho Panza (his commander in Spain, Marshal Murat) for territorial losses. He promises America to Murat in compensation, but she proclaims: 'America will be an enchanted Dulcinea that you will never possess.'

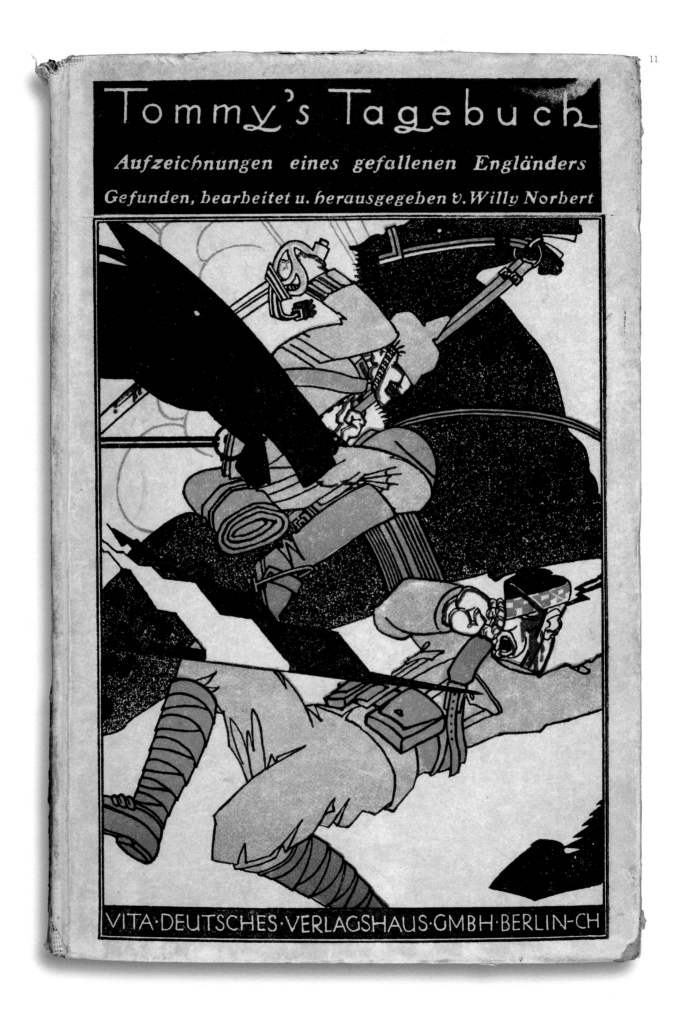

Tommy's Tagebuch

Aufzeichnungen eines gefallenen Engländers

Gefunden, bearbeitet u. herausgegeben v. Willy Norbert

VITA·DEUTSCHES·VERLAGSHAUS·GMBH·BERLIN-CH

11 *Tommy's Tagebuch*, a German anti-British propaganda publication, translates as 'Tommy's Diary—Record of a Dead Englishman'. The front cover evokes traditional representations of George and the Dragon, as widely used by the British in their own propaganda; but here 'George' is a German cavalry officer slaying the 'Dragon' in the shape of a soldier from a Scottish regiment.

12 A French propaganda postcard (1916) entitled *La Fessée!* ('The Spanking!'), in which the British and French unite to deliver some punishment to the Germans. It provides a wartime twist on the notion of *Entente Cordiale*. Many postcards of the First World War were highly stylised and staged, having been posed and shot in photographic studios for their full propaganda effect.

12

■ The propaganda century

It was, however, between 1914 and 1918 that the wholesale employment of propaganda as an organised weapon of modern warfare served to transform the popular understanding of its meaning into something sinister. By now, media such as daily newspapers and weekly magazines, and the novelty of film, had created something new: a mass audience. The means thus existed for governments to mobilise entire industrial societies for warfare, and to disseminate information (or propaganda) to large groups of people within relatively short time spans. Once it was realised that the war was going to be an all-embracing and long drawn out struggle—not apparent in the first months of 1914—the governments and militaries of the belligerent countries saw the necessity of a sustained propaganda campaign to bolster the Home and Fighting fronts, as well as to try and sap the enemy's will and garner support from non-belligerent nations—for Britain, primarily the United States. Accordingly, the press, leaflets, posters and the new medium of film were exploited, censored and coordinated (arguably for the first time) in order to propagate officially approved themes. One consequence of the emergence of the mass media (over the whole period, 1870 to 1939) was that international affairs increasingly became the concern of peoples everywhere, and governments knew they could not afford to neglect the ever more powerful press. But there was now more than just printed material to contend with. During the 1920s and 1930s the exploitation of, particularly, film and radio for political purposes became more commonplace—most strikingly in the new authoritarian regimes of the Soviet Union, Fascist Italy and Nazi Germany. It should, however, also be noted that Leon Blum's short-lived French Socialist government of 1938 retained a 'Ministry of Propaganda'. As a new global war approached, the French government of Édouard Daladier revealingly chose, in July 1939, to rebrand the ministry as the less transparent *Commissariat de l'Information*.

The gradual replacement of cables by wireless as the chief means of propaganda was a significant development. The international potential of radio broadcasts provided governments with an ideal instrument of political propaganda in the age of the politicised masses. Such technology had been employed during the First World War, but its impact was limited because transmissions were largely confined to morse code. In the 1920s, radio was used for propaganda purposes in a number of international disputes, for example in the 1923 Franco–Belgian occupation of the Ruhr—an attempt to enforce German compliance with reparations responsibilities. The German government was quick to realise the value of radio as a means of enabling those Germans separated from their homeland by the terms of the Versailles Treaty—such as in the 'Free City' of Danzig (modern Gdansk), surrounded by Poland—to keep in touch and retain their sense of identity.

In the 1930s the lofty ideal of the British Broadcasting Corporation (BBC) that 'Nation Shall Speak unto Nation' had given way, in the larger world, to a more aggressive type of nationalistic broadcasting. This development had first become apparent when the Soviet Union developed the world's first short-wave station, Radio Moscow (established in 1922, and greatly extended in 1925). For Bolshevik leader Lenin, radio was a 'newspaper without paper—and without boundaries'. With the rise to power of the Nazis in 1933, radio propaganda was exploited to spread the doctrine of National Socialism and to make the regime more respectable abroad, before the regime's initiation of an expansionist foreign policy. Radio was also used to great effect in the 1935 plebiscite held in the League of Nations-administered Saarland, whose citizens voted to rejoin Germany, and it was to prove a crucial feature of the German propaganda assault on Austria between 1934 and the eventual German annexation (*Anschluss*) of the country in 1938. For the 1936 Olympic Games in Berlin, the Nazis constructed the world's largest shortwave radio transmitter, and by the end of 1938 the Germans were broadcasting more than 5,000 hours a week in more than 25 languages. Things had developed to such serious proportions by the mid-1930s that, for example, the British government established (in 1934) the British Council, to propagate British culture abroad, and in 1938 inaugurated the BBC foreign-language broadcasts, all in an attempt to combat the totalitarian challenge to democracy.

Revealingly, out of the 30 European national broadcasting systems in existence in 1938, 14 were state owned and operated, 9 were government monopolies operated by autonomous public bodies or partially government-controlled corporations, 4 were actually operated by government—and only 3 were privately owned or run. The special qualities that made radio such an effective instrument

13 **A Nazi poster proclaiming that 'All Germany listens to the *Führer* with the People's Radio.' Under the Nazis, German radio became the 'voice of the nation'. To increase the number of listeners, the Nazis produced one of the cheapest wireless sets in Europe, the VE 30131 or *Volksempfänger*** ('people's radio'). By the beginning of the war over 70 per cent of German households owned a wireless set, the highest percentage anywhere in the world. There was a catch: radios were designed with a limited range, which prevented Germans from receiving foreign broadcasts.

13

14 The massacre of Russian citizens by tsarist Cossacks on the Odessa Steps, at the Black Sea port of Odessa, is the most famous scene from Sergei Eisenstein's film *Battleship Potemkin* (1925). Although historically unverified, the scene (and the film) had a powerful propaganda effect. It was an early example of the power of film to create a poetry of unforgettable images to convey the Bolshevik message of the oppression of the masses and their eventual liberation and resurrection.

> radio was capable of reaching large numbers of people, regardless of geography, borders, literacy, political and ideological affiliations ...

of international propaganda were simple. It relied upon the spoken word and was thus more direct in approach and personal in tone than any other available medium. It was also immediate and extremely difficult to stop by means of jamming. Moreover, radio was capable of reaching large numbers of people, regardless of geography, borders, literacy, political and ideological affiliations or social status; it allowed the propagandists of one nation to speak directly and immediately to large numbers of people in another country, from the outside.

Radio was not the only medium used for international propaganda purposes, though arguably it was the most important. The press remained powerful—indeed, during his meeting with the British Foreign Secretary Lord Halifax in November 1937 Hitler maintained that nine-tenths of all international conflicts were caused by the press. The captive press in the Third Reich increasingly reflected official state policy. In the democracies, where vague notions of free speech were cherished, direct control was more difficult. The French press, however, was notoriously prone to political influence, including subsidies from foreign governments. In Britain the situation was less extreme, although Fleet Street was clearly amenable to government influence. But given the nature of British newspaper proprietorship during the 1930s, the press generally shared common interests with the government on foreign-policy issues. This was particularly the case regarding the Franco-British 'appeasing' of German demands: revealingly, only one popular British newspaper proved critical of Prime Minister Neville

Chamberlain's foreign policy and the 1938 Munich Agreement that handed Germany the Czech Sudetenland. (It was the *News Chronicle*, owned by the Cadbury family with a circulation of 1,320,000 drawn mainly from the lower middle class.) By and large, it is fair to say that governments tended to resent criticism in the foreign press and frequently dismissed such criticism as jingoistic propaganda.

Film, which was in its infancy during the First World War, emerged to become *the* mass medium of the interwar period. It certainly was an effective means for delivering international propaganda. As with the press, national film industries acted as propaganda merchants for the endorsement of their country's way of life. The Bolsheviks were quick to seize upon film, Leon Trotsky referring to it as a 'spectacular innovation' that had 'cut into human life with a successful rapidity never experienced in the past', rivalling the 'beer-house and the Church as indispensable institutions'. And Lenin maintained that 'of all the arts for us the cinema is the most important'.

The role of feature films (and to a lesser extent, newsreels and documentaries) in international propaganda during the period is perhaps best illustrated by the example of Hollywood, which promoted America's culture, commerce and political ethos abroad. In 1923, no less than 85 per cent of films shown in France were American. In Britain, 25 per cent of films shown in cinemas in 1914 were British, but by 1925 this figure had fallen to a mere 2 per cent. By 1939, the United States owned approximately 40 per cent of the worldwide total of cinemas. This global distribution network ensured the projection of American society and culture, as seen through the eyes of Hollywood, and was to have significant commercial repercussions. 'Trade follows the film' became a popular maxim for economic expansionists during the 1920s and 1930s. As a result, European countries, with their less well-developed film industries, soon began to express concern at what they saw as the significant and unfair advantages provided by Hollywood for American commerce, and struggled throughout the interwar period to combat this dominance by introducing quota systems and later import licensing schemes. At the same time, they attempted to bolster their own native film industries with varying degrees of success.

The technological and communications developments of the 1920s and 1930s, such as film and radio, took place against the background of a deteriorating international situation, in which the fragile safeguards that the League of Nations had implemented to secure peace and collective security, in the aftermath of the First World War, were increasingly undermined amid political polarisation. The League could do nothing to prevent the outbreak of the Spanish Civil War in July 1936, and less than a year later, in April 1937, the Basque city of Guernica was destroyed by German bombers sent to assist General Franco's Nationalist rebels. The event—as captured by the realism of the newsreel cameras, and later commemorated in art by Pablo Picasso—provided a frightening glimpse of the horrors of total war and a sobering reminder that cities like London and Paris were equally vulnerable to squadrons of modern bombers. For some historians, it was these brutal images that spurred the policies of appeasement,

as democratic governments sought to spare their own populations such misery and suffering.

That attempt, of course, failed, and global catastrophe beckoned—along with what Philip M. Taylor has described as 'the greatest propaganda battle in the history of warfare'. All the participants in the Second World War used propaganda on a scale that dwarfed that of other conflicts, and in all phases of the war official propaganda and the commercial media played key roles. This was a struggle between mass societies, and in many respects a war of political ideologies, in which propaganda was a significant weapon.

The war witnessed a vast proliferation of media production, from state-sponsored posters, pamphlets, radio and films (including newsreels) to commercial newspapers, comics and military newspapers. The Soviet Union boasted no less than 757 separate military titles by 1945, and as for radio, the BBC increased its foreign-language services from 10 in 1939 to 45 by 1943. The US government inaugurated the multilingual Voice of America network in 1942, for external broadcasting, while at home the amount of radio airtime devoted to news rose from 5 per cent to 20 per cent—with 9 out of 10 Americans listening to 4 hours of radio daily. Towards the end of the war, the Nazi government was also trialling television for a limited German audience.

The extraordinary levels of propaganda during the Second World War were sustained after 1945 during the long period of the Cold War and the communist/capitalist ideological divide, a contest characterised in 1950 by US President Harry S Truman as a 'struggle above all else, for the minds

15 **A Spanish Civil War poster (1936), attributed to Juan Antonio Morales, portrays stereotypes of General Franco's Nationalists ('Los Nacionales') and their foreign supporters: an Italian Fascist, a cardinal, a Nazi businessman and North African troops. The place-names Burgos and Lisbon allude to the principal** Nationalist stronghold and to the pro-Nationalist stance of Portugal respectively, while a map of suffering Spain hangs from the gallows. The war, and its propaganda, testified to the deep Left–Right divide tearing Europe apart.

Arriba
España

ESPAÑA

JUNTA DE BURGOS
LISBOA

Los Nacionales

16 **A musically themed Soviet poster (1960s) depicting an American capitalist literally conducting propaganda. Instead of a podium he stands astride a bank, and instead of a baton he waves a missile. An extraordinarily complex series of comic images shows various sections of (white) American society, the 'Orchestra of Psychological Warfare', all singing to his tune.**

17 **President Ronald Reagan, a notable Cold Warrior, broadcasts on the Voice of America radio station. At the time of its 60th anniversary in 2002, the VOA was providing over 900 hours of weekly radio, television and internet programming in 53 languages, to an estimated audience of 91 million people.**

17

of men'. The Soviet leadership under Joseph Stalin, untroubled by the negative connotations evoked by 'propaganda', viewed the role of the media as mobilising and legitimising support for expansionist policies. Stalin's determination to control the countries 'liberated' by the Soviet armies at the end of the Second World War led to a growth in arms production and to strident anti-capitalist propaganda, which contributed to the growing tensions. The Department of Agitation and Propaganda (Agitprop) of the Central Committee of the Communist Party fed official propaganda to the media, which were already closely scrutinised by the Soviet censors. Meanwhile, from September 1947 the Communist Information Bureau (Cominform) began systematic campaigns, masterminded by Agitprop, to bring the newly independent countries of the Third World under Soviet influence and to marshal international support for Moscow against the West.

In the United States, the Smith–Mundt Act (1948) created the legal framework for a permanent overseas information effort, using the media, exchange programmes and exhibitions to counter the massive disinformation campaigns launched from Moscow by the KGB to discredit the United States. From the mid-1950s, US policymakers believed that cultural diplomacy would successfully complement 'psychological warfare' (*see below*) and might, in the long term, prove more effective. From this decade the export of American culture and lifestyle was heavily subsidised by the US government and coordinated by the United States Information Agency (USIA), which operated from 1953 to 1999. Cultural exchange programmes, international trade fairs and exhibitions, and the distribution of Hollywood movies were some of the activities designed to extract propaganda value from the appeal of America's way of life, particularly its popular culture and material success.

From the 1960s the Voice of America took advantage of the popularity of American rock music with audiences behind the Iron Curtain to boost the standing of the United States. While radio remained an important weapon in Cold War terms, broadcasting was also seen by the American authorities as a means to win 'hearts and minds' throughout the world, as part of a long-term process of cultural propaganda.

Throughout the Cold War, the United States was also able to call upon the reach of private 'philanthropic' and multinational concerns with an increasingly high visibility, such as Coca-Cola, McDonalds, Levi's jeans and so on. The universal popularity of these American icons testified to the success of such 'cultural imperialism', having the effect of homogenising the world into a global village dominated by American values.

The spread of television as a mass medium, from the 1950s, opened up the possibility of a radical new level of exposure of civilian populations to the 'realities' of war. The television coverage of the Vietnam War in the 1960s and early 1970s weakened public support for US war aims in the region and exposed the contradictions in American foreign policy. During the First Gulf War in 1991, the term 'media war' came into common usage, a reflection of the fact that the conflict was not just being fought hour by hour, but was being portrayed and watched as it unfolded. In the Kosovo War (1999), both sides in the conflict—the Serbs and the Kosovar Albanians (eventually supported by NATO airstrikes)—understood the importance of manipulating such real-time news to their own advantage. Moreover, Kosovo witnessed the first systematic use of the internet to disseminate propaganda, including by non-governmental players; it highlighted the sheer pace of change between the Second World War and today's globalised information environment.

The 9/11 al-Qaeda terrorist attacks on the United States in 2001 were, their sheer destructive aspect notwithstanding, planned for their media impact as acts of 'propaganda by deed'. For decades terrorism had been about gaining the 'oxygen of publicity' for causes and to exert pressure on governments—indeed, it used to be said that a terrorist's ideal *modus operandi* gained maximum publicity with minimum violence. But the adoption of mass casualties as a terrorist strategy, when targeted at the United States, provoked a furious response. Unsurprisingly, propaganda became a major feature of the resulting 'Global War on Terror' that followed. The 2003 invasion of Iraq to topple Saddam Hussein was portrayed as part of the campaign against international terrorism and the threat of tyrannical regimes holding weapons of mass destruction, but it also became a plan for the 'liberation' of Iraq by 'Coalition Forces', the latter a propaganda term devised to place the US and British military in a flattering light and to give the impression of a broader group of participating nations than the actual make-up suggested. Media coverage of this war, and the war's psychological dimension, are of particular interest in propaganda terms. It witnessed a number of media innovations, notably the decision to 'embed' reporters and television journalists as actual members of the invasion forces, on the one hand allowing an immediacy never before possible, while on the other introducing a new intensity of information overload.

Today, in the early 21st century, we inhabit a complex 'media-scape', with blurred distinctions between different technologies. There is much that is new, while the 'traditional' media of the 20th century—the newspaper press, radio, film and television—have demonstrated remarkable resilience in adapting to a changing environment and increased globalisation.

Kosovo witnessed the first systematic use of the internet to disseminate propaganda, including by non-governmental players; it highlighted the sheer pace of change

■ Censorship and propaganda

If today's multimedia world has spread the scope for propaganda, it has also multiplied the possibilities for subversion of official messages, and for evading attempts to manage the message. Yet control of the message in the form of *censorship* remains the essential twin of propaganda.

Censorship—the suppressing of information or opinion offensive to the values of the authority represented by the censor—has been referred to as a negative form of propaganda. Without some form of it, propaganda, in the strictest sense of the word, would be difficult to imagine. Censorship and propaganda remain two sides of the same coin, both involving the manipulation of opinion. But censorship is of little value unless it selectively blends fact and opinion in order to deceive its intended audience. In this respect, the propagandist must work closely with the censor. In wartime, censorship chiefly affects the supply of news, while in peacetime it impacts on the expression of opinion—although in totalitarian states this distinction does not apply as news is censored on a daily basis.

Censorship in practice may be described as either the selection of information to support a particular viewpoint or the deliberate manipulation (or doctoring) of information to create an impression different to that originally intended. In the West, the first type of censorship can be traced back to the Middle Ages, with the most obvious example being ecclesiastical censorship, whereby the main channel for the dissemination of news and opinion was by word of mouth, particularly from the pulpit. Censorship tended to manifest itself as the suppression of heretical views. In

the early modern era, ecclesiastical censorship generated the celebrated (or notorious) *Index Librorum Prohibitorum,* dating from the 16th century, which listed all the published works and authors considered pernicious to the Roman Catholic Church, including numerous thinkers and theologians. Astonishingly, it was augmented right up to the middle of the 20th century.

By contrast, an example of the second type of censorship, through doctored information, would be Otto von Bismarck's famous 'Ems telegram' of 1870. Released to the newspapers, it edited and spiced up a conversation between King Wilhelm I of Prussia and the French ambassador, and became the pretext for the Franco-Prussian War.

In wartime, governments have typically established censorship to prevent the enemy from acquiring sensitive information and to bolster the morale of their soldiers and citizens. Yet again the First World War set the tone, as the first modern war in which all the belligerents deployed the twin weapons of censorship and propaganda to rigidly control public opinion. Most nations considered it vital, for national security reasons, to control the means of communication—and in 1914–18 that meant primarily the press. Such was the pervasiveness of official censorship and propaganda that a huge gap was manufactured between those fighting the war and the civilian Home Front that supported them. In Germany the justifications for tight censorship were to uphold the domestic political truce and to respond to the fear that newspapers might publish sensitive military information. There was little to support this fear, for the only wire service in Germany was the 'official' Wolff Telegraph Bureau

(WTB), which, at the outbreak of war, became the German newspapers' sole source of official war news, with all sensitive material first being cleared by the German Foreign Office.

In Britain, under the Defence of the Realm Act (DORA) from 1914, a system of censorship so severe was created that it continues to have implications for British society to this day. Technically all press censorship was voluntary; editors were entitled to submit for advance consideration any material that was likely to violate DORA. The Press Bureau was to provide official war news and the war correspondents were expected to publish its communiqués without comment. The willingness of the newspaper proprietors to accept self-censorship and their cooperation in disseminating propaganda

18

sol.764

OPIS AMATORSKIEJ ANTENY KIERUNKOWEJ
/PRZECIWZAGŁUSZENIOWEJ/

1. Przeznaczenie anteny

Antena służy do polepszenia jakości odbioru programów radiowych nadawanych na falach krótkich w pasmach od 16 do 41 m. w warunkach ich zagłuszania. Antena taka sprawdza się szczególnie w dużych miastach i umożliwia czytelny dla ucha odbiór audycji w tych miejscach, gdzie zagłuszanie czyni odbiór całkowicie niemożliwym, oraz umożliwia znaczną poprawę jakości odbioru w tych miejscach, gdzie odbiór /bez dodatkowej anteny/ był możliwy, ale zniekształcony zagłuszaniem.

2. Materiały potrzebne do wykonania anteny

- kabel telewizyjny okrągły współosiowy /tzw. koncentryczny/ - ck. 2 m plus odległość /przewidywana/ anteny od odbiornika;
- listewki /drewniane lub z materiału izolacyjnego/ o orientacyjnych wymiarach 2x3x48 cm oraz 2x3x65 cm plus materiały na podstawę do anteny;
- kondensator nastawny 200 pF z dielektrykiem stałym;
- płytka/cienka, z materiału izolacyjnego/ o wymiarach ok. 3x6 cm / do zamocowania kondensatora/;
- pałeczka /lub rurka/ z materiału izolacyjnego o orientacyjnej długości 10 cm /do przedłużenia osi pokrętła kondensatora/.

3. Ogólny opis anteny

Schematyczny widok ogólny anteny przedstawiono na rysunku 1. Na konstrukcji podtrzymującej w kształcie krzyża rozpięte są dwa obwody kabla koncentrycznego uformowane w okręgi i leżące na płaszczyźnie krzyża. Większy obwód /okrąg o śre-

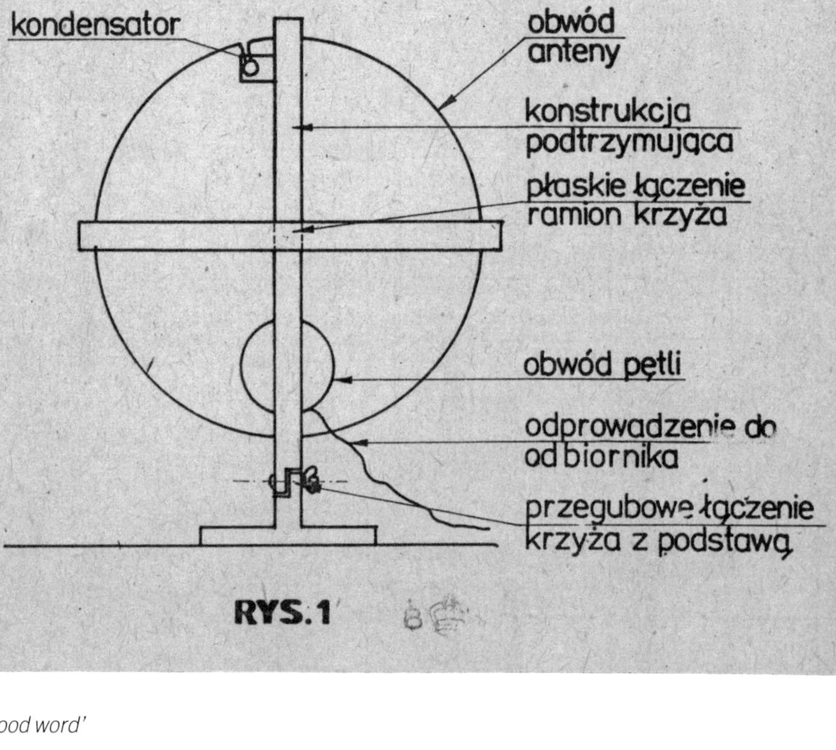

kondensator
obwód anteny
konstrukcja podtrzymująca
płaskie łączenie ramion krzyża
obwód pętli
odprowadzenie do odbiornika
przegubowe łączenie krzyża z podstawą

RYS.1

18 Instructions (in Polish) on how to create an anti-jamming antenna that would allow listeners in the Soviet Bloc to receive broadcasts from the West by, for example, Radio Free Europe and Voice of America. Such extraordinary documents would have been distributed by hand within the Polish underground.

19 The News Division of the Ministry of Information typing D-Day invasion stories (6 June 1944). A 'voluntary' pre-censorship, which proved effective for propaganda purposes, operated in Britain during the Second World War. Compulsory censorship was sometimes threatened but never imposed.

19

ultimately undermined public trust in the press. British war correspondents identified with the armies in the field and largely shielded the government and the military leadership from public criticism by withholding accounts of military setbacks and focusing on the camaraderie of life in the trenches. The United States, once in the war from 1917, set up its own propaganda organisation, the Committee on Public Information (CPI), with responsibility for censorship.

During the interwar period the growing popularity of the commercial film industry attracted increasing censorship. There was a widespread fear, both in the United States and elsewhere, that film's persuasive power might be used for harmful ends. The international dominance of Hollywood movies ensured that the restrictions contained in the Motion Picture Production Code (or Hays Code) shaped the films that the rest of the world saw. From 1934 until the 1950s the Code, formulated following a series of Hollywood controversies and scandals and backed by the Production Code Administration (PCA), heavily influenced the content of American films.

In the opening phase of the Second World War, Britain attempted to repeat the experience—and inadvertently therefore the mistakes—of the First World War, when censorship and propaganda had been conducted separately. Once again censorship was to be on a 'voluntary' basis. Beginning

in January 1940, when Sir John Reith (late of the BBC) became its head, the Ministry of Information began to assert itself, and by 1941 the system was operating so effectively that most observers were unaware that a sophisticated form of pre-censorship was in force, even within the BBC. This explains why Britain's wartime propaganda gained its reputation for telling the truth when, in fact, the whole truth could not be told.

During the Cold War, censorship continued to play a dominant role in the prolonged ideological conflict; but the censorship/propaganda relationship reached a new peak in the 1980s. The Falklands War (1982) revealed just how much the British had learned from their experience in the propaganda war against the Provisional IRA (Irish Republican Army) in Northern Ireland and also from the American experience in Vietnam. During the war the British government established near total control of information flowing out of the war zone (*see below* and Chapter 3), and this media management provided a model for US military–media relations subsequently, notably the invasion of Grenada (1983) and the intervention in Panama (1989). Restrictive media management has been a key feature in subsequent conflicts, even though the wars in the Persian Gulf, Bosnia, Kosovo, Iraq and Afghanistan have been reported on a global scale, with extensive and virtually instantaneous coverage, and huge audiences.

■ 'Propaganda'—a contested word

With the 20th and 21st centuries' rapidly changing technology, definitions of propaganda themselves have undergone change. One result of the Second World War and the Cold War was the emergence of new political and sociological theories on the nature of Man and modern society—particularly in the light of the rise of totalitarian states. Some writers, such as the American sociologist Daniel Bell, talked about an 'end of ideology'. In the bleakest views, society was made up of the undifferentiated and malleable masses, rather than individuals, and apocalyptic visions of this mass society emphasised such factors as the feelings of alienation caused by work, the collapse of religion and family ties, and a general decline in moral values. This perspective also regarded culture as reduced to the lowest common denominator for a mass consumption, and, politically, the masses were generally seen as apathetic yet prone to ideological fanaticism, vulnerable to manipulation through the media—particularly the new medium of television—and by the increasingly sophisticated methods of propagandists. According to such views, propaganda assumed the status of a metaphorical 'magic bullet' or 'hypodermic needle', capable of injecting opinions and behaviour and thereby controlling the people.

This pessimistic set of views was challenged by a number of American social scientists, including Harold Lasswell, one of the pioneers of the study of propaganda, and Walter Lippmann. They argued that within the context of a fragmented, 'atomised' mass society, propaganda was a mechanism for engineering public opinion and consent and thus acted as a means of social control (what Lasswell referred to as the 'new hammer and anvil of social solidarity'). More recently, the French sociologist Jacques Ellul took this idea a stage further and suggested that modern technological society had conditioned people to a 'need for propaganda'. In Ellul's view, propaganda was most effective when it reinforced already held opinions and beliefs.

The 'hypodermic' theory has thus been largely replaced by a more complex 'multi-step' model, which acknowledges the influence of the mass media but also recognises that individuals seek out opinion-leaders from within their own class and gender for confirmation of their ideas and in forming attitudes. Nowadays, writers tend to agree that propaganda confirms rather than converts—or at least that it is more effective when the message is in line with the existing opinions and beliefs of its consumers, reinforcing and sharpening them. (It is not, of course, an entirely new conclusion. Writing in 1936, Aldous Huxley observed that 'the propagandist is a man that canalises an already existing stream; in a land where there is no water, he digs in vain'.) This shift in emphasis highlights the common misconception that propaganda implies *only* the art of persuasion, in an attempt to *change* attitudes and ideas. That is undoubtedly one of its aims, but often a limited and subordinate one.

A second basic misconception is the belief that propaganda consists only of lies and falsehood. Rather, it operates with many different levels of

20a&b **Two British Ministry of Information postcards, exploiting the association of Hitler with duplicity and the 'big lie'. In one, an angelic exterior is cast aside and trodden underfoot, while German promises of good will evaporate amidst the realities of Nazi oppression. In the other, 'truthful' news wins an easy victory over 'ridiculous German claims', as a German family listens with rapt attention to the BBC.**

20a

1. *Mein Kampf* 'The great masses of the people are more easily victimised by a large than a small lie.' HITLER

2. RIDICULOUS GERMAN CLAIMS

BUT THE BIG LIE CANNOT

3. TRUTHFUL B.B.C. NEWS

STAND UP TO THE TRUTH!

4. *Das Reich* AUGUST 15, 1941 We introduce the death penalty for listening in to the B.B.C. GOEBBELS

J.X

20*b*

truth—from the outright lie, to the half-truth, to the truth out of context. Many writers on propaganda see it as essentially appeasing the irrational instincts of man, and this is true to a certain extent; but because our attitudes and behaviour are also the product of rational decisions, propaganda must appeal to the rational elements in human nature as well. The preoccupation with the former ignores the basic fact that the act of propagandising is ethically and morally neutral—it may be put to good or bad use.

We tend to think of propaganda pejoratively, but there can be all kinds of legitimate and functional uses. Citizens need to be more informed and must arm themselves with a greater understanding of the nature and process of the Information Age. In all political systems policy must be explained, the public must be convinced of the efficacy of government decisions (or at least remain quiescent), and rational discussion is not always the most useful means of achieving this, particularly in the age of mass society, so instead messages are disseminated. In recent years, for example, the British public have been reminded of the 'Dunkirk'

and 'Falkland' spirits, asked to consider 'who governs Britain' at a time of industrial unrest; it has been assured that the rate of inflation can be 'reduced at a stroke', and has been encouraged to think of itself as part of the 'Big Society' or as 'One Nation'. Propaganda plays its part as an essential component of the whole political process. In modern times, governments (and interest groups and organisations) have sought to come to terms with the mass media, to control them and to harness them, particularly in times of crises, and to ensure that as often as possible they have acted in 'the national interest'.

Today, the most obvious reason for the increasing importance ascribed to propaganda and its assumed power over opinion is the broadening base of politics, which has dramatically transformed the nature of political participation. Of course, the means of communication have correspondingly proliferated. We are now witnessing the explosion of 'information superhighways' and digital data networks, and legitimate concerns have been expressed about the nature of media proprietorship and access, and about the extent to which information flows freely in an age where it becomes possible to marshal resources to obtain (in Edward S. Herman and Noam Chomsky's phrase from the 1990s) the 'manufacture of consent'. Propagandists have been forced to respond to change; they must assess their audience and use whatever methods they consider to be most effective.

Interestingly, and in contrast to ideas of propaganda as a form of mass brainwashing, there is the fact that, as we are realising, propaganda is essentially limited in its effects. A great deal of recent research on the subject has forced us to reappraise previous simplistic assumptions by looking at 'resistance' or 'immunity' to propaganda. In the short term propaganda may carry its audience on a wave of fervour, like the patriotic surges that can accompany the outbreak of war. In the longer term, however, it becomes less effective, because the audience has had both the time and opportunity to question its underlying assumptions.

As Goebbels remarked, 'Propaganda becomes ineffective the moment we are aware of it.' The key here is that communication between human beings relies on a mixture of reason and emotion for its effect. If propaganda is too rational, it can be boring; if it is too emotional, too strident, it can become transparent and laughable. As in other forms of human interaction, propaganda has to strike the right balance.

Propaganda is, as we have suggested (and as described in the chapters to follow), shape-changing, it can take many forms. We usually think of the conventional media—radio, television, the press, etc.—but propaganda as an agent of reinforcement is not confined to these. Few would deny that the presence of Hitler's head on the stamps and coinage of the Third Reich is an example of propaganda, though more might be surprised at the suggestion that the same conclusion may be reached with regard to the monarch's head on British postage stamps and coins. The role of commemoration in reinforcement propaganda is also often overlooked: what better way of reinforcing the present and determining the future could there be than commemorating the glories of the past? It is no coincidence that London has its Waterloo Station and Paris its Gare d'Austerlitz, both of them testaments to respective Napoleonic-era victories. We need to think of propaganda in broad terms, for wherever public opinion is deemed important, there we shall find an attempt to influence it, whether in the form of a building, a flag, a coin—even a government health warning on a cigarette packet. Widening our terms of reference and divesting propaganda of its 'gut-reaction' pejorative associations will better reveal propaganda's significance as an intrinsic part of the whole political process in the modern age. As Goebbels maintained, 'In propaganda, as in love, anything is permissible that is successful.'

21

21 A Falkland Islands stamp (1964) marking the 50th anniversary of the Battle of the Falklands (1914) between British and German ships. The Battle Memorial depicted was unveiled in 1927, and has since appeared widely on stamps and postcards, an important aspect of Falkland Island identity and an example of the significance of commemoration in building national identity. Queen Elizabeth's head, though a standard feature, quietly asserts British sovereignty.

■ Propaganda: does it work?

But, how do we *measure* 'successful' when it comes to propaganda? It is a recurring issue, and as the scale of mass communications has proliferated, so have the means by which governments have attempted to measure public opinion. The historian A.J.P. Taylor once famously said, in the context of the First World War, that you 'cannot conduct a gallup poll amongst the dead'. Nevertheless, even during that war most governments did possess some limited feedback on public opinion by means of police reports and letters to newspapers and magazines. In Germany, for example, monthly public-opinion reports (*Monatsberichten*) were compiled by the military, who established a national network of monitoring stations. The copious evidence received from these reports, together with those from the police and from the *Büro für Sozialpolitik* (Office for Social Policy), provided the German Imperial government with feedback on the 'pulse of the people'. But measuring public opinion was still in its infancy.

During the interwar period, totalitarian fascist and communist states not only monopolised the means of communication, but also established agencies to monitor closely both public reaction to their policies and factors affecting public morale. This process operated largely in 'closed' societies away from foreign opinion and influences. It may surprise some people to learn that Goebbels impressed on all his staff at the Propaganda Ministry the imperative necessity of constantly gauging the public mood. He therefore regularly received (as did all the Nazi elite) extraordinarily detailed reports (*SD Berichte*) about this from the secret police of the Nazi Security Service

(*Sicherheitsdienst*). At the outbreak of the Second World War all the major belligerents had in place organisations providing detailed information on popular attitudes. In Britain, Mass Observation (MO) worked for the Ministry of Information, which also used the Home Intelligence Reports, and in the United States the Office of Government Reports (OGR) provided 'opinions, desires and complaints of the citizens' for the Office of War Information.

In the Second World War's aftermath, the gathering and analysis of public opinion became much more sophisticated by means of highly structured opinion polls (at least in the democracies). In recent times, the 'new media' such as the internet, mobile phones and social networks have added a new dimension to our understanding of popular opinion. They have empowered individuals and groups to become propagandists in their own right—often with the capacity to subvert state propaganda and mobilise civilian unrest. This new capability, triggered by 'bottom-up' protest, was clearly evident during the events that led to the Arab Spring (*see* Chapter 6).

In the chapters to come, although limited space does not permit elaboration on the detailed feedback evidence available to historians of propaganda, this aspect has been taken into consideration, wherever possible, in selecting the case studies of propaganda.

The varieties of propaganda

The chapters that follow look at propaganda in a range
of (chiefly) 20th- and 21st-century manifestations, in
both wartime and peacetime, and the reader may find it
useful to retain at the back of his/her mind some useful
categories, which are described here. In the popular
view, propaganda is commonly associated with the idea
of the 'big lie', but in fact it operates on many different
levels. It may be overt or covert, truthful or mendacious,
serious or humorous, rational or emotional; especially
in times of war it may be 'black', but it may also be 'grey'
or 'white'. And when it comes to conflict, actual warfare
may be bolstered by 'psychological warfare'.

The big lie

F ROM ATROCITY STORIES about the Saracens during the Crusades to stories of babies being used in the manufacture of soap during the First World War, the 'big lie' or falsehood has always been part of the propagandist's stock-in-trade. The big lie can be defined as the intentional distortion of the truth, especially for political purposes.

Adolf Hitler believed implicitly in the big lie, claiming that propaganda for the masses had to be simple and target the lowest level of intelligence. Indeed, for him the bigger the lie the better, for 'the great mass of people will more easily fall victim to a big lie than to a small one' as he opined in *Mein Kampf*. His propaganda minister Goebbels, despite being referred to in Allied propaganda as the 'Big Liar', took a different view, claiming that propaganda should be as accurate as possible.

It is true that after 1918 propaganda was widely associated with lies and falsehood. In Arthur Ponsonby's influential book *Falsehood in Wartime* (1928), which reflected public opinion at the time, the author wrote that 'when war is declared truth is the first victim ... Falsehood is the most useful weapon in case of war.' As a result of the innumerable lies, deliberate or otherwise, that were disseminated and believed during the First World War, propaganda was inexorably associated with falsehood and viewed by many as something to be ashamed of. The Allies, in particular, quickly disbanded agencies that had been established for propaganda purposes, though other less democratically inclined nations viewed propaganda in a radically different light and were attracted by the allure of using the new communications technologies to manipulate mass opinion. Partly as a reaction to this, in the interwar period British government officials even considered banishing the word 'propaganda' from the diplomatic vocabulary, the implication being that whereas fascist or communist regimes resorted to lies, democracies told the truth.

The big lie does not, of course, go away as part of a propagandist's toolbox, and there are always examples to be observed of inventing stories about adversaries, falsifying statistics and 'creating' news. But there is an interesting discipline about its use. From the propagandist's point of view, lies must only be told about *unverifiable* facts. For example, in the First World War the German Admiralty continued to exaggerate the successes achieved by German U-boats even after they had reached their peak of effectiveness; they could do this only because it was relatively safe to disseminate such news without fear of contradiction. If, however, the public always *associates* propaganda with lies, then the propaganda will never achieve any credibility and, as such, becomes counter-productive.

To explain this contradiction, Jacques Ellul made a distinction between facts and intentions (or interpretations), or, put differently, between material and moral elements. According to Ellul, the truth that pays off is in the realm of facts. The necessary falsehoods, which also pay off, are in the realm of intentions and interpretations. In the light of Lenin's dictum earlier in the century, that 'in propaganda, truth pays off', the dissemination

> In the interwar period British government officials even considered banishing the word 'propaganda' from the diplomatic vocabulary ... <u>democracies told the truth</u>

of false news can create its own problems. And propagandists have discovered that it is better to reveal bad news oneself than to wait until it is revealed by the enemy.

It is now a generally accepted norm in the field of propaganda that, with the exception of harmful and unbelievable truths, wherever possible the truth should be told. When Sir John Reith was appointed British Minister of Information in 1940, he laid down two of the ministry's fundamental axioms for the balance

Black propaganda

of the war: that news equated to the 'shock troops of propaganda' and that propaganda should tell 'the truth, nothing but the truth and, as near as possible, the whole truth'. In its propaganda manual, the Supreme Headquarters Allied Expeditionary Force (SHAEF), which organised the D-Day landings in June 1944, recommended that:

> … when there is no compelling reason to suppress a fact, tell it. Aside from consideration of military security, the only reason to suppress a piece of news is if it is unbelievable … When the listener catches you in a lie, your power diminishes … For this reason, never tell a lie which can be discovered.

This view has to be qualified by a recognition that the public cannot accept an undiluted diet of bad news. One of the skills of the propagandist is clearly therefore the manner in which 'facts' are presented. The publication of a 'true' fact is not in itself dangerous. However, if it would be dangerous to make it public, the propagandist would prefer to hide it, to say nothing rather than to lie. So silence can be preferable, and it has been estimated that approximately one-fifth of all press directives given by Goebbels during the war were orders to simply remain silent concerning events. Silence—even when the facts are known—becomes a means of preventing the proper understanding of those facts by modifying the context. This propaganda technique, known as 'selection', leads to an effective distortion of reality and in the process becomes yet another example of the big lie.

SOMETIMES THERE IS complete openness about the source of a piece of propaganda. However, on other occasions it is necessary to conceal the source's identity in order to achieve certain objectives. 'Black' propaganda (sometimes referred to as 'covert' propaganda) tries to conceal its own identity by purporting to emanate from someone or somewhere other than the true source. It is therefore often quite difficult to detect black propaganda until after all the facts are known.

During the early phase of the Second World War, the Nazis operated at least three radio stations that sought to give the impression that they were broadcasting somewhere in Britain. One was called Radio Free Caledonia and claimed to be the voice of Scottish nationalism; another referred to itself as the Workers' Challenge Station and disseminated unorthodox left-wing views; a third, the New British Broadcasting Station, provided news bulletins and comments in the style of the BBC but with a concealed pro-German bias. None of these stations reached large audiences, and they only broadcast for a few hours a day. The aim of this black propaganda was to undermine the morale of the British people, particularly during the Battle of Britain in 1940.

The Nazi regime used similar techniques on French soldiers serving on the Maginot Line between 1939 and 1940. Radio broadcasts from Stuttgart were fronted by a Frenchman named Paul Ferdonnet, who pretended to broadcast from within France. His transmissions were designed to weaken the French soldiers' morale by comparing the poor conditions of the ordinary foot soldiers in the Maginot Line with the luxurious lifestyle of French officers enjoying the delights of Paris. Ferdonnet also described in lurid detail the behaviour of British soldiers billeted in French towns who, because they earned higher pay than their French counterparts, were seducing French women. The broadcasts found an audience not necessarily because the French soldiers were deceived by the 'black' nature of the broadcasts, but more often because they were simply more entertaining than official French broadcasts.

Later in the war the British (who sometimes conflated black propaganda with 'political warfare', i.e. psychological warfare) set up their own 'black' radio station, which claimed to be an official German station run by German soldiers for those on the Western Front. At the same time leaflets in the form of newspapers were dropped over the German lines purporting to originate from (non-existent) German resistance organisations. Fake ration cards and other ingenious devices were also employed.

Black propaganda, by definition, seeks to deceive and encompasses all types of deception, meaning not only leaflets, posters and radio stations, but also including postage stamps, television stations, and now even the internet. This type of propaganda consequently receives the most attention when it is revealed. The success or failure of it largely depends on the receiver's willingness to accept the authenticity of the source and the content of the message. For black propaganda to achieve its aims, great care has to be taken to place the message within the social,

> the British set up their own 'black' radio station, which claimed to be an official German station run by German soldiers

political and cultural experiences of the target audience, and to take similar care with the manner in which it is disseminated.

One of the most successful examples of the genre was Radio Free Hungary, which began broadcasting after the unsuccessful Hungarian Uprising against Soviet authority in 1956. The radio station called for intervention from the United States and graphically detailed Soviet atrocities committed during the crushing of the Uprising. In fact, Radio Free Hungary was a Soviet KGB operation designed to embarrass the United States by showing that the latter could not be relied upon to help smaller countries opposing Soviet communism. Radio Free Hungary was even able to deceive the American CIA, which did not recognise the source until after it had stopped operating.

Radio figured prominently during the 1982 Falklands War too, when a BBC-fronted programme began broadcasting under the guise of an Argentinian radio station. The British government invoked an obscure clause in the BBC charter that allowed the government to requisition the BBC transmitters in time of crisis. One of the programmes broadcast was called *Ascension Alice*, in which a sexy female announcer attempted to undermine the morale of the Argentinian troops stationed in the Falklands. For example, the announcer (Alice) would claim that the Argentinian president had stated on television that he was prepared to sacrifice 40,000 men to defend the Falklands. The radio station also played sentimental Argentinian ballads in an attempt to divert the soldiers' attention to loved ones back home. It even played classics like 'Under Pressure' by the rock group Queen, as well as a fictitious request programme from Argentinian mothers, who made emotional appeals to their sons to look after themselves and return home safely. Following the end of the conflict, the British government was criticised for compromising the BBC's reputation for objective and accurate reporting. The authorities, for their part, felt that the propaganda war justified such draconian measures, provided the source of the radio station remained concealed. (*See also* Chapter 3.)

In the 21st century, black propaganda was supposedly part of the responsibility of the US Office of Strategic Influence (OSI), the body established at the Pentagon as the 'Global War on Terror' got underway in 2001. In early 2002 the White House proposed retaining this office as a component of the broader US psychological war on terrorism, and it exists to this day.

White propaganda

As its name suggests, white propaganda is conceived of as the opposite to black propaganda, that is, something that is open, above board and makes no attempt to conceal its origins. As mentioned above, the establishment of a Ministry for Popular Enlightenment and Propaganda in Nazi Germany made no secret of the name nor, indeed, of the task that it would perform. And Goebbels openly declared in one of his first speeches that the new ministry would be responsible for 'the mobilisation of mind and spirit in Germany'. The source

> The information in the message tends also to be accurate … since any suggestion that the message might be false would undermine the credibility of the source.

here was known, the aims and intentions were identified, and the public knew that an attempt was being made to influence it—all attributes of white propaganda.

By the 1930s there was a growing recognition that it was important to distinguish between overt, or information-based, propaganda—the output representing the official policy of the government, which needed to be truthful (that is, factually accurate)—and the type of covert propaganda seeking to achieve immediate results by any, and all, means, and whose essential requirement (apart from effectiveness) was that it should not be traceable back to its source. In other words, the distinction between white and black propaganda was well understood. Hugh Carleton Greene of the BBC defined white propaganda as 'to tell the truth within the limits of the information at our disposal and to tell it consistently and frankly … It is a strategic weapon and must not deviate from the truth for tactical reasons.'

The emphasis on truth and credibility was shared by the future politician Richard Crossman when he was assistant chief of Psychological Warfare Division at SHAEF (*see* 'Psychological Warfare' *below*). He gained the reputation of a propaganda genius, thanks to his almost clairvoyant ability to transport himself into the mind of the enemy.

White propaganda tends to be conducted by an identifiable government agency. The information in the message tends also to be accurate (although not necessarily verifiable), since any suggestion that the message might be false would undermine the credibility of the source. The message is usually intended to convince an audience of the superiority and justness of a particular regime or ideology. Thus, while the message disseminated is largely truthful, it is slanted to favour the value system of the propagandist. During the Cold War, the broadcasts of the Voice of America and Radio Moscow employed this type of white propaganda in order to establish credibility with an audience that might prove useful at some point in the future.

Grey propaganda

GREY PROPAGANDA falls, unsurprisingly, somewhere between white and black propaganda. The source may or may not be identified, and the accuracy of the information is uncertain. During the First World War, Britain's War Propaganda Bureau, better known as Wellington House (where it was headquartered), conducted its major campaign in the then neutral United States through an American branch headed by Sir Gilbert Parker, a Canadian-born writer and British Member of Parliament. British propaganda, aimed at sustaining a benevolent neutrality rather than explicitly persuading America to join the Allies, targeted America's elite with material about which they might make up their own minds, in the belief that this would, in turn, influence the larger public.

An educated or elite audience likes to believe that it can spot propaganda when confronted by it, and then duly dismiss it as 'propaganda'. British propaganda therefore required delicate handling, and Wellington House had to disseminate material that did not *appear* to be propaganda—or at least not all the time. Rather, it had to take the form of reasoned argument based on the facts—although not necessarily *all* the facts—which was presented in an objective manner. Some of it came directly from Wellington House (white), while other portions were disguised (grey). For this purpose, a clandestine publishing operation produced material that was distributed under the imprint of famous commercial publishing houses, such as Hodder and Stoughton, John Murray and Macmillan. (For more on Wellington House's activities, *see* Chapter 3.)

In the Second World War, Britain's Political Warfare Executive (PWE) produced grey propaganda as well as black, an example being the highly praised newspaper for German troops entitled *Nachrichten für die Truppen*, which was delivered by air. Its contents could not possibly be reconciled with official German authorship, but the failure to disclose its true origin permitted the newspaper to express views that might have been embarrassing if attributed to an official British source. In the early Cold War era, Western powers attached great importance to psychological warfare, employing propaganda measures to sway international opinion to support the Free World and, ultimately, to bring about the disintegration of communist regimes. In 1948 the British Foreign Office sponsored a peacetime covert propaganda agency, the Information Research Department (IRD), which was intended to counter Soviet and communist propaganda and defend Western liberal democracy. The IRD was formed in the aftermath of the communist coup in Prague, Czechoslovakia, and increasingly hostile Soviet propaganda. Supported by Foreign Minister Ernest Bevin, the approach adopted was secretive and aggressive, designed to take the initiative away from the enemy. IRD was in many respects a peacetime PWE. Its task was not black propaganda, which was the preserve of the Secret Intelligence Service (that is, MI6), but rather grey propaganda, in this case biased information emanating from an indeterminate source. The target was

> When the Soviet Union invaded Afghanistan in 1979, Radio Moscow employed grey propaganda when it attempted to justify its actions

communist Russia and the task was to attack and expose this ideological enemy and offer 'something better'. Grey propaganda was adopted because it was more direct and aggressive than white but less likely to offend the Soviet Union quite as much as black propaganda.

At one level, IRD material consisted of in-depth confidential studies on aspects of Soviet communism designed for high-level consumption by senior Allied politicians. On a less classified level, radio broadcasts, pamphlets, articles, letters and speeches were directed at policymakers in Eastern Europe, who could

Psychological warfare

use such material as factual background in their general work without the need for attribution. To distinguish its activities from those of the Americans, the IRD concentrated on the areas of Eastern Europe threatened by communism. The ability of IRD to disguise its sponsorship of cultural activity until the late 1970s points to the reason for its success, namely, the fact that much of it was not generally recognised as propaganda.

When the Soviet Union invaded Afghanistan in 1979, Radio Moscow employed grey propaganda when it attempted to justify its actions. A television documentary entitled *Afghanistan: The Revolution Cannot Be Killed* was broadcast on Christmas Day, 1985, which deliberately gave the impression that the conflict had been started by other powers. Iran and Pakistan were specifically implicated, and captured mercenaries claimed that they had been sent to Afghanistan by the CIA. The film ended with pro-Soviet troops being cheered by Afghan crowds. The source of the message was not in question, but the information was largely inaccurate.

In the wake of the 9/11 terrorist attacks against New York and Washington, DC, the United States prepared the population of Afghanistan for a planned US air and land war by dropping food containers and radios that could only pick up one signal. The US-run radio station—another example of grey propaganda— simply referred to itself as 'Afghan FM', and sandwiched between some lively Afghan music an announcement was broad-cast 'for the attention of the noble people of Afghanistan'. The announcer then proceeded to explain that American forces would be passing through the area and that their aim was not to harm the people but rather to arrest al-Qaeda leader Osama bin Laden and those who supported him.

THE PLANNED USE of propaganda to influence enemy audiences in times of war is the essence of psychological warfare, a concept that the British pioneered during the First World War. In 1950 one official document defined it as 'activities, other than physical combat, which communicate ideas and information intended to affect the minds, emotions, and actions of the enemy, for the purpose of disrupting his morale and his will to fight'.

Psychological warfare can be distinguished from other forms of external propaganda in that it is directed at an enemy rather than at peoples of neutral or friendly nations. Sometimes known as 'combat propaganda', psychological warfare has gradually come to have wider applications at the strategic and political levels, no longer being confined to formal war situations, which is why psychological operations ('psyops') is now the preferred term. Like propaganda in general, psychological warfare can assume black, white and grey forms, and it became a character-istic of conflict in the 20th century, figuring not only in the cent-ury's 'hot' wars, but also the Cold War and counter-insurgency conflicts of the kind that the British undertook in Kenya and Malaya during the 1950s. But its attributes go much further back.

Pre-literate ages used frightening sounds and images, and rumours spread by word of mouth, to weaken an enemy's morale. During the American Revolution (War of Independence), American forces encouraged British troops to desert by wrapping messages around stones and throwing them behind the British lines. Printed leaflets aimed at Hessian mercenaries, fighting for the British, proved particularly effective and may have accounted for the high level of desertion among these soldiers—by some estimates 5,000 or 6,000 of the 30,000-strong force.

The modern period can be said to have begun with a 'paper war': the dropping of millions of leaflets by balloon and aircraft over enemy lines during the First World War (*see* Chapter 3). At the conclusion of the war, victors and losers alike made extensive claims for the effectiveness of psychological warfare. In 1919 the *Times* concluded that 'good propaganda probably saved a year of war, and this meant the saving of thousands of millions in money and probably at least a million lives'. General Erich von Ludendorff, the German chief of staff, claimed that 'we were hypnotised by the enemy's propaganda as a rabbit is by a snake'. General Hindenburg, German commander-in-chief, wrote that 'besides bombs which kill the body, his [the enemy's] airmen throw down leaflets which are intended to kill the soul … Unsuspectingly many thousands consume the poison.' Both men claimed that psychological warfare was a principal factor contributing to the final collapse of Germany in November 1918, a conclusion with which Hitler came to concur. Of course, they each had good reasons for blaming the defeat of Germany on causes other than either the military conduct of the war or the fighting abilities of German soldiers.

In 1920, some military historians were predicting that in the future physical combat would be replaced by a purely psychological warfare, wherein weapons would not be used nor battlefields sought. A new factor after 1918 was the emergence of Soviet Russia, followed by Fascist Italy and then Nazi Germany, ushering in a new era of ideological warfare, which lasted, through the Cold War, until 1989. These circumstances made psychological warfare a permanent feature of international relations; and it was often conducted by newly emerging secret intelligence services. The British called it 'that aspect of intelligence in which information is used aggressively to manipulate opinion or to create special conditions by purely intellectual means'. The Germans preferred the term *Geistige Kriegsführung* ('intellectual warfare').

During the Second World War, the British government continued to use the term 'political warfare'—based on its Political Warfare Executive—until the Americans joined in after 1941, when the preferred US term 'psychological warfare' replaced it. Allied Psychological Warfare branches were established in the various theatres of action, the largest of which was set up in North Africa in November 1942. As part of the preparations

for the invasion of Europe, the Psychological Warfare Division was established at Supreme Headquarters Allied Expeditionary Force (PWD/SHAEF). Although this suggested greater inter-Allied cooperation than was, in fact, the case, the British and Americans were united in their overall approach to psychological warfare, which was based on a distinction between white and black propaganda.

A group of fictitious radio stations ostensibly broadcast conversations between underground cells of disaffected German soldiers. They were, in fact, broadcast by a secret transmitter in Britain, codenamed 'Aspidistra', and this constituted the principal black propaganda technique employed by the Allies, reinforced by secret agents disseminating false rumours. Since it was purportedly coming from within occupied Europe, the black propaganda did not have to worry about lies or false promises. For example, following the Casablanca Conference of 1943,

> The British called it 'that aspect of intelligence in which information is used aggressively to manipulate opinion …'

Allied policy was one of demanding unconditional surrender, which implied that negotiation would not be possible even if the German people rose up against their Nazi rulers. Black propagandists, on the other hand, could suggest that if 'we' got rid of 'Hitler's gang', then 'our' situation might well improve.

Most post-1945 views of psychological warfare assumed that it was both a necessary and legitimate response to the growing political, military and ideological threat posed by international communism. Following North Korea's invasion of South Korea in 1950, President Truman established the Psychological Strategy Board in the White House to coordinate the wider effort, both overt and covert. A bolstering of the white propaganda machinery occurred first within the State Department in the form of the International Information Administration (IIA). In 1953 President Eisenhower, who had seen the potency of psychological warfare on the battlefields of Europe, established the autonomous United States Information Agency (USIA), with the Voice of America as its white broadcasting arm. The CIA funded Radio Free Europe and Radio Liberty as grey broadcasting organs. The degree to which the activities of these groups were effectively coordinated is doubtful, though, with each branch going its separate way, until the 'Bay of Pigs' disaster in 1961—which attempted to topple Cuba's Fidel Castro—exposed the myth of a coordinated psychological effort.

Psychological warfare ('psywar') was used episodically in Vietnam, but with the defeat of the United States it fell into disrepute in Western military thought. The Soviet Union retained its faith in it, however, describing it blandly as 'active measures' and scoring some notable Cold War successes, in particular the campaign surrounding the neutron bomb and later campaigns accusing the United States of manufacturing the AIDS virus in a biological warfare lab. President Reagan revived US psychological warfare in the 1980s in the form of the Department of Defense's 'psyops master plan' of 1985, and in the years thereafter 'psyops' have played a role in US interventions in Panama, the Gulf War, Bosnia, Kosovo and the Global War on Terror (*see also* Chapter 6).

'One people, one nation, one leader!'

The propaganda of nationhood and leadership

2

**B**UILDING AND SUSTAINING a sense of national identity is an important goal of most states. The means by which they do this, and spread messages about their people and histories, constitute a rich seam in the story of propaganda.

But first we must ask: what *is* a nation? The modern concept stems from the 18th century during which, in the West, Enlightenment ideas and revolutionary movements were destroying the legitimacy of monarchical, hierarchical authority. Indeed, a number of academic 'historicist' writers on the subject, such as Ernst Gellner and Eric Hobsbawm, have regarded the concepts of nation and nationalism as products of modernity, *created* as means to political and economic ends.

The nation has been defined as an 'imagined political community', and nationalism as a form of patriotism based on the identification of a group of individuals with that nation. This sense of an imagined community differs from an actual community, because it is not based on everyday, face-to-face interaction among its members. Instead, members hold in their minds a mental image of their community and the symbols, norms and values that bind them to it. Academic studies have demonstrated that a person's national identity stems from a myriad of 'common points' in people's daily lives: national symbols, language, national colours, the nation's history, national consciousness, blood ties, culture, music, cuisine, radio, television, and so on. That sense of belonging and shared identity (nationhood) felt with other members is often foremost when the imagined community is under threat or otherwise pitted against another community, as in war or sport. On such occasions, the political affiliations, diverse ethnic identities, inequalities and other internal differences may be put aside, as individuals come together under this larger umbrella of the 'nation'. (Traditionally, the media too have created imagined communities, usually through targeting a mass audience or generalising and addressing citizens as 'the public'.)

The types of propaganda that support the assertion of national identity are wide-ranging. Prominent among them are the overt national symbols such as flags, anthems and memorials. Achievements demonstrating prowess, for example in technology, space exploration or on the sporting field, can contribute. And of course there is the role of a great leader in a nation's history. Creating the sense of nationhood, of belonging, is imperative for any state in order to justify political and economic policies to its citizens—especially when it comes to the collecting of taxes and other unpalatable activities.

The concept of citizenship is therefore an important glue binding people to the nation and the state. In countries under colonial rule—which perhaps disregard local traditional groupings— or countries ruled by a dictatorship, very often a sense of national identity has to be 'artificially' constructed. In other scenarios, such as post-Soviet Russia and post-apartheid South Africa, there has had to be a *recreation* of the idea of the nation, in which the need for reconciliation forms a major plank in the process.

The stories that state propaganda uses to foster this sense of nationhood might look to the past, drawing on history or myth, but they might

22 Marianne, a national emblem of France and one of the most prominent symbols of the French Republic. She is an allegory of liberty and reason; but the French flag—the tricolour (here draped over Marianne)—remains the only *official* emblem permitted under the French Constitution.

also look to a utopian future. States have often attempted to use or shape public perceptions of identity, character and history to justify official actions or build support for new institutions or change. This can be seen most clearly at times of national upheaval or radical change, as in political revolutions or the transfer of power that accompanies decolonisation; but it is evident, too, in times of economic hardship or in the attempts to found new transnational institutions, such as the League of Nations and the United Nations, and in the evolution of the European Union.

22

"LA MARSEILLAISE"

créée à Strasbourg par Rouget de l'Isle, en 1792 y rentre triomphalement, en 1918, à la tête des Armées Alliées!

JACQUES CARLU

Allons donc enfants de la Patrie allons achever de libérer les peuples...»

(G. Clémenceau)

DEVAMBEZ, IMP. PARIS. Visa 12.498.

■ The propaganda of national symbols

One tactic at a state's disposal is the use of iconic figures to strengthen a particular point about national identity. They might be real people presented in a mythologised form as national heroes, such as William Shakespeare or Che Guevara, or they can come from old myths or popular folklore: John Bull and Britannia; Uncle Sam in the United States; or Marianne, the national emblem of France and an allegorical encapsulation of liberty and reason. They can even be entirely new creations by the state, a good example being the cults of ideal workers as propagated in the 20th century by communist and socialist regimes.

An alternative strategy is the use of material symbols of nationhood. Indeed, a state might have numerous opportunities at its disposal to create narratives and circulate images favourable to its preferred national story—in everyday items such as coins, banknotes and postage stamps, or symbolic structures such as statues, monuments and buildings. Two of the most overt and powerful symbols that allow citizens to express their affinity with the state are the nation's flag and its anthem.

THE NATIONAL ANTHEM

Music lends itself to patriotic appeal since the latter depends on, at root, an emotional response, and music is inherently well suited to that. Unsurprisingly then, national anthems appear in a wide array of contexts, from state funerals to sporting competitions, and by definition they are compositions intended to evoke and eulogise, or at least encompass, the history of a nation.

One of the most rousing in the Western tradition remains France's 'La Marseillaise'. Its words and music were composed in 1792 by Claude Joseph Rouget de Lisle, an officer in the French Army of the Rhine. The new revolutionary government in Paris had just declared war on Austria, and as the army mustered in Strasbourg for an advance into the German states, the mayor of that city noted that they lacked any appropriate marching songs. He commissioned Rouget de Lisle, whose musical skill he admired, to write something suitable. The result was originally entitled 'The War Song of the Army of the Rhine' but was renamed after being used in action, when a battalion from Marseilles stormed the Tuileries Gardens in Paris during August 1792. Its simple tune and rousing words ('Come, children of the fatherland / The day of glory is here!') made it an infectious propaganda vehicle for the spirit of the French Revolution. It went on to feature, famously, in the 1942 film *Casablanca*, where it symbolised the defiant spirit of French resistance in the Second World War, and was heard in 1967 in The Beatles' 'All You Need is Love', played on *Our World*, the first live global television link, and watched by 400 million in 26 countries.

As a direct response to 'La Marseillaise', Franz Joseph Haydn composed the Austrian national anthem in 1797, whose tune was so good that when the states of Germany were unified into one nation, they adopted it for their own national anthem, 'Deutschland, Deutschland über Alles'.

In the United States, 'The Star-Spangled Banner' only became the official anthem in 1931. It combines a stirring text by the 19th-century lawyer and poet Francis Scott Key with

23 A French poster (1918) from the First World War, in which Prime Minster Georges Clémenceau paraphrases 'La Marseillaise' to rally the nation: 'Come, children of fatherland, let's achieve the liberation of the people.' The figure urging the nation on derives from a painting of the anthem's creator, Rouget de Lisle, singing the song for the first time.

the popular English drinking song 'Anacreon in Heaven' by John Stafford Smith. Although millions of individuals can sing the simple melody of England's 'God Save the Queen' with ease, the US national anthem has a melody with notes so high that few can sing it properly—including the amateur soloists who open many a sporting event.

THE NATIONAL FLAG

Perhaps the most striking symbol of nationhood is the national flag. In the United States, for example, the idea of the flag is fundamental to the Oath of Allegiance: 'I pledge allegiance to the Flag of the United States of America, and to the Republic for which it stands, one Nation under God, indivisible, with liberty and justice for all.' In times of war or other crises, citizens are encouraged to 'rally around the flag'; in times of national elation such as a sporting event, the national flag becomes the proud symbol of prowess.

Flags represent a powerful force that cements people together; but, conversely, for those who are not included they can foster a sense of isolation and 'apartness'. On the one hand such symbols may simply represent the visible part of an accepted, and acceptable, patriotism—the simple expression of national identity; on the other hand, they can be a dangerous component of ideological doctrine and a powerful weapon of a regime's propaganda, perhaps the most obvious example being the Nazi swastika.

The choice of a national flag becomes especially important at the birth of a nation. The experience of India as it reached independence is particularly illustrative. Prior to the 1947 independence, and with no national flag (other than one imposed by its British colonial master) and no national emblem, the Indian subcontinent would occasionally adopt the symbol of the tiger, which featured also in the campaign for independence. Mohandas K. ('Mahatma') Gandhi, who had first proposed a flag to the Indian National Congress in 1921, reputedly said: 'It will be necessary for us Indians—Hindus, Muslims, Christians, Jews, Parsis and all others to whom India is their home—to recognise a common flag to live and die for.' At independence, such a flag was adopted on 22 July 1947, and it was made up of elements with specific meanings. A horizontal rectangular tricolour of saffron, white and green, it contains at its centre the Ashok Chakra, a 24-spoke wheel, in navy blue. The saffron colour represents courage and sacrifice, while white implies truth, peace and purity, and green indicates prosperity. The Ashok Chakra represents the continuing progress of the nation and the importance of justice in life. India's founding prime minister, Jawaharlal Nehru, called it 'a flag not only of freedom for ourselves, but a symbol of freedom for all people'.

Historically, national flags originated as military standards, used as field signs worn on a combatant's clothing to show the difference between friend and foe or a combatant and a civilian. The practice of flying flags indicating the country of origin, outside of the context of warfare, emerged with the maritime flag, introduced in the early 17th century, denoting a ship's country of registration. In the West, the rise of nationalist sentiment from the

24

24 **A proof for the first stamp of postcolonial Ghana (1957) is full of the promise of a new nation: it boasts not only its new flag but also a statue of Kwame Nkrumah, its first president and prime minister, and an optimistic sunrise suggesting a bright future.**

25a&b **Symbols of India. In the first (a), from a Second World War pamphlet, the nation is transformed into a ferocious tiger at the service of the Allies, trampling on the flags of Germany and Japan. Below (b), India's first post-independence stamp issue (released on 21 November 1947) celebrates the new flag. Gone is the British 'king emperor' head from the country's stamps, to be replaced by an assertion of new identity in the tricolour of saffron, white and green, with the circular Ashok Chakra at the centre.**

25a

25b

late 18th century transformed the status of the flag, and increasingly national flags were displayed in civilian contexts. The flag of the United States, the Stars and Stripes, was originally adopted as a naval ensign in 1777, and after the American Revolutionary War it began to be displayed as a generic symbol of the new United States. The flag has become an extremely powerful symbol, at home and abroad, of the nation and of American values. It has been deployed in war and peace, to bring Americans together following a disaster such as Pearl Harbor in 1941 or the terrorist attacks of 9/11, and to record American achievements. In all of the successful moon landings, starting with the Apollo 11 mission, American astronauts have felt compelled to plant the Stars and Stripes on the lunar surface. For foreign opponents of the United States and US policies, and sometimes for internal dissenters too, burning the 'Stars and Stripes' has been a familiar, symbolic gesture of anger. Indeed, the United States and other countries have periodically enacted laws prohibiting citizens from desecrating the national flag.

As the US experience shows, a common objective of nationalistic propaganda is to make people feel attached to 'the flag', leading to its widespread display and use in both solemn and celebratory rituals—the most obvious examples including jubilees, state funerals and the ceremonies of a state's armed forces. At different times, in different places, this *cult of the flag* has become magnified and obsessive—as in the cases of Nazi Germany, the Soviet Union and Kim Il-Sung's North Korea. Such examples serve to remind us of the correlative to the feeling of attachment, in that those 'not covered' by the flag are implicitly excluded.

26

... *we here highly resolve that these dead shall not have died in vain* ...

REMEMBER DEC. 7th!

26 **A patriotic US poster from the Second World War. To galvanise the rage that Americans felt after the Japanese attack on Pearl Harbor, the US government produced this, one of the most stirring propaganda posters ever made. It unites a determination to 'Remember December 7th' with expressions of resolve from President Lincoln's Gettysburg Address. With the haunting image of a tattered Stars and Stripes swaying against a burning black sky, it perfectly captured the emotion of its intended audience.**

27 **Astronaut Buzz Aldrin, saluting the US flag on the moon during the Apollo 11 mission (1969). Apart from its feats of science, technology and human endurance, the moon landing restored pre-eminence to the United States in the space race with the Soviet Union. A similar flag was planted on each of the five sub-sequent successful moon landings, as symbolic gestures of national pride in achievement.**

27

As the US experience shows, a common objective of nationalistic propaganda is to make people feel attached to 'the flag'

28

NATIONAL MONUMENTS

Memorials, statues and monuments have been used to foster a sense of national history and patriotic pride since Ancient times, whether to mark great victories and discoveries, celebrate the lives of great men and women, or to commemorate moments of great stress, sorrow or loss. Indeed, memorials are an extremely important propaganda medium, capable of imparting a wide range of messages. It is perhaps surprising, though, to note how remark-ably little they have changed in their essential design and function over the centuries.

Ancient Egyptian and Assyrian civilisations both built memorials, and their traits can be seen in the memorials of other early civilisations. The Romans were enthusiastic monument builders, using them to illustrate battles and mark great victories. Columns became a favourite device for relating the stories of war campaigns. Some are still extant, one of the most important being Trajan's Column in Rome, built in the 2nd cent-ury AD to commemorate the Roman Emperor Trajan's victories. The Romans also built arches and gates to mark important events. Triumphal

arches, like columns, provided narrative friezes to commemorate the accomplishments of emperors and generals. All of these devices were passed down to European civilisation. However, the medieval world did not show quite the same reverence for memorial architecture. The commemoration of martial prowess was more often embodied in the architecture of the tombs of leading figures: great kings and princes were frequently entombed beneath effigies of themselves in full armour.

The Renaissance period, with its revival of interest in the Classical world, inspired a return to greater diversity in the use and design of mem-orials. And following the Great Fire of London in 1666, Sir Christopher Wren adopted the Classical column to provide a memorial to mark the event. The base of the Monument (as it is simply known) contains inscriptions relating the story of the fire. One panel contains a bas-relief of the reigning monarch, Charles II, in Roman dress, directing the relief of the sick and the destitute, and linking him with Christian charity and the wisdom and power of the Ancient world. Another panel, added

in 1681, was deliberately aimed at maintaining England's Protestant ascendancy by implying that the fire had been started by Catholics.

By the 18th century, and the growth of Enlightenment culture, memorial architecture not only mirrored the diversity and ubiquity it had achieved in the classical world but was just as dedicated to the dissemination of messages and images. Columns and arches proliferated, such as the column honouring Britain's maritime hero Horatio Nelson, which dominates London's Trafalgar Square, and the Arc de Triomphe in Paris. Such patriotic edifices—Buckingham Palace is another example—have, over time, come to represent not just the city in which they are situated but the nation as a whole. Amply illustrative of this is Paris's Eiffel Tower, named after the engineer Gustave Eiffel, whose company designed and built the tower. Erected as the entrance arch to the 1889 World's Fair, this 'temporary' structure has become both a global icon of France and one of the most recognisable in the world. A latter-day attempt in 1999/2000 to capture the *zeitgeist* in the form of London's Millennium Dome backfired and proved a major political embarrassment for the Labour government, although the building subsequently re-invented itself.

In the 19th century, monumental public statuary constituted a sort of open-air museum of national history seen largely through the perspective of great men—with a few notable female exceptions, such as Thomas Thornycroft's *Boadicea* near London's Westminster Pier and Emmanuel Frémiet's statue of Joan of Arc at the Place des Pyramides, Paris.

The two global wars of the 20th century and the growing importance of the nation-state turned war memorials into potent symbols of the political landscape. Smaller memorials built at the community level tended to stress the elements of grief and loss, whereas larger schemes expressed pride in victory and the glory of war. Before the First World War had concluded, Britain had instituted an Imperial War Graves Commission (1917). It employed the finest architects in the Empire to create cemeteries and memorials that reflected imperial glory, dignity and power. After the Second World War the Commission completed a new set of memorials and cemeteries. Now renamed the Commonwealth War Graves Commission, the organisation continues to care for such sites across the globe.

Memorials elsewhere, such as that to the US Marine Corps in Arlington, Virginia, fulfil a similar purpose. Based on the famous 1945 photograph showing Marines hoisting the Stars and Stripes over the conquered Japanese island of Iwo Jima, the memorial was intended as a powerful reminder of the might and resolution of the United States. In complete contrast is the Vietnam Veterans Memorial in Washington, DC, completed in 1982. The memorial, designed by the Chinese American Maya Lin, attempted to heal the deep wounds created by the war in American society by remaining simple, dignified and rather austere. Consisting of a reflective black surface, the wall contains the names of the 58,000 US war dead and missing.

In recent years Britain has erected a number of memorials that commemorate different aspects of the Second World War. In 1973, a bronze statue

> The Soviet Union erected statues to its revolutionary heroes—leaders and workers—with extraordinary enthusiasm.

of Winston Churchill was unveiled in London's Parliament Square to commemorate his statesmanship, and in 2005 the National Monument to Women in World War II was opened to the north of the Cenotaph in Whitehall, to celebrate the 60th anniversary of the end of the conflict. The bronze monument stands 22 feet (6.7 metres) high, 16 feet (4.9 metres) long and 6 feet (1.8 metres) wide. Its lettering replicates the typeface of wartime ration books, and there are 17 individual sets of clothing and uniforms around the sides, symbolising the numerous jobs women undertook in the war. Baroness Betty Boothroyd, the former Speaker of the House of Commons, dedicated the memorial with the words: 'This monument is dedicated to all the women who served our country and to the cause of freedom, in uniform and on the Home Front. I hope that future generations who pass this way will ask themselves: "what sort of women were they?" and look at our history for the answer.'

On 28 June 2012, and after much controversy and campaigning, an extraordinary memorial intended to recognise the role played, and the sacrifice made, by the Royal Air Force's Bomber Command in the Second World War was dedicated and unveiled by Queen Elizabeth II. (Bomber Command lost 55,000 men.) The large bronze sculpture consists of seven figures, 9 feet (almost 3 metres) tall, and represents a bomber's aircrew at 'the moment when they get off the aircraft and they've dumped all their heavy kit onto the ground', as described by the creator Philip Jackson.

After the Second World War, some communist states—notably the Soviet Union, China and North Korea—maintained an unqualified attachment to public statuary, including giant monuments surrounded by figures of workers, peasants, soldiers and by military arms. The Soviet Union erected statues to its revolutionary heroes—leaders *and* workers—with extraordinary enthusiasm. In the 1930s, too, totalitarian states were using memorials as reminders and imparters of specific ideologies, mobilising the national past on their behalf, and mythologising or inventing it where necessary. In more recent time, memorials were ubiquitous in Saddam Hussein's Iraq. The destruction of a giant statue of Saddam, seen worldwide on live television, became a defining image of the US victory in the Iraq War of 2003 (*see* Chapter 6). Similar images of monuments toppled defined the collapse of communist power in the former Soviet Bloc in the early 1990s.

■ The propaganda of national achievement

Stories about success are important in building or maintaining morale, at an individual and organisational level, and also in sustaining the legitimacy of a state. They help build international support and, conversely, establish superiority over other lower-achieving nations, and many a state seeks to 'speak' through its achievements to these ends. Statements about achievements, and celebration of achievement, are thus among the most common forms of state propaganda, but they take on particular urgency during times of conflict and hardship. During the Cold War, scientific innovation and technological advances were seen as symbolic

30 Homage to a leader.
North Koreans bow before
a statue of Kim Il-Sung,
the founder of North
Korea, who is considered
the eternal president of
the country. There are
over 500 statues of Kim
Il-Sung in the country,
a testament not only to
his long rule (1948–94)
but to one of the most
assiduously cultivated
personality cults of
modern times.

barometers of the strength and health of the US and Soviet superpowers, most notably in space technology. When the Soviet Union launched the first satellite (*Sputnik*) in October 1957, it shocked the United States, shattering assumptions about America as *the* technological superpower. It goaded the United States into a more aggressive stance in the emerging space race, which culminated with the successful moon landing in 1969.

International gatherings provide propaganda challenges and opportunities for countries wishing to showcase their achievements and attempt to overawe their rivals. In the modern era two examples are of particular interest: the Olympic Games, which, during the Cold War, provided a ritualistic stage on which sporting prowess was used to exhibit superpower strength (to domestic audiences and, equally importantly, to Cold War alignment blocs and the politically neutral countries); and world fairs for trade and innovation, which can project a state's achievements in a variety of areas.

WORLD FAIRS AND EXHIBITIONS

Since the success of the 1851 Great Exhibition in London, exhibitions and world fairs have provided a major opportunity for promoting national pride and achievements through demonstrations of trading clout, industry, art and knowledge. They have been used to celebrate historical events, giving the host countries an opportunity to stress national culture and achievements. They have also served to underscore a nation's superiority over its rivals, thereby, strictly speaking, violating the original spirit behind the concept.

The inspiration for the Great Exhibition came from the prince consort, Prince Albert. Very much a man of his time, his idea for a grand celebration of the industry of nations reflected 19th-century concepts of liberalism, whereby, it was thought, Free Trade and free discourse would help foster peace in the world. Joseph Paxton's Crystal Palace, specially built for the event, promoted this idealism while simultaneously celebrating British architectural and engineering innovation. With Britain as the world's greatest industrial and imperial power at the time—the so-called 'workshop of the world'—the vast bulk of the exhibition was given over to British and imperial products, encouraging a sense of imperial unity. From the very outset, therefore, such exhibitions were strongly connected with national pride and the promotion of national or imperial culture.

The second half of the 19th century witnessed further imperial fairs in Sydney (1879–80), Melbourne (1880–81), Calcutta (1883–84), London again (1886) and Adelaide (1887–88). In 1911, Sydenham, the home of the Crystal Palace after its removal from Hyde Park, witnessed a Festival of Empire. Huge military tattoos, re-enactments of famous imperial battles, and other entertainments all served to stress the idea of a powerful, united empire. The culmination of these celebrations occurred in 1924–25 at Wembley, North London, where the centrepiece of the exhibition was the new Empire Stadium. King George V opened the exhibition in a lavish ceremony involving representatives from across the far-flung Empire. Large crowds attended— as they did at the Glasgow Festival of Empire in 1938—proving that the appeal of Empire was much greater than has sometimes been suggested.

During the 1920s and 1930s, when the British Empire was actually still expanding, the British

31 **The front page of the Soviet satirical magazine** *Krokodil*, **celebrating Yuri Gagarin's achievement as the first human to journey into outer space when his Vostok spacecraft completed an orbit of the Earth on 12 April 1961. The drawing shows all sections of Soviet society cheering Gagarin's feat.**

Рисунок И. СЕМЕНОВА.

Ю. А. ГАГАРИН: — Полет продолжается нормально. Состояние невесомости переношу хорошо.

КРОКОДИЛ

№ 11 (1625)   ГОД ИЗДАНИЯ 39-Й   20 АПРЕЛЯ 1961

32

PRINTED FOR H.M. STATIONERY OFFICE BY EYRE & SPOTTISWOODE L.ᵀᴰ H.M. PRINTERS, LONDON.

32 A typical poster (by H.S. Williamson, 1928) of the kind commissioned by Britain's Empire Marketing Board, showing a grocer's shop—'John Bull & Sons'—selling a multitude of imperial and domestic goods. No explicit references were made in the posters to the potential military advantages of an extended imperial economic market. Instead, the dominant images are of peaceful harmony and an abundance for all, summed up in the shop-window's assertion that 'The Empire is your garden'.

government set up a new department, the Empire Marketing Board (1926–33), to promote British trade and prestige across its imperial holdings. The First World War had accelerated Britain's relative economic decline and the British economy, highly dependent on export markets, was particularly vulnerable when foreign nations imposed tariff barriers to protect their home markets, while remaining at liberty to export their own products to the still largely free-trading home and colonial markets of Britain. Britain's once supreme position as the leading industrial nation was now under threat and many imperial enthusiasts looked to the British Empire overseas for salvation. The work of the Empire Marketing Board was built on the premise that 'trade will follow the flag' ('follow the flag in all your purchases'), and it attempted to consolidate imperialistic ideals and an imperial worldview as part of British popular culture. One distinctive feature of its work was its poster campaigns.

For other nations, too, trade and industrial fairs provided an opportunity to promote national pride and culture. Between 1890 and 1914 Belgium hosted a cluster of fairs and exhibitions reflecting its growing wealth and confidence as an industrial and colonial power: at Antwerp (1894), Brussels (1897), Liège (1905), Brussels (1910) and Ghent (1913). The French revealed themselves to be even more infatuated by the concept. After a hugely successful fair in 1867, Paris hosted exhibitions in 1878, 1889 and 1900. The 1889 centenary of the French Revolution proved to be a particularly spectacular affair, with the completion of the Eiffel Tower. The 1900 exhibition occurred at a time of international rivalries: British and French tensions had recently been high over their imperial competition in Africa, while the Germans had wanted to host the exhibition and so were determined to outshine the French, in which effort they succeeded. Meanwhile, the United States and Japan put on strong displays, causing a certain amount of French national introspection. The Paris exhibition of 1925 served as a moment of rehabilitation, giving Soviet Russia the chance to make its presence felt on the international stage. In the depths of economic depression in 1931, France seized the moment once again to promote its empire, holding a successful 'Exposition Coloniale Internationale', in which French culture and its civilising influence on the globe were the main themes.

The most politically volatile of the Parisian exhibitions occurred in 1937. It was already clear that Nazi Germany and the Soviet Union were planning to use the occasion for maximum competitive propaganda effect. Albert Speer designed an imposing German pavilion, with two 23-foot statues representing family and comradeship topped by an enormous German eagle with the swastika in its claws. Visitors were able to view Leni Riefenstahl's famous film of Nazi triumphalism, *Triumph of the Will* (1935; *see also below*). The Soviet Union, meanwhile, erected an equally imposing pavilion, topped by two workers brandishing the hammer-and-sickle. The 1937 exhibition was dominated by these structures, huge and deliberately symbolic, which confronted each other across the mall, pitting fascist ideology against communism. Politics manifested itself

33 **Communism versus Nazism, in the confrontation of the pavilions at the Paris Exhibition of 1937. Albert Speer, designer of the German pavilion (*left*), later revealed that he had secretly seen drawings of the Soviet pavilion, and he had designed the German pavilion to represent a bulwark against communism.**

elsewhere, too. Other exhibits at the exhibition included Picasso's anti-war painting *Guernica* (1937), lamenting the victims of German aerial bombing in the Spanish Civil War.

Two years later, the British pulled out all the stops for a massive propaganda effort at the New York World's Fair of 1939. Aiming to win US sympathy on the eve of the Second World War, the British sought to stress the common heritage of the British and American people. (The king and queen travelled to the United States on a related visit.)

Postwar, with the emergence of the Cold War divide, political rivalries continued. At the 1959 American National Exhibition held in Moscow and sponsored by the US government, Vice President Nixon became embroiled with Soviet leader Nikita Khrushchev in their infamous 'kitchen debate' in which each of the leaders extolled the virtues of their respective economic and political systems in a model American kitchen. The exhibition was clearly viewed by the administration of President Eisenhower as an important propaganda tool, a form of cultural diplomacy critiquing the Soviet way of life. The Soviet regime, on the other hand, wanted to exploit the event to extol its superiority in the space race. Tass, the Soviet news agency, famously remarked of the US display: 'There is no more truth in showing this as the typical home of the American worker than, say, in showing the

Taj Mahal as the typical home of a Bombay textile worker.' It was all a far cry from any noble ideals that informed the Great Exhibition a century before.

OLYMPIC COMPETITION

International sport, like war, invariably heightens a sense of nationalism, and the Olympic Games pits more nations against one another than any other event. The modern Games coincided with the rise of mass entertainment and above all a mass sporting culture, with which came an increase in the number of public spaces and structures for the expression of mass emotion and spectacle— potentially fertile territories for propaganda.

The first modern Games were held in Athens in 1896. They were largely the brainchild of a Frenchman, Baron Pierre de Coubertin, who certainly had a political agenda in mind. He saw the revival of the ancient Olympics as a way of promoting peace among nations through a friendly sports competition. His ideas reflected the coming together of a number of 19th-century ideals, notably the liberal belief in free and unbridled discourse among nations, which, it was hoped, would promote peace, happiness and progress worldwide; and the development of 'muscular Christianity', which encouraged the idea of 'manly' godliness whereby 'Christian gentlemen' sought

34 **A collage of images from Soviet displays for the International Press Exhibition in Cologne (1928). Each country created a pavilion within the exhibition highlighting its innovation in graphic design and mass media output. El Lissitzky's Russian pavilion featured photomontage, film and new construction materials like Plexiglas and cellophane, creating a dynamic and ground-breaking experience of spectacle and propaganda for Stalin's regime.**

34

to improve and test themselves in the pursuit of physical excellence. The Games were consequently full of symbolic import, reflecting the dominant ideals of the Western world at the time.

The first few Olympic Games remain rather hazy affairs. Although competitors were nominally connected with national teams, there was a greater feeling than now of individual effort and competition. By the 1908 London Games, the concept of the national team was beginning to take shape. The Olympics now became an important stage for propaganda, and hence were more highly politicised as nations sought to stress their own virtues. The International Olympic Committee (IOC) and the various national Olympic committees have always denied this combination of sport and politics, but the conjunction of the two is difficult to ignore. The impact of television satellite communications, creating a global mass audience, has served only to increase the event's political and propaganda potential.

In 1920 the Games took place in Antwerp, marking the recovery of Belgium after the devastation of the First World War. But the legacy of war was still strong, for the IOC banned the former wartime Central Powers of Germany, Austria, Hungary and Bulgaria from competing. However, Germany returned in 1928 for the Amsterdam Games. After the Second World War, international politics and the Olympics became even more intimately linked. The 1964 Games were awarded to Tokyo, marking Japan's return to the fold as a rehabilitated nation and showcasing the Japanese economic miracle. This was also the year in which South Africa was banned in response to its

apartheid laws. The next Games, held in Mexico in 1968 and Munich in 1972, were also used as overt propaganda platforms.

Perhaps the most overtly political and propagandist Games in modern times were those held in Berlin in 1936. The Nazi government invested vast sums in them, believing they would provide an excellent test of Nazi racial theories. Meticulously stage-managed in order to maximise their propaganda potential, the Games brought a significant innovation: Dr Carl Diem had the idea of bringing the Olympic torch from Mount Olympus itself. So, in July 1936, 15 Greek maidens, clad in short tunics to evoke the priestesses' robes of Ancient Olympia, gathered at dawn on the plain by Mount Olympus. The rays of the morning sun, reflected off a concave mirror, lit the torch, which was then conveyed by a relay of runners to Berlin. The imagery was unmistakable: Nazi Germany was claiming for itself the legacy of Ancient Greece as the new home of civilisation and defender of Western ideals. The Games were given added propaganda value by Leni Riefenstahl in her extraordinary documentary *Olympia* (1938). Today the Games are best remembered for the performance of African American athlete Jesse Owens, who won four gold medals and almost single-handedly deflated Nazi racial arrogance.

From 1945, the Olympics became a stage for Cold War one-upmanship, though the Soviet Union only joined in as late as 1952, in Helsinki. At times it appeared as though the Games' sole purpose was to pit the United States against the Soviet Bloc, and it was clear that media interest lay mostly in this aspect. In 1956 the conduct of the Melbourne Games was dominated by the Soviet invasion of Hungary, which led to the first boycott in modern Olympic history, when the Dutch, Spanish and Swiss teams refused to take part. The 1968 Olympics, held in Mexico City, were marked by the Black Power salute made by the African American athletes Tommie Smith and John Carlos during their medal ceremony, in order to highlight the problems of racism in US society. As they turned to face their flags and hear the 'Star-Spangled Banner', they each raised a black-gloved fist – and kept it raised until the anthem had finished. Both men, as well as Australian silver medallist Peter Norman, also wore human rights badges on their jackets. This controversial act was one of the most overtly political statements in the history of the modern Olympics, and many believed that it constituted an act of betrayal of both the United States and the Olympic spirit. The official International Olympic Committee website carries an ostensibly bland statement that is open to interpretation: 'Over and above winning medals, the black American athletes made names for themselves by an act of racial protest.'

If 1968 witnessed the most overt political act, then four years later the Munich Games witnessed the most tragic. In 1972 pro-Palestinian terrorists kidnapped members of the Israeli team. Nine Israelis died as a result of the kidnap attempt and a bungled rescue attempt. Cold War tensions reached their nadir in 1980, when the United States led a boycott of the Moscow Games in response to the Soviet invasion of Afghanistan. Sixty-three nations stayed away, including West Germany,

Japan, China and Canada. At the opening ceremony many countries made a propaganda statement about Olympic ideals, by using the Olympic flag instead of their national flag and by performing the Olympic hymn instead of their national anthem during the medals ceremonies.

The tit-for-tat response came in 1984 when much of the Soviet Bloc boycotted the Los Angeles Games. These Games were notable for their showy razzmatazz and promotion of the American way of life; many of the European nations, in particular, complained that the US press and television did not appear to notice that any other nation was taking part. The whole event, with a very high visibility for its corporate sponsors, appeared to be a triumph of the Reagan era's confident capitalism and patriotism. Controversy had still not died down by 1988, when the next Games were held in South Korea, a state much of the communist world did not recognise, though most of its member countries did attend. The Seoul Games sought to reproduce the success of Tokyo in 1964, but the result actually had more in common with the Mexico Games, as pro-democracy activists staged protests, using the media attention to their advantage.

The millennial Games were held in Sydney in September 2000. The choice marked the importance of the Pacific Rim to the world economy and also gave Australia an opportunity to project a new multicultural image. The IOC awarded the 2004 Games to Athens, and in 2001 it voted to hold the 2008 Games in Beijing. The decision offered a propaganda coup for the Chinese government, but

35

35 **African American athletes Tommie Smith and John Carlos subverting the usual Olympic decorum of national pride by performing their Black Power salute at the 1968 Summer Olympics in Mexico City. The salute was one of the most overtly political statements by individual athletes in the modern Games.**

36 **Political solidarity in the Cold War. An English-language publication offers support from the German Democratic Republic (communist East Germany) for the Moscow Olympics (1980), following a boycott of nations initiated by the United States in protest at the Soviet invasion of Afghanistan.**

We Greet the Olympic City of Moscow and its Guests

Manfred Ewald,
President of the German Sports and Gymnastics Union and of the National Olympic Committee of the German Democratic Republic

The flame for the Games of the XXIInd Olympiad of modern times is now burning in Moscow, the capital of the USSR.

This traditional symbol of peace and of the world-embracing Olympic idea calls on the best athletes from throughout the world to vie with each other in peaceful and fair competition. These XXIInd Olympic Games will go down in the annals of the Olympic movement, because it is the first time that the capital of a socialist country plays host to this greatest sports event in the world.

Since it first participated at Olympic Games, the Soviet Union has contributed much to developing the Olympic movement by its striving for détente and peace and by the outstanding performances of its athletes. The noble humanitarian aims of the Olympic movement—to foster peace, understanding, mutual respect and recognition, equality and friendship between the people and nations—is also at the root of the consistent peace policy pursued by the CPSU, the government and the people of the USSR.

It is the aim being pursued when physical culture and sport are developed, in the Soviet Union as much as in all the socialist countries, for the benefit of the whole population.

Therefore, we strongly oppose the dangerous attacks launched by the US Carter Administration in cooperation with the governments of several other countries against the foundations of the International Olympic movement and the Olympic Games. We express our sympathy with all men and women athletes in those countries who wanted to take part in the Moscow Olympics, but were barred from doing so under political pressure from their governments.

We, the members of the GDR Olympic team, as the representatives of the first socialist German state and millions of sports enthusiasts in this country, want do develop and expand friendly contacts with peaceloving athletes the world over.

It is our deep desire in this way to contribute to the safeguarding of peace and the promotion of the Olympic movement.

As in the other participating countries, athletes in the GDR have prepared well for the Olympic events. In fair competition with the world's sporting elite they will contend for victories and medals and do their utmost to represent their socialist homeland well through good sports performances. Good conditions exist for that in the Soviet capital and at all the Olympic venues.

Our Soviet friends have done all they could to ensure the success of the competitions and a pleasant stay in a truly Olympic atmosphere for all the athletes and tourists. We thank them sincerely for this.

In this spirit we greet everyone involved in the work, from the organisers to all working people in Moscow and throughout the fraternal Soviet Union.

We greet the Olympic teams from throughout the world, wishing the Olympic Games success for the benefit of the Olympic movement.

We are certain that the 1980 Olympic Games in Moscow will be a triumph for sport, promote international friendship and decisively contribute to the worldwide striving for détente, understanding and peace.

The participants at the VI. Sports and Gymnastic Festival of the GDR in Leipzig in 1977 formed this living picture in honour of the Olympic city of Moscow in 1980

it also prompted a storm of criticism concerning China's human rights record.

The costs of hosting the Games, with their lavish opening and closing ceremonies, have escalated incrementally. The opening ceremony in particular has become an opportunity for nations to propagandise their historical, political and cultural achievements, and the presentations have generally grown in scale, extravagance and complexity as successive hosts attempt to outshine their predecessors in terms of memorability. The mass choreographed opening ceremony of the Beijing Games reportedly cost $100 million and was watched by an estimated global audience of almost 1 billion people. London could not compete in terms of sheer scale, but instead opened the 2012 Games with a quirky multimedia narrative entitled 'Isles of Wonder', designed by the film director Danny Boyle. The ceremony, described in the British press as a 'love-letter to Britain' and by one newspaper as 'brilliant, breathtaking, bonkers and utterly British', celebrated with exuberance, humour and eccentricity the host nation's history, art and culture.

■ The propaganda of leadership

In the 20th century, the personality cults attached to national leaders were not in themselves new phenomena; but the arrival of the mass media, in conjunction with the rise of communist and fascist states, highlighted them as a means to legitimise regimes. Dictators seeking to alter or transform their nations according to radical ideas have invariably used the mass media and propaganda to create idealised, heroic public images of themselves. Such an approach to leadership has been defined by Max Weber as 'charismatic authority', and the cult of the leader, surpassing any normal level of trust in political leadership, is central to an understanding of the appeal of dictatorships—of both the Right and the Left—and is undoubtedly the most important theme cementing their propaganda together.

Certainly, propaganda plays an important role in the projection of all leader-figures. But at the head of a dictatorship stands a usually charismatic leader embodying the nation's will and aspirations. Italy's Benito Mussolini, a former journalist, was arguably the first fascist dictator to appreciate the value of propaganda and the tools of paramilitary display—uniforms, flags, parades (along with his frenzied balcony speeches)—to create a sense of belonging among his followers. Once he was in power, Italian propaganda depicted *Il Duce* as a protean superman whose powers were unlimited. Mussolini was well aware of the importance of the role and played up to such an image. He despised what he considered to be the effete liberal Italy that had emerged in the late 19th century and longed for the glories of Ancient Rome. In a series of impassioned speeches he offered his countrymen

the possibility of a Third Roman Empire, in which he would perpetuate the glorious tradition of the Roman emperors.

Italian Fascism claimed to be a movement of youth. In fact, it established a multiplicity of organisations for every age group. When the Fascists took office in Italy they immediately reformed the school and university curricula, emphasising Italy's role in world affairs, the importance of strong leadership and the need for discipline and sacrifice. One of the most popular propaganda posters of the time showed Mussolini in a formal Fascist paramilitary uniform. The bombastic pose was struck in countless newsreels and photographs and at national rallies – chin and stomach out, arm outstretched demanding authority from above and obedience from below, the whole summed up in the poster's slogan: 'Believe/Obey/Fight'.

When Adolf Hitler came to power in Germany in 1933 he promised the German people that the Nazi Reich would last a thousand years. A propaganda slogan of the period called upon the nation 'to awake' (*Deutschland Erwache!*). Just as National Socialism needed its enemies, so it also required its heroes. For their concept of the heroic leader the Nazis turned to the German *völkisch* (meaning roughly 'racial') philosophy of 19th-century Romanticism and the notion of the 'leadership principle' (*Führerprinzip*), centred on a mystical figure embodying and guiding the nation's destiny in a similar fashion to *Il Duce*. The leadership principle required a very special personality, who had the will and power to actualise the 'racial state' (*Volkstaat*), a man

37 Benito Mussolini in typical bombastic pose, in a poster of 1938. *Il Duce* is shown in formal Fascist Party paramilitary uniform addressing a mass rally, with the Party symbols—the *fasces* (rods bound with an axe-head)—visible on either side of him. Official posters like this, together with countless propaganda news-reels and photographs, embodied the Fascists' image of themselves. The movement's demand is expressed in the Italian formula 'Believe/Obey/Fight'.

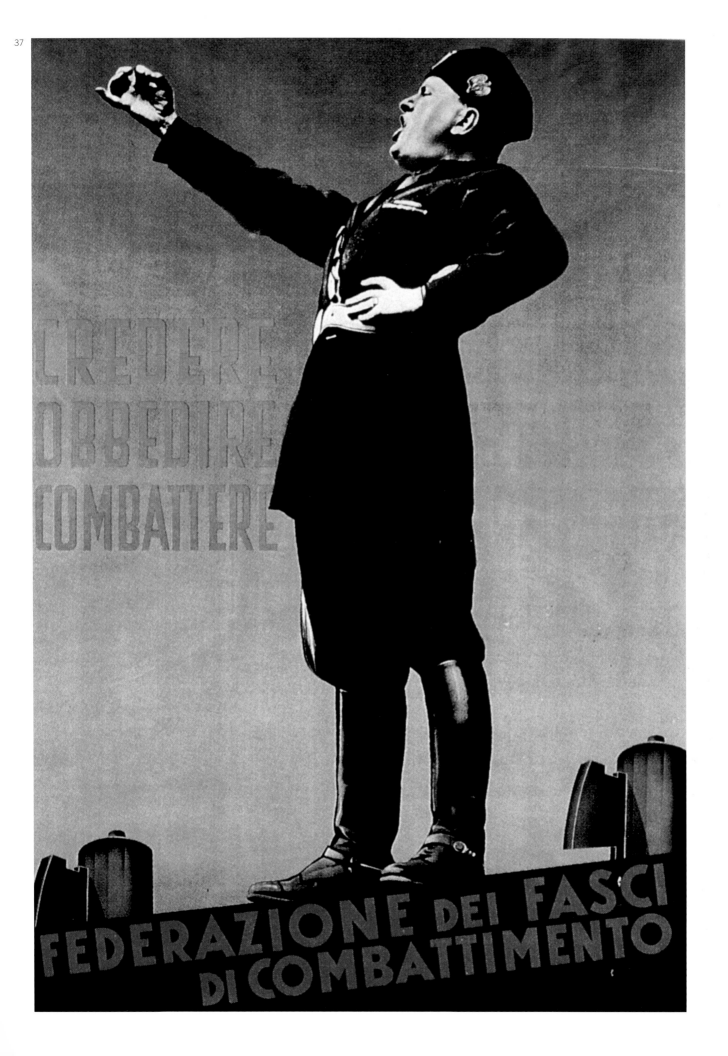

of destiny—resolute, dynamic and radical—who would destroy the old privileged and class-ridden society and replace it with the ethnically pure and socially harmonious 'national community' (*Volksgemeinschaft*). Hitler's tenure on absolute power was therefore justified not so much by virtue of his constitutional position as chancellor and head of state but more in charismatic terms as *Führer* of the German *Volk*—not a state, but a German nation as a racially determined entity. As the custodian of the nation's will, Hitler's authority eschewed constitutional limitations. The '*Heil Hitler!*' greeting would subsequently replace, by law, the traditional greeting *Guten Tag!* Adults were made to greet each other with the new acclamation, and children in school used it at the start of each new lesson. It was accompanied by the familiar, stiff right-arm salute.

In 1935, Leni Riefenstahl's documentary film *Triumph of the Will* (*Triumph des Willens*), based on the previous year's Nazi Party rally at Nuremberg, projected the image of the strong modern leader to a German audience that had come to associate the country's previous weak Weimar Republic and the humiliating terms of 1919's Treaty of Versailles with a feeling of national ignominy. She portrayed Hitler as a statesman of genius, who had single-handedly rebuilt the nation and staunchly defended Germany's territorial rights. Nazi Party rallies were carefully staged theatrical events, devised to create the impression of national unity. This also explains why the Nazis repeatedly staged 'national moments' (*Stunden der Nation*), when Hitler's speeches would be broadcast simultaneously throughout the Reich on the cheap 'people's radios' (*Volksempfänger*) that were affordable to all citizens. On such occasions life would come to a standstill, demonstrating the sense of national community. The idea was that the individual participant in the ritual, moved by Hitler's rhetoric and swayed by the crowd, would undergo a metamorphosis, turning—in Propaganda Minister Goebbels' famous phrase— 'from a little worm into part of a large dragon'.

Like Italian Fascism, National Socialism demanded authority from above and obedience from below. A famous poster of the period showed Hitler in Renaissance pose above the propaganda slogan 'One People, One Nation, One Leader!' ('*Ein Volk, ein Reich, ein Führer!*'). Other slogans

38 The cover of *Jugend um Hitler* ('Youth around Hitler', 1934) with a montage by the photographer Heinrich Hoffmann, showing a clutch of young Aryan girls idolising Hitler. One section of the population that proved particularly receptive to the notion of a 'national community' was German youth. From June 1933 all youth organisations were replaced by the Hitler Youth (*Hitlerjugend*) and its female counterpart, the League of German Girls (*Bund deutscher Mädel*).

39 Leader, citizens and country fuse into one in this portrait of Hitler with the slogan that translates as 'One People, One Nation, One Leader'. In cultivating the *Führer* cult, the depiction of Hitler was both essential and sensitive. Photographs of Hitler appeared regularly and provided day-to-day contact between leader and people; but artists, film-makers, poets and musicians were commissioned to depict Hitler in a more stylised fashion, illustrating different aspects of the *Führer*'s work, his moods and his 'genius', in accordance with official Nazi art policy.

Ein Volk, ein Reich, ein Führer!

39

40

40 Stalin mythologised. Here, a young Stalin is presented as a cultured figure keenly absorbing his heritage. He is reading the Georgian national poet, Shota Rustaveli (1172–1216).

41 Stalin mythologised again, this time in more typical fashion, in a poster whose slogan proclaims: 'Long Live the Victorious Nation! Long Live Our Dear Stalin'. The symbol of the Communist Party shines with a sun-like radiance, while a carefully selected, diverse group of types represent 'the people'. Centrally, the god-like figure of Stalin rises high above his people, reflecting the culmination of his dictatorial infallibility following the Soviet Union's victory over Nazism in the 'Great Patriotic War'.

included: 'The Hand that Guides the Reich', 'Youth Serves the *Führer*' and 'Hitler is Victory'. The creation of the *Führer*-myth turned Hitler into the most vital legitimising force within the regime, and in so doing bestowed upon him the halo of infallibility.

Joseph Stalin's infallibility took rather longer to cultivate within the Soviet Union. When Lenin died in January 1924 it was widely believed that Leon Trotsky would take over as leader, but a complex power struggle developed from which Stalin finally emerged as undisputed leader by 1929. One could say that creation of the image began when—to use his real, Georgian name—Joseph Djugashvili took the name 'Stalin', meaning 'man of steel', some time after joining the Bolsheviks in 1904. But the Stalin cult is generally thought to have taken off in a significant way on the occasion of his 50th birthday in December 1929, when Soviet cities were decorated with flags, portraits, banners, balloons and so forth, and tributes were widely paid to the rapidly emerging 'leader of the international proletariat'. As the first statues of him began to be commissioned, the new slogans became 'Stalin is the Lenin of Today' and 'Stalin, Man of Steel'.

Stalinist policies included the fostering of 'socialism in one country', rapid industrialisation, a centralised state, the collectivisation of agriculture, and the subordination of interests of other communist parties to those of the Soviet Party. Stalin insisted that rapid industrialisation was needed because the country was economically backward in comparison with others, and that it was needed in order to challenge internal and external enemies of communism. And industrial transformation was the overriding aim of the series of Five-Year Plans. The first (1928–32) concentrated on heavy industry as did the second (1933–37), which also provided for increases in consumer goods. Realising (and surpassing) production targets became as much a psychological stimulus, a promise of better things to come, as an opportunity to show solidarity with the Party and its leader. Propaganda eulogising the achievements of the regime had an important function in mobilising enthusiasm and pride in the modernisation of Russia. Posters in particular had a significant role to play, carrying exhortations to workers: 'Work, build, and no complaining', 'Let's storm the production targets!', or—in reference to the prize-winning and target-exceeding miner Aleksei Stakhanov—'Long Live the Stalinist Order of Heroes and Stakhanovites!' In the arts, 'Socialist Realism', supposed to serve political imperatives, became the order of the day. Heroic, optimistic images intended to mirror everyday life were a feature of Soviet art in the 1930s and part of the wider cultural revolution that Stalin forced though as an important corollary of economic changes. Ritual gratitude was often in evidence ('Thanks to the Party, Thanks to Dear Stalin for a Happy, Joyful Childhood'). It should always be remembered that the propaganda was supplemented with a large dose of terror and coercion.

СЛАВА НАРОДУ-ПОБЕДИТЕЛЮ!
СЛАВА РОДНОМУ Сталину!

In 1936, in the midst of the purges that constituted the so-called 'Great Terror', a new Soviet constitution was introduced, which gave the illusion of being more democratic. While Karl Marx's 'dictatorship of the proletariat' remained enshrined in it, in practice Stalin now assumed more power than Lenin had ever had. Thus, although Stalin still needed the memory of Lenin to provide ideological legitimacy for his actions, the cult of personality was such that he could now rewrite Soviet history in his own image.

It was, however, only during and after the Second World War—in Soviet parlance, the Great Patriotic War—that Stalin's image displaced that of Lenin, the 'Father of the Revolution'. To increase popular enthusiasm for the war, Stalin reshaped his domestic policies to heighten the patriotic spirit. Nationalistic slogans and appeals for patriotic unity replaced much of the communist rhetoric in official pronouncements and the mass media ('Stalin in the Kremlin Cares for Each of Us', 1940). The endurance of the cities of Leningrad and Stalingrad became physical embodiments of Stalin's will to resist—and thus propaganda gifts reinforcing the Soviet Union's moral right to victory. Stalin was able to take credit for the defeat of Nazism and the emergence of the Soviet Union as a 'superpower' with an unprecedented empire in Eastern Europe. Stalin's 70th-birthday celebrations in December 1949 were the high point of his cult, the culmination of dictatorial infallibility.

The other extraordinary communist leader of the 20th century, and the focus of his own personality cult, was China's Mao Zedong (Mao Tse Tung), commonly referred to as Chairman Mao. In 1949 Mao finally won China's long civil war to establish the People's Republic of China, which, among other things, maintained direct control over the mass media and the educational system. He understood the importance of propaganda and put considerable effort into disseminating communist ideology. The Party used a wide range of propaganda techniques—including mass meetings, posters, musical compositions and theatre—to communicate an easily understandable message that became closely identified with the leader. A personality cult around Mao, 'the Great Helmsman', soon followed. Large quantities of politicised art circulated, with Mao at the centre. Numerous posters, badges and musical works referenced Mao in the phrase 'Chairman Mao is the red sun in our hearts' and a 'Saviour of the people'.

By 1960 the country was in the grips of a disastrous famine, a consequence of the policies of the so-called 'Great Leap Forward' and partly a result of Mao's proclivity for believing his own propaganda. After being briefly sidelined, Mao re-launched himself in the mid-1960s by reaching out first to the army and then to China's youth with an anthology of his writings, *Quotations from Chairman Mao* (better known as the *Little Red Book*). Party members were encouraged to carry a copy with them, and indeed possession became almost mandatory as a criterion for membership. Posters of Madame Mao (Jiang Quing) holding the *Little Red Book* carried slogans such as: 'The invincible thoughts of Mao Zedong illuminate the stages of revolutionary art!' The *Little Red Book* helped fuel the radical ideological fervour of Mao's

42 **Mao mythologised. A highly romanticised painting shows the young Mao Zedong, prophet-like, in 1921, kindling the flames of revolution in Anyuan.**

Chairman Mao Tse-tung Goes to Anyuan

In autumn 1921, our great teacher Chairman Mao went to Anyuan and personally kindled the flames of revolution there.

A collective work by students of Peking universities and colleges. Painted by Liu Chun-hua and others.

'Cultural Revolution', which was unleashed in 1966 and was marked by successive waves of violence and propaganda.

This was, however, the first Chinese government successfully to make use of modern mass-propaganda techniques, adapting them to the circumstances of a nation that had a largely rural and illiterate population. Mao set up a state propaganda apparatus that used the mass media of the press, radio and film together with group meetings (in which a very precise form of language grew in importance) to transmit the leadership's line. During this period Mao's personality cult grew to immense proportions, and over the years his image became ubiquitous—displayed in homes, offices, schools, shops and public spaces. There was an interesting exception: his image never appeared on Chinese banknotes, which preferred, instead, to portray China's minorities. In 1968 a poster encouraged the people to 'respectfully wish Chairman Mao eternal life'. It was not to be; but by the time of Mao's death in 1976, his significance as a propagandist was being felt far beyond China.

An interesting spin-off was the personality cult of North Korea's founding leader, Kim Il-Sung. Although based on the ideas of Marx and Lenin, North Korean ideology and propaganda parted company with the rest of the communist bloc and became an idiosyncratic projection of the 'Great Leader' and 'Sun of the Nation' Kim. He acquired the usual trappings of the personality cult (massive statues, portraits, coins, stamps and so forth) while establishing his own version of Marxist Leninism known as *Juche*, which emphasised the importance of the leader-figure—to the extent that he established a ruling dynasty, with power passing to his son and then to his grandson. Just as the ruling family has stayed the same, the propaganda disseminating the unquestioning cult of the leader has remained largely unchanged.

The propaganda of personality cults may loom large in totalitarian states, where leaders have sought to impose revolutionary ideas and change on a nation. But leader-figures can assume extraordinary and charismatic impact in the history of democratic nations too. One only has to think of Winston Churchill's wartime premiership or the legacy of President Kennedy, revealingly referred to simply by his initials JFK (his hold on the American imagination encapsulated in such phrases such as 'Ask not what your country can do for you; ask what you can do for your country.'), or Nelson Mandela's reconciling leadership in post-apartheid South Africa. More recently, there was also the extraordinary public outpouring of affection for Elizabeth II during her Diamond Jubilee in 2012.

Churchill was a consummate propagandist and notable wordsmith, but he is said to have preferred deeds to words. After the resignation of Neville Chamberlain as prime minister in the spring of 1940, Churchill rallied the British nation with his leadership and particularly the radio broadcasts of his speeches, which expressed the defiant spirit of the nation following the fall of France in June 1940: 'We will fight them on the beaches; we will fight them in the fields and on the landing grounds, and we will never surrender.' The war was Churchill's stage, and it was a case of 'cometh the hour cometh the man'; as war drew to a close, he was unceremoniously voted out of office, suggesting the

Mao set up a state propaganda apparatus that used the mass media of the press, radio and film together with group meetings to transmit the leadership's line.

43

43 Mao mythologised again. A Chairman Mao badge was an icon of his cult of personality. Wearing these badges, which were ubiquitous in China at the time of Mao, was a visible means of political and ideological identification with the leader.

limitations of leader-figures in democracies. Looking back on the war period at the end of his life, he commented that 'the British people were the lion … I just provided the roar'. However, in 1965 he received the rare honour of a state funeral, accompanied by the kind of extraordinary pomp and ceremony normally only bestowed upon a British monarch. (JFK's grave is lit with an 'eternal flame'—funerals and burials of leaders provide yet other examples of propaganda associated with nationhood.)

The death in 2013 of President Hugo Chavez of Venezuela prompted an outpouring of grief

from his supporters. As mass crowds queued to pay their last respects, it was announced that his body would be embalmed and put on permanent display 'like Lenin and Mao Zedong'. Chavez famously had a Twitter account with more than 3 million followers, which he claimed he used for 'revolutionary purposes' in that it allowed the people to bypass bureaucracy and gain direct access to their president.

Nelson Mandela offers a particularly interesting example of a leader-figure, because here is someone who was imprisoned in his own country (as was Chavez) as a militant activist, supporting an armed struggle, yet who on his release became a symbol of reconciliation and peace in a new democratic nation. As we have mentioned, creating a sense of 'the nation' and a national identity are important goals of the state, even if not always conscious or deliberate ones. For post-apartheid South Africa the challenge was to transform its identity from a long colonial history and from white-minority rule. Such a transfer of power can be fraught where the previous rulers have pursued a policy of divide and rule. But, after his release (1990) and his election as president of a new multiracial South Africa (1994), Mandela's demeanour and stature—together with the priority he gave to reconciliation—did much to foster what he called 'the rainbow nation'. In 2009, *Newsweek* summed up the power of his image: 'Mandela rightly occupies an untouched place in

the South African imagination. He's the national liberator, the saviour, its Washington and Lincoln rolled into one.' A figure of global significance, his birthday (18 July) became 'Mandela Day' in November 2009, after a vote by the United Nations General Assembly, celebrating his contribution to world freedom.

From Mussolini to Mandela clearly covers a lot of ground. But be they dictators of the Right or Left, or wartime democratic leaders or the father of a new nation, all have exerted influence over the mass media in order to disseminate their propaganda and project their images. This is not *necessarily* a bad thing. But, taken together, these examples are testament to the ways in which the modern state can become synonymous with the magnification of its leader's image.

44

44 **Hero worship, Chinese style.** Young girls in Canton brandish copies of the *Quotations from Chairman Mao* in front of a poster of Mao (18 January 1967). Published from 1964 to 1976, the *Quotations* contained selected statements from Mao's speeches and writings, and they were widely distributed during the Cultural Revolution. The most popular versions were printed in small sizes that could be easily carried and were bound in bright red covers, begetting the informal name the *Little Red Book*. It became one of the most printed books in history.

'Your country needs you'

The propaganda of war

3

ONE OF THE MOST significant lessons emerging from the experience of war in the 20th century was that public attitudes could no longer be ignored by governments. Unlike previous conflicts, the First World War (1914–18) was a 'total war', the first of its kind, in which whole nations and not just their armed forces were locked together in struggle. Although the American Revolutionary War and Napoleonic Wars had foreshadowed this development through their levels of popular involvement, the world wars of the 20th century were markedly different.

Before 1900, the impact of the new media—newspapers and photography—in the conduct of war propaganda was comparatively small. The Crimean War (1853–56), where British, French and Turkish forces fought the Russians, was, though, a sign of things to come. Here, newspaper reports of living conditions from the theatre of war—relayed by steamship and telegraph—caused a scandal in London, particularly those sent to the *Times* by the first person ever to be called a 'war correspondent', William Howard Russell. His criticisms led the *Times* to denounce the government of Lord Aberdeen, playing a part in its fall, and encouraged a climate of reform after the war. This and other demonstrations of the power of the press forced subsequent British governments to take the media and war reporting seriously. Russell's account of the charge of the British light cavalry brigade at the Battle of Balaclava in 1854 inspired the poet Tennyson to write 'The Charge of the Light Brigade'. While appalled at the losses in the charge, Tennyson, like Russell, stressed the heroism and sense of duty of the men. His poem

45 War reporting. A Japanese print depicts the Sino-Japanese War (1894–95) with the slogan 'Long Live the Great Japanese Empire!' In this scene of the attack on Songhwan, near Seoul, journalists can be seen hiding among the trees. Artistic representations of warfare remained popular in Japan.

became a cornerstone of propaganda, stressing an ethic of self-sacrifice, and it was recited in British schoolrooms for the next hundred years.

Whereas previous British colonial wars had been covered by a handful of reporters, the Anglo–Boer War (1899–1902) involved some two-hundred journalists at its height. The war witnessed new forms of press accreditation and censorship, which laid the foundations for the much greater control of the media during the 20th-century conflicts. In general, the British press was willing to cooperate with the authorities, and the recently founded daily

newspapers and illustrated weekly newspapers in particular benefited from the war. Developments such as the creation, in 1896, of Britain's first mass-circulation newspaper (the *Daily Mail*), the inauguration of the imperial penny post in 1898, and the establishment by 1899 of a worldwide British telegraph cable system meant that this war was reported—and propagandised—in new ways. Contributing to those was new technology, in the shape of lightweight cameras and an early form of the cine-camera—the 'Biograph'.

Both the First and Second world wars served to increase the level of popular interest and participation in the affairs of state. The gap between the soldier at the Front and civilian at home narrowed substantially, in that the entire resources of the state—military, economic and psychological—had to be mobilised to the full. This was the logic of the new circumstances of 'total war'. The statistics alone are telling. In the First World War, where, for

example, civilians had their first experience of aerial bombing, 14 per cent of war deaths were civilians. This increased to a massive 67 per cent in the Second World War (not including the Holocaust).

■ The First World War

For the British people, as for the people of other nations, the First World War was therefore a matter for every member of the population. In Britain, the introduction of conscription, the recruitment of women into the munitions factories and the Land Army, Zeppelin and bomber raids over England and the attempts of German submarines to starve Britain into submission—these were all new, often traumatic, experiences for a nation learning the rules of modern warfare against a powerful European enemy. In such a struggle, civilian morale came to be recognised as a significant military

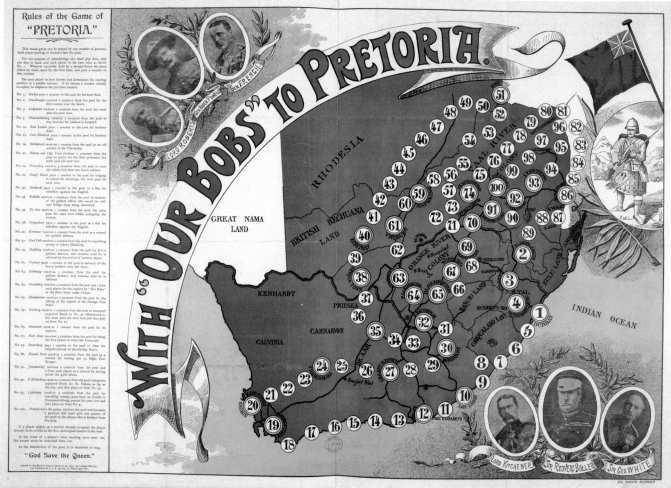

46 'With "Our Bobs" to Pretoria', a single-sheet game (1900) to accompany the Second Anglo-Boer War. It was a simple jingoistic game, which encouraged British children to identify with heroic British military leaders and their victories over the Boers.

47 War Secretary Lord Kitchener's unavoidable glare, in the first incarnation (5 September 1914) of the most famous recruitment image of the war. Its stark simplicity makes it all the more effective, and it inspired countless imitations. By the time conscription was introduced in Britain in 1916, this image had helped to recruit over 1 million men.

47

factor and propaganda began to emerge as the principal instrument of control over public opinion and an essential weapon in the national arsenal.

The war still holds a unique position as the benchmark against which the heroism, brutality and futility of modern industrialised warfare has come to be measured. Once it began, the belligerents rapidly began publishing accounts of how it had been caused. They did so because the issue of responsibility was the key element in the propaganda battle. Propaganda was directed towards the home population to support the war, towards neutral countries as a means of influence, and towards the enemy as a weapon.

The armies of continental Europe were made up of conscripts, and they really had little choice about going to war. In 1914 the British Army, by contrast, was much smaller and made up of professionals (the original British Expeditionary Force) and then volunteers; and the government was not sufficiently confident to introduce conscription to prosecute the war. The British authorities placed immense reliance, therefore, on propaganda to justify the war to the people, to help promote recruitment

into the armed forces and to convince the population that their sacrifices would be rewarded. Immediately following the declaration of war on 4 August 1914, the British government, like all the belligerents, claimed that its actions were just, that it would be a short war and would be all over by Christmas.

One of the most enduring images of the war—much copied and parodied since—remains the distinctive recruitment poster of Lord Kitchener's heavily moustachioed face and intimidating finger imploring the British population that 'Your Country Needs YOU'. Kitchener had been appointed War Minister on 5 August 1914 and was already a war hero among the public for his military exploits in the Sudan. The poster, deriving from a magazine cover, came to be regarded as a symbol of the national resolve and will to win; its message testified to the realisation of what would be required by way of human resources in an age of mass industrial warfare. The official Parliamentary recruiting campaign for Kitchener's 'New Armies' was colossally successful, and by January 1915 about a million men had enlisted.

The First World War was the first war in which the mass media played a significant part in disseminating news from the Fighting Front to the Home Front, as well as the first war to target *systematically* produced government propaganda at the general public. In order to encourage all citizens to contribute to the war effort, both the Home and Fighting fronts needed to be persuaded of the importance of their collective effort to securing ultimate victory.

Britain, like all the belligerents, was therefore compelled to recognise that it had to justify the righteousness of its cause. Tracing this evolution is particularly interesting, because it was conducted by a democracy still coming to terms with the idea that ordinary people, and not simply elites, were demanding a voice in the political process as *quid pro quo* for their participation in the war effort. Until 1918, no women could vote, and neither could men who were not property-owners, a category including vast numbers of soldiers. Out of these tensions, Britain evolved an extraordinary approach to the conduct of propaganda that would help secure ultimate victory but would leave British public opinion with a bitter after-taste in the period following the peace settlements.

It is surprising to discover, therefore, that Britain's first steps in setting up its propaganda machinery were tentative and uncertain. There is little evidence, for example, that there was any pre-war planning of how propaganda should be organised. In Germany, on the other hand, the entry of the civil government into the field of propaganda began in the 19th century under Otto von Bismarck's chancellorship, with the establishment of the Press Office (*Presseamt*),

an early example of an official bureau set up to monitor news coverage and to release information favourable to the government. Owing to extensive pre-war preparations, Germany, unlike Britain, was not caught by surprise at the outbreak of hostilities and responded with extraordinary vigour. Posters, pamphlets, leaflets and other forms of pro-German propaganda poured out from Berlin to Europe and the rest of the world—notably the United States.

Given the social tensions that existed in Britain in the years leading up to 1914—a mixture of industrial unrest, an Irish crisis, Suffragette militancy and constitutional troubles—one of the first tasks of the British government was to justify to an apparently divided nation the efficacy of the government's war aims. The German invasion of neutral Belgium was the pretext for an anti-German campaign that rapidly mobilised widespread support among all sections of the population. Belgium was depicted as a defenceless child or as a woman ravaged by a brutal Prussian militarism (*see also* 'The Hun and the Prussian bully' in Chapter 5). The violation of Belgian neutrality represented a moral issue of the kind to which British liberalism would habitually respond. The war now became a crusade.

The emotional appeal of a violated Belgium was expressed in many forms. Stereotypes deeply embedded in national sentiment were invoked to justify Britain's entry into the war and British propaganda posters often employed the religious symbolism of St George slaying the (German) dragon. One of the most popular songs of 1914 was 'Three Cheers for Little Belgium' (sung by Violet Lorraine). A hardline German policy against those

48 **A British recruiting poster (1914), which traded on the surge of popular pro-Belgian feeling at the time. Propaganda posters—often showing images of women and children needing protection—played a key role in the campaigns to persuade men to sign up as soldiers. By the end of August 1914, around 30,000 British men were enlisting every day.**

Belgian civilians deemed to be adopting guerrilla tactics delivered a propaganda coup to the Allies, and the popular press needed no encouragement from the government to publish stories of German atrocities.

When war broke out, the relationship between the government and the press continued along the lines set out in the 1906 Commission of Imperial Defence. It was a relationship of voluntary liaison, whereby the press committed itself to self-censorship. In 1914, Winston Churchill, responsible for such matters, announced the formation of the Press Bureau, which essentially performed the negative function of providing 'trustworthy information' supplied by the War Office. Then in April 1915, six journalists were allowed to France to report the war and syndicate their stories back to Fleet Street. They were, however, denied the opportunity to gather news from the Front, and as a result sent back optimistic reports of British and French victories that came straight from military GHQ. This rebounded on the government when the *Times* published reports of the first Allied defeats in 1915—which clearly shocked the people (as did the 'great shells scandal' over insufficient munitions, in May 1915).

By 1916, with no easy victory in sight, the government started to prepare for a long war and for the strengthening of morale. Increasingly it began to rely on censorship and the provisions of the Defence of the Realm Act (DORA), introduced in August 1914 and supplemented several times thereafter (*see also* Chapter 1). By the terms of DORA, any newspaper publishing unauthorised news, or speculating about future strategy, ran

the risk of prosecution. It proved a formidable weapon, later memorably described by historian A.J.P. Taylor as an 'elderly lady, the symbol of restriction'.

Like Britain, Germany on the eve of war was beset by numerous internal tensions. When war was declared, a 'State of Siege' was announced, placing the military hierarchy in charge of the country, and the normally competing social and political groupings resolved to work for victory by means of a political truce (*Burgfrieden*). This proved a fruitful theme in German propaganda. The belief that the war was foisted upon Germany as a result of enemy encirclement—principally in the shape of the Franco-Russian Entente—persuaded all sections of the community to put aside their differences. However, maintaining the *Burgfrieden* depended on a swift victory. As the conflict dragged on, tensions resurfaced. Eventually the German Imperial authorities' failure to respond to genuine grievances and demands for political reform stretched the political truce beyond bearable limits and, by the end of 1917, it had lost its credibility as a unifying theme.

At the start of the war most countries had only embryonic propaganda organisations. Institutions developed piecemeal, beginning as local initiatives that were later centralised as the war progressed. In Germany, the High Command (*Oberste Heeresleitung*, or OHL) established a Supreme Censorship Office (*Oberzensurstelle*) and the War Press Office (*Kreigspresseamt*) to facilitate cooperation between the military and civilian authorities and to control the flow of information as tightly as possible. In Britain, two organisations were set up.

> The British campaign was almost invisible, deliberately targeting American elite opinion ... in contrast to the strident and public German campaign.

At the Foreign Office, a News Department had been established shortly after the outbreak of war to respond to the increased demand for war news from Allied and neutral correspondents in London. The second organisation was the Neutral Press Committee (NPC), formed under the aegis of the Home Office in connection with the Press Bureau, the government's principal wartime censorship organisation.

Having set up the machinery to deal with foreign opinion there was an even greater need to convince the British public, the Empire and neutral countries (especially the United States) of the justice of the British case. The Cabinet was particularly alarmed at the virulence of the German propaganda campaign in the United States, and it became apparent that immediate counter-measures were urgently required. As a result, the War Propaganda Bureau (known as Wellington House) was established under the leadership of Charles Masterman, and it operated as Britain's principal propaganda department for the initial two-and-a-half years of the war. Masterman has been described as 'one of the inventors of twentieth-century propaganda'. And he was arguably the most important government propagandist in Britain during the war, although lords Beaverbrook and Rothermere would later take much of the credit.

Masterman's brief at the Bureau was to put Britain's case for entering the war and to justify wartime policies to neutral countries and to the Dominions (of Canada, South Africa, Australia and New Zealand) that were fighting alongside Britain. There was, however, neither precedent nor blueprint for such an experiment, yet Masterman distinguished himself by the speed with which he addressed the task and the manner in which he formulated general principles for his work, which largely endured until the end of the war. They were, in essence: the need for secrecy in order to disguise the source of the propaganda; that propaganda should be based on accurate information and measured argument; and that propaganda should be directed towards opinion-makers rather than at the masses. With the help of some of the greatest writers of the day—including J.M. Barrie, Arnold Bennett, G.K. Chesterton, Arthur Conan Doyle, John Galsworthy, Thomas Hardy, John Masefield, Gilbert Murray, G.M. Trevelyan, H.G. Wells and Rudyard Kipling—Masterman set about winning the hearts and minds of neutral opinion, particularly in the United States, the chief neutral target of Allied propaganda. The British campaign was almost invisible, deliberately targeting American elite opinion (where the British were able to exploit their common language), in contrast to the strident and public German campaign. (*See also* 'Grey Propaganda' in Chapter 1.)

Wellington House's American campaign had, in fact, been greatly assisted by an action that had been undertaken before a shot had been fired. This was the cutting by the *Telconia* of the direct transatlantic cables from Germany to the United States, all within hours of Britain's ultimatum to Germany expiring on 4 August 1914. The British had recognised the importance of controlling the flow of raw information through the development in the 19th century of a global communications network. Now, all news from Germany, with the exception of wireless reports, had to proceed via London, the cable centre of the world.

One of the most important consequences of this action can be seen in 1917 when the British intercepted, deciphered and leaked to the US press the infamous Zimmermann Telegram—the diplomatic proposal from the German Foreign Minister that Mexico make war on the United States. It stands as a perfect example of intelligence and propaganda working hand in hand and did much to bring the United States into the war. This recognition of the relationship between propaganda, censorship, and intelligence-gathering provided Wellington House with an important advantage in the battle for hearts and minds, in that it meant that the majority of news reaching America was disseminated through British filters, not German. Almost instinctive at the time, such an approach established the blueprint for how a modern state should go about a global propaganda campaign, in a changing world already witnessing a version of what we now call the globalisation of mass communications.

Having formulated a number of operational ground rules, Masterman set about applying them in pursuit of certain key objectives such as the righteousness of Britain's cause, mobilising hatred of the enemy, maintaining the friendship of Allies and, as mentioned, procuring the cooperation of neutrals. Under his direction, Wellington House developed into the most active of all propaganda departments, arranging for the production and dissemination of books, pamphlets and periodicals as well as films, photographs, lantern slides, cartoons and picture postcards. For the United States—and recognising the counter-productive effects of the German approach, which was to bombard US public opinion with pro-German propaganda—Wellington House decided to eschew exhortation in favour of explanation; and, as mentioned, to target American opinion-makers, individuals who were in a position to influence others, to encourage 'a right view of the actions of the British government since the commencement of the war'. In the event, the British campaign did play a significant part in US entry into the war, its scope and success even causing a scandal among American isolationists when it was revealed after the war.

In early 1918 a centralised British propaganda organisation, the Ministry of Information (MOI), was established under Lord Beaverbrook, owner of the *Daily Express*, to look after home and Allied morale through propaganda. An Enemy Propaganda Department was also created at Crewe House in London. It was headed by the founder of modern popular journalism, Lord Northcliffe, owner of the *Daily Mail* and the *Times*.

The basic British approach, known as 'the propaganda of facts', was developed, by which the official propaganda presented events as accurately as possible but with an interpretation that was favourable to British war aims. Beaverbrook considered propaganda to be 'the popular arm of diplomacy' in which 'the *munitions of the mind* [my stress] became not less vital for victory than fleets or armies'.

Upon entering the war in 1917, the United States copied the British policy of stressing facts whenever possible, by establishing its own Committee on Public Information (CPI), known also as the Creel Committee after its director George Creel. CPI activities were intended to 'sell the war to the American people' and included poster campaigns and war-bond drives.

49 **A British leaflet (1917) dropped over German lines. It reports deteriorating conditions in Germany and quotes the Prussian hero Frederick the Great: 'I wouldn't have any soldiers, if they began to think.' Printed in German gothic font, these leaflets were extremely information heavy. This one also announces its mode of delivery:** *durch Luftballon* **('by balloon').**

Contrary to received opinion, the German government had developed, from an early stage in the conflict, a sophisticated notion of propaganda …

Deutsche Zeitungsausschnitte.

Also sagt Friedrich der Große, König von Preußen: „Wenn meine Soldaten anfingen zu denken, bliebe nicht einer in den Reihen."

Der Krieg und die Facharbeiter.

„Es kann noch gar nicht übersehen werden, wie stark der Krieg die Zahl der Ungelernten vergrößert und die Zahl der gelernten Facharbeiter vermindert hat. Die Lehrlingszahl ist namentlich in den Großstädten, aber auch auf dem Lande ganz erstaunlich ersunken."—(Hugo Hillig.) Vorwärts.

Deutschlands Platz am Hasse.

„Stellen wir fest; England hat den Krieg nicht gewollt, bloß nicht verhindert, der Krieg war in England nicht populär (wie in Rußland und Frankreich auch nicht). Trotzdem ist er populär geworden, die ganze Welt hat sich in Haß gegen uns geeinigt bis über den Atlantischen und den Stillen Ozean."—Vorwärts.

Der Fall Daimler im Reichstag.

„Hier handelt es sich nicht um Einzelfälle, sondern um das System des Kapitalismus. Für die Kapitalisten ist der Krieg die beste Verdienstgelegenheit. Dabei ist es nur menschlich, wenn sie den Krieg verlängern, ja ihn hervorrufen wollen. Wo kein Verdienst winkt, hört für sie der Patriotismus auf."—(Abg. Hencke.) Vorwärts.

Das letzte Hemd hergegeben.

„Das Berauner Lokalblatt meldet: Eine Frau, der man die Kriegsleiden ansah, war Kartoffeln einkaufen gewesen. Für Geld war nichts zu haben, ein jeder wollte ein Tauschgeschäft machen. Verzweifelnd kam sie in ein Bauerngut, wo man ihr 15 Kilogramm Erdäpfel gegen ein Hemd anbot. In der Furcht, daß sie auf andere Weise ihren Kindern nichts heimbringen würde, zog sie ihr Hemd aus, um Erdäpfel hierfür einzutauschen."—Arbeiter-Zeitung.

Wahlrechtsfeinde und Annexionisten.

„Die Auflösung des russischen Heeres bot Deutschland die Gelegenheit zu Eroberungen im Osten. Der Imperialismus erhob wieder sein Haupt. Der Einfluß der Alldeutschen erstarkte; die bürgerlichen Parteien begannen von dem Verständigungsfrieden abzurücken; der Reichstag hat seine berühmte Resolution für den Verständigungsfrieden vergessen und er bleibt stumm, wenn Hindenburg den „weichen Frieden" im Westen ablehnt und Hertling die Angliederung Estlands und Livlands an das Reich ankündigt. Und mit dem Imperialismus nach außen erstarkte auch wieder die Reaktion im Innern. Wir haben sie wüten gesehen bei der Niederwerfung des Waffenstreits; wir sehen sie wirken in der Ablehnung des gleichen Wahlrechtes. Es ist derselbe Feind in beiden Fällen: das preußische Volk wird die Wahlrechtsfeinde nur dann bezwingen, wenn es mit den Feinden des Verständigungsfriedens fertig werden kann. Der Gedanke der Demokratie ist unteilbar; Eroberungspolitik nach außen kann sich nicht mit demokratischer Politik im Innern paaren."—Arbeiter-Zeitung.

Bestattung der Toten mit Papierkleidern.

„Aus München wird gemeldet: Eine Ministerialverordnung weist die Stadt- und Gemeindevertretungen an, dahin zu wirken, daß die Toten nur noch mit Kleidern aus Papiergeweben bestattet werden. Die Leichenfrauen werden angewiesen, dort, wo Tote mit Tuchkleidern bestattet werden sollen, diese Kleider an die Gemeindevertretungen abzuliefern, wofür ihnen Kleider aus Papier eingehändigt werden."—Arbeiter-Zeitung.

Prophezeiungen.

„Am 1. Februar 1917, als die folgenschwere Entscheidung des verschärften U-Boot-Krieges gefallen war, hat der damalige Staatssekretär Helfferich in der Budgetkommission des Reichstages gesagt:

„Wie die Dinge liegen, besteht für mich keine Hoffnung, daß Amerika in die Lage kommen wird, überhaupt noch in den Krieg effektiv einzutreten."

Und der Staatssekretär der Marine, Herr v. Capelle, erklärte:

„In militärischer Hinsicht erachte ich die Störung durch den Eintritt der Vereinigten Staaten in den Krieg auf Seite unserer Gegner für Null. Es müssen erst einmal die oft genannten Hunderttausende von Freiwilligen in Amerika gefunden werden. Meinetwegen sollen Hunderttausende von Leuten in den Vereinigten Staaten aufgestellt werden; wie wollen sie nach England herüberkommen? Wenn sie sie wirklich zusammenbrächten — eine bessere Jagdbeute für unsere Unterseeboote auf der hohen See könnten wir uns doch gar nicht vorstellen."—Arbeiter-Zeitung.

51

51 A subversive leaflet distributed by the Indian Independence League to Indian regiments fighting in France, trading on images of colonial cruelty as reasons for them to revolt: 'Drive out these British Devils'.

50 *On les aura* ('We Will Get Them!'), a French poster (1916) designed by Jules Abel Faivre for the Second War Loan, with a slogan coined by General Pétain. The soldier's pose recalls a group sculpted by François Rude on the Arc de Triomphe. The restrained assertion of patriotic faith as symbolised in the searching eyes and the outstretched hand, urging the people on, reflected the nation's mood and shows the potency of posters in mobilising nationalist sentiment.

By comparison, the German approach was controlled largely by the army. Contrary to received opinion, the German government had developed, from an early stage in the conflict, a sophisticated notion of propaganda and its reception by different publics, and had established a national network of monitoring stations to provide feedback on the 'pulse of the people'. But, having constructed the means to read the mood of the people, the German authorities failed to act upon what was discovered. Moreover, as a result of the militarisation of German society, its propaganda was too closely tied to military success.

The British separation of home/Allied propaganda on the one hand and enemy propaganda on the other allowed, for the first time, a distinction between the conduct of propaganda—persuasion, largely at the strategic level—and psychological warfare, conducted largely at the tactical level. Put another way, it distinguished between propaganda, which was directed at civilian audiences, and psychological warfare, directed at enemy soldiers; there was, as yet, no effective means for reaching the German civilian population, located so far from the frontlines. In respect of enemy soldiers, a 'paper war' involved the dropping of millions of leaflets by balloon and aircraft over enemy lines. Pamphlets and trench newspapers, written in all the enemy languages, also featured as ways to play up political and ethnic differences. The

intention was to undermine the will of the enemy to continue to fight, to sow doubts about his government's aims and honesty, sap his morale and ultimately to induce desertion, defection and even insurrection. Pioneered by the British, who referred to it generally as 'political warfare', it was adopted in 1917 by the US Army, using the now more familiar term 'psychological warfare' (*see also* 'Psychological warfare' in Chapter 1).

HOME FRONTS IN THE FIRST WORLD WAR
Once it became clear in 1914 that the war would not be 'over by Christmas', it was imperative to remind people, both at home and in the trenches, of what they were fighting for. The major themes included a call to arms and a request for war loans, and efforts to encourage industrial activity, to explain national policies, to channel emotions such as courage or hatred, to urge the population to conserve resources, and to inform the public of food and fuel substitutes.

The novel concept of the 'Home Front' was actually introduced in Britain in 1915. It was based on government intervention, on a massive scale, in order to restructure the country's economy and society for war, with corresponding sacrifices from the civilian population. The French equivalent was known as the Sacred Union (*Union Sacrée*), an alliance between government, industry and civilians. The German version, introduced in late

1916, was the Hindenburg Programme, named after leading general Paul von Hindenburg. Control of the mass media and propaganda were both seen as essential in maintaining national support. Until almost the end of the war, civilians in the most developed and cohesive belligerent nations—Great Britain, France and Germany—generally supported their respective country's war efforts and continued until the end to fight for final victory.

Once the initial euphoria ('war fever') had subsided, British recruitment posters changed in tone, from the appeal to an individual's honour to 'mobilisation by shame'. Savile Lumley's famous poster of 1915 depicted two young children asking their father about his military prowess after the war: 'Daddy, what did YOU do in the Great War?' The emotional blackmail of using children to shame their elders into fighting was, in fact, employed by most of the belligerents. Women were also assigned the responsibility for ordering men into war. Another notable poster of the time asked women: 'Is your "Best Boy" wearing khaki? If not don't YOU THINK he should be? ... If a young man neglects his duty to his King and Country—time may come when he neglects his duty to YOU!' Perhaps the most well known in this genre is E.V. Kealy's 'Women of Britain Say—"GO!"' (1915).

The need to raise money to pay for the war by means of war bonds (or 'Liberty Bonds' as they were known in the United States) provided one of the most important propaganda themes for posters and for the new medium of film. A recurring, related theme was the portrayal of money (coins and banknotes) as an active force in military engagement, for example: 'Turn Your Silver into Bullets—at the Post Office'. In Britain, one poster (by D.D. Fry, 1915) urged the population to 'Lend Your Five Shillings to Your Country and Help Crush the Germans'. In this poster, the five-shilling piece flattens a German soldier, leaving St George triumphant. In France, a similar poster, designed by Jules Abel Faivre in 1915, depicted a large gold coin with a Gallic cockerel on it crushing a German soldier, with the slogan: 'Deposit Your Gold for France—Gold Fights for Victory'. It

52

52 Slain by St George. In this 1915 poster, distributed by the Parliamentary War Savings Committee, a German soldier is defeated by a five-shilling coin bearing the image of St George, the moral being that money is also a powerful weapon.

53 For the greater good. Pride, honour and trepidation mingle in this well-known British recruitment poster (1915) by E.V. Kealy. It cleverly balances a male patriotic imperative of enlistment with a sense of sacrifice by women and children, urging their menfolk to leave them for the larger cause.

WOMEN OF BRITAIN SAY — "GO!"

Published by the PARLIAMENTARY RECRUITING COMMITTEE, London.   Poster No. 75   Printed by HILL, SIFFKEN & Co. (L.P.A. Ltd.), Grafton Works, London, N.   W. 13741 25 M. 3/15

55

54 **Patriotic payments.** The advent of the tank in 1916 may not have transformed the battlefield, but it caught the British public imagination and, as a piece of expensive new technology, provided more reasons to support the war effort financially.

55 **A US War Bond stamp (1918).** As with the poster of the same design, American propaganda was able to exploit the ready-made monumental symbol of American values that is the Statue of Liberty in the cause of fundraising.

encouraged French citizens to trade their gold for paper money, as gold was needed to pay for foreign imports. The most notorious of all war-bonds posters was 'Put Strength in the Final Blow—Buy War Bonds' (1918), designed by Frank Brangwyn. It is a superb example of the lithographer's approach, and unusual in that it actually portrays the viciousness of war. Brangwyn's brutal image, which shows a British soldier bayoneting a German over a precipice, shocked the National War Savings Committee, who had commissioned it for their autumn 1918 loan drive. Nevertheless, they overcame their initial reservations and published it, agreeing that no image was too extreme in the fight against Germany. The poster captures the message that by investing in war bonds, citizens were making a real contribution to the defeat of the enemy.

All sides, therefore, supplemented their military engagement with propaganda aimed at stimulating national sentiment, maintaining Home Front morale, attempting to win over neutral powers and spreading disenchantment among the enemy population. The British in particular were credited with having carried out these objectives more successfully than any other belligerent state, and indeed skilful propaganda and censorship have been viewed by historians as helping to maintain the wartime consensus despite major tensions.

■ Propaganda between the wars

After the war, in contrast with the war experience itself, a deep mistrust developed on the part of ordinary British citizens , who realised that conditions at the Front had been deliberately obscured by patriotic slogans and by atrocity propaganda based on obscene stereotypes of the enemy. The population also felt cheated that their sacrifices had not resulted in the promised homes and a land 'fit for heroes', as promised by Prime Minister Lloyd George in a speech of November 1918. Propaganda was now associated with lies and falsehood. Even politicians were sensitive to these criticisms and as a result the Ministry of Information was immediately disbanded. The British government regarded propaganda as politically dangerous and even morally unacceptable in peacetime. It was, as one official wrote in the 1920s, 'a good word gone wrong—debauched by the late Lord Northcliffe'. Indeed, the impact of propaganda on political behaviour had such a profound effect that in the Second World War, when the British government attempted to educate the population about the existence of Nazi extermination camps, it was not immediately believed. A similar reaction against what was interpreted as propaganda took root in the United States in the wake of the wartime experience. In 1920 George Creel published an account of his achievements as director of the CPI, and in so doing contributed to the public's growing suspicion of propaganda. This atmosphere created a major obstacle for propagandists attempting to rally American support against fascism in the late 1930s and 1940s.

Fledgling dictators in interwar Europe, however, viewed the propaganda of the First World War in a different light. The perceived success of British propaganda provided the defeated Germans with a fertile source of counter-propaganda aimed at the postwar peace treaties and the ignominy of the Weimar Republic that followed the toppling of the Kaiser. Writing in *Mein Kampf*, Adolf Hitler devoted two chapters to propaganda. By maintaining that the German army had not been defeated in battle but had been forced to submit because of disintegration of morale from within German society, accelerated by skilful British propaganda (*see also* 'Psychological warfare' in Chapter 1), Hitler—like other right-wing politicians and military groups—was providing historical legitimacy for the 'stab-in-the-back' theory. Regardless of the *actual* role played by British (or Soviet) propaganda in helping to bring Germany to its knees, it was generally accepted that Britain's wartime experiment was the ideal blueprint on which other governments might subsequently model their own propaganda apparatus. Convinced of propaganda's essential role in any political movement set on obtaining power, Hitler saw it as a vehicle of political salesmanship in a mass market.

The task of propaganda, Hitler argued, was to bring certain subjects to the attention of the masses. Propaganda should be simple, concentrating on a few essentials, which then had to be repeated many times, with emphasis on such emotional elements as love and hatred. Through the sustained uniformity of its application, propaganda, Hitler concluded, would lead to results 'that are almost beyond our understanding'. The Nazis did not make a distinction in their terminology between agitation and propaganda, unlike the Bolsheviks. In Soviet Russia, agitation was concerned with influencing the masses through ideas and slogans, while propaganda served to spread the ideology of Marxist-Leninism. The distinction dates back to Marxist theorist Georgi

56 A Soviet Agit Prop train. The term 'agitprop' originated from the Soviet *Agit*ation and *Prop*aganda Section of the Central Committee Secretariat of the Communist Party, set up to mobilise public opinion. Armed with public speakers, writers, books, pamphlets, posters, films and even printing presses, these trains travelled to remote areas, circulating Bolshevik propaganda.

56

Plekhanov's famous definition, written in 1892: 'A propagandist presents many ideas to one or a few persons; an agitator presents only one or a few ideas, but presents them to a whole mass of people.' The Nazis, on the other hand, did not regard propaganda as merely an instrument for reaching the Party elite, but rather as a means for the persuasion and indoctrination of all Germans.

■ The Second World War

The outbreak of a new global war would see the belligerent states employing propaganda on a scale that dwarfed that of all previous conflicts. Modern participatory democracies and totalitarian dictatorships had both emerged from the First World War, and, among other things, the outbreak of hostilities in 1939 was a testimony to their mutual incompatibility. There followed a 'total war' even more all-encompassing than the First World War (as the figures for civilian dead mentioned above confirm), reflecting mass societies, ideological and racial conflicts, and an even wider global reach; and once again propaganda was a significant weapon. It was also arguably, from the Allied point of view, a morally justified war, thus invalidating humanitarian 'protest' literature and art.

During the Second World War, authorities appropriated and controlled all forms of communication by means of strict censorship in order to requisition them for propaganda process. In the totalitarian states such as Italy, Germany, Japan and the Soviet Union this posed few problems, as the media—indeed the arts in general—had

become part of the apparatus of the state. In the liberal democracies, on the other hand, the effort proved more problematic. Nevertheless, on the propaganda front Britain appeared to be better prepared than in the First World War. A new Ministry of Information (MOI) had been mooted and planned for some time, and came into being within a matter of days after the declaration of war in 1939. But when set up, it was, to some extent, making up for lost ground. Morale would obviously be a crucial factor in enduring civilian bombing or a war of attrition, and the MOI would have to compete with a German propaganda machine already in existence for several years, under Joseph Goebbels.

The MOI handled propaganda intended for home, Allied and neutral territory, and the Political Warfare Executive (PWE) dealt with enemy territory. The programmes of the BBC earned Britain a powerful reputation for credibility that proved an asset long after the war ended. When Sir John Reith, the former Director General of the BBC, was appointed Minister for Information in 1940, he laid down his two fundamental axioms: that 'news is the shock troops of propaganda' and that propaganda should tell 'the truth, nothing but the truth and, as near as possible, the whole truth'. By contrast, Hitler, as we have seen, believed implicitly in the concept of the 'big lie'; but Reith had an unlikely fellow-traveller in the shape of Goebbels and his view that propaganda should be as accurate as possible.

With the Reich Ministry for Popular Enlightenment and Propaganda (*Reichsministerium für Volksaufklärung und Propaganda*) established in

57 A collection of Allied propaganda leaflets dropped by aeroplane during the Second World War. The conflict saw a massive use of leaflets by all of the major belligerents. To be effective, leaflets needed (and still need) to speak directly, in idiomatic language and readily understandable images.

A LAST APPEAL TO REASON

BY

ADOLF HITLER

Speech before the Reichstag, 19th July, 1940

I have summoned you to this meeting in the midst of our tremendous struggle for the freedom and the future of the German nation. I have done so, firstly, because I considered it imperative to give our own people an insight into the events, unique in history, that lie behind us, secondly, because I wished to express my gratitude to our magnificent soldiers, and thirdly, with the intention of appealing, once more and for the last time, to common sense in general.

If we compare the causes which prompted this historic struggle with the magnitude and the far-reaching effects of military events, we are forced to the conclusion that its general course and the sacrifices it has entailed are out of all proportion to the alleged reasons for its outbreak — unless they were nothing but a pretext for underlying intentions.

The programme of the National-Socialist Movement, in so far as it affected the future development of the Reich's relations with the rest of the world, was simply an attempt to bring about a definite revision of the Treaty of Versailles, though as far as at all possible, this was to be accomplished by peaceful means.

This revision was absolutely essential. The conditions imposed at Versailles were intolerable, not only because of their humiliating discrimination and because the disarmament which they ensured deprived the German nation of all its rights, but far more so because of the consequent destruction of the material existence of one of the great civilized nations in the world, and the proposed annihilation of its future, the utterly senseless accumulation of immense tracts of territory under the domination of a number of States, the theft of all the irreparable foundations of life and indispensable vital necessities from a conquered nation. While this dictate was being drawn up, men of insight even among our foes were uttering warnings about the terrible consequences which the ruthless application of its insane conditions would entail — a proof that even among them the conviction predominated that such a dictate could not possibly be upheld in days to come. Their objections and protests were silenced by the assurance that the statutes of the newly-created League of Nations provided for a revision of these conditions; in fact, the League was supposed to be the competent authority. The hope of revision was thus at no time regarded as presumptuous, but as something natural. Unfortunately, the Geneva institution, as those responsible for Versailles had intended, never looked upon itself as a body competent to undertake any sensible revision, but from the very outset as nothing more than the guarantor of the ruthless enforcement and maintenance of the conditions imposed at Versailles.

All attempts made by democratic Germany to obtain equality for the German people by a revision of the Treaty proved unavailing.

World War Enemies Unscrupulous Victors

It is always in the interests of a conqueror to represent stipulations that are to his advantage as sacrosanct, while the instinct of self-preservation in the vanquished leads him to reacquire the common human rights that he has lost. For him the dictate of an overbearing conqueror had all the less legal force, since he had never been honourably conquered. Owing to a rare misfortune, the German Empire, between 1914 and 1918, lacked good leadership. To this, and to the as yet unenlightened faith and trust placed by the German people in the words of democratic statesmen, our downfall was due.

Hence the Franco-British claim that the Dictate of Versailles was a sort of international, or even a supreme, code of laws, appeared to be nothing more than a piece of insolent arrogance to every honest German, the assumption, however, that British or French statesmen should actually claim to be the guardians of justice, and even of human culture, as mere stupid effrontery. A piece of effrontery that is thrown into a sufficiently glaring light by their own extremely negligible achievements in this direction. For seldom have any countries in the world been ruled with a lesser degree of wisdom, morality and culture than those which are at the moment exposed to the ragings of certain democratic statesmen.

The programme of the National-Socialist Movement, besides freeing the Reich from the innermost fetters of a small substratum of Jewish-capitalistic and pluto-democratic profiteers, proclaimed to the world our resolution to shake off the shackles of the Versailles Dictate.

Germany's demands for this revision were a vital necessity and essential to the existence and honour of every great nation. They will probably one day be regarded by posterity as extremely reasonable. In practice, all these demands had to be carried through contrary to the will of the Franco-British rulers. We all regarded it as a sure sign of successful leadership in the Third Reich that for years we were able to effect this revision without a war. Not that — as the British and French demagogues asserted — we were at that time incapable of fighting. When, thanks to growing common sense, it finally appeared as though international co-operation might lead to a peaceful solution of the remaining problems, the Agreement to this end signed in Munich on September 29, 1938, by the four leading interested States, was not only not welcomed in London and Paris, but was actually condemned as a sign of abominable weakness. Now that peaceful revision threatened to be crowned with success, the Jewish capitalist war-mongers, their hands stained with blood, saw their tangible pretexts for realizing their diabolical plans vanish into thin air. Once again we witnessed a conspiracy by wretched corruptible political creatures and money-grabbing financial magnates, for whom war was a welcome means of furthering their business ends. The poison scattered by the Jews throughout the nations began to exercise its disintegrating influence on sound common sense. Scribblers concentrated upon decrying honest men, who wanted peace, as weaklings and traitors, and upon denouncing the opposition parties as the Fifth Column, thus breaking all internal resistance to their criminal war policy. Jews and Freemasons, armaments manufacturers and war profiteers, international business-men and Stock Exchange jobbers seized upon political hirelings of the desperado and Herostrates type, who described war as something infinitely desirable.

It was the work of these criminal persons that spurred the Polish State on to adopt an attitude that was out of all proportion to Germany's demands and still less to the attendant consequences.

In its dealings with Poland, the German Reich has pre-eminently exercised genuine self-restraint since the National-Socialist régime came into power. One of the most despicable and foolish measures of the Versailles Dictate, namely, the severance of an old German province from the Reich, was crying out aloud for revision. Yet what were my requests?

I name myself in this connexion, because no other statesman might have dared to propose a solution such as mine to the German nation. It merely implied the return of Danzig — an ancient purely German city — to the Reich, and the creation of a means of communication between the Reich and its severed province. Even this was to be decided by a plebiscite subject to the control of an international body. If Mr Churchill and the rest of the war-mongers had felt a fraction of the responsibility towards Europe which inspired me, they could never have begun their infamous game.

It was only due to these and other European and non-European parties and their war interests, that Poland rejected my proposals, which in no way affected either her honour or her existence, and in their stead had recourse to terror and to the sword. In this case we once more showed unexampled and truly superhuman self-control, since for months, despite murderous attacks on minority Germans, and even despite the slaughter of tens of thousands of our German fellow-countrymen, we still sought an understanding by peaceful means.

What was the situation?

One of the most unnatural creations of the Dictate of Versailles, a popinjay puffed up with political and military pomp, insults another State for months on end and threatens to grind it to powder, to fight battles on the outskirts of Berlin, to hack the German armies to pieces, to extend its frontiers to the Oder or the Elbe, and so forth. Meanwhile, the other State, Germany, watches this tumult in patient silence, although a single movement of her arm would have sufficed to prick this bubble inflated with folly and hatred.

On September 2, the conflict might still have been averted — Mussolini proposed a plan for the immediate cessation of all hostilities and for peaceful negotiations. Though Germany saw her armies storming to victory, I nevertheless accepted his proposal. It was only the Franco-British war-mongers who desired war, not peace. More than that, as Mr Chamberlain said, they needed a long war, because they had now invested their cap in armaments shares, had purchased machinery and required t for the development of their business interests and the amo zation of their investments. For, after all, what do these "citi of the world" care about Poles, Czechs or such-like peoples?

On June 19, 1940, a German soldier found a curious docum when searching some railway trucks standing in the station of Charité. As the document bore a distinctive inscription, immediately handed it over to his commanding officer. It was t passed on to other quarters, where it was soon realized that had lighted on an important discovery. The station was subjec to another, more thorough-going search.

Thus it was that the German High Command gained possess of a collection of documents of unique historical significance. T were the secret documents of the Allied Supreme War Council, included the minutes of every meeting held by this illustrious b This time Mr. Churchill will not succeed in contesting or lying ab the veracity of these documents, as he tried to do when docum were discovered in Warsaw.

These documents bear marginal notes inscribed by Messi Gamelin, Daladier, Weygand, etc. They can thus at any time confirmed or refuted by these very gentlemen. They further y remarkable evidence of the machinations of the war-mongers war-extenders. Above all, they show that those stony-hea politicians regarded all the small nations as a means to their e that they had attempted to use Finland in their own interests; they had determined to turn Norway and Sweden into a the of war; that they had planned to fan a conflagration in the Balk in order to gain the assistance of a hundred divisions from t countries; that they had planned a bombardment of Batum Baku by a ruthless and unscrupulous interpretation of Turk neutrality, who was not unfavourable to them; that they inveigled Belgium and the Netherlands more and more comple until they finally entrapped them into binding General S agreements, and so on, ad libitum.

The documents further give a picture of the dilettante met by which these political war-mongers tried to quench the b which they had lighted, of their democratic militarism, which part to blame for the appalling fate that they have inflicte hundreds of thousands, even millions of their own soldiers, of barbarous unscrupulousness which caused them callously to f mass evacuation on their peoples, which brought them no mil advantages, though the effects on the population were outrageo cruel.

These same criminals are responsible for having driven Po into war.

Eighteen days later this campaign was, to all intents and purp at an end.

Britain and France Considered Understanding a Crime

On October 6, 1939, I addressed the German nation for the se time during this war at this very place. I was able to in them of our glorious military victory over the Polish State. A same time I appealed to the insight of the responsible men in enemy States and to the nations themselves. I warned them n continue this war, the consequences of which could only devastating. I particularly warned the French of embarking war which would forcibly eat its way across the frontier and w irrespective of its outcome, would have appalling consequences the same time, I addressed this appeal to the rest of the w although I feared — as I expressly said — that my words woul be heard, but would more than ever arouse the fury of the inter war-mongers. Everything happened as I predicted. The respon elements in Britain and France scented in my appeal a dange attack on their war profits. They therefore immediately beg declare that every thought of conciliation was out of the ques nay, even a crime; that the war had to be pursued in the of civilization, of humanity, of happiness, of progress, and leave no stone unturned — in the name of religion itself. For purpose, negroes and bushmen were to be mobilized. Victory, then said, would come of its own accord, it was, in fact, within easy reach, as I myself must know very well and have know a long time since, or I should not have broadcast my appea peace throughout the world. For if I had had any justificatio

58 An English translation of Hitler's speech demanding British surrender, as dropped in large numbers over England and Wales in August 1940, during the Battle of Britain. The Welsh owner of this example remembers his parents telling him that they resembled midsummer snowfall.

59 Goebbels' demand for 'total war' at the Berlin Sportpalast (27 February 1943). In a carefully planned propaganda campaign, Goebbels posed ten questions. After the 'spontaneous' assent from his audience, he concluded by declaring: 'Therefore let the slogan be from now on: "People arise, and storm break loose!" '

59

March 1933, the exigencies of war now demanded of Goebbels a more intense concern with the tactics of propaganda and greater flexibility to respond to changing military situations. His directive entitled 'Guidelines for the Execution of NSDAP [Nazi] Propaganda', issued at the outbreak of war, outlined the means he expected his staff to employ, which included the use of radio and newspapers, films, posters, mass meetings, illustrated lectures, and 'whisper' or word-of-mouth propaganda (*Mundpropaganda*). During the course of the war, the changing military fortunes dictated four major German propaganda campaigns—on the themes of the *Blitzkrieg*, the campaign against the Soviet Union, total war and the need for strengthening morale, and promises of retaliation or revenge (*Vergeltung*).

From 1942 onwards, Nazi propagandists were forced to shift their focus away from the initial euphoria of the *Blitzkrieg* victories to account for a rapidly deteriorating military situation. The impact of the Nazi defeat at Stalingrad on the morale of the German people cannot be over-estimated: it affected their attitude towards the war

and created a crisis of confidence in the regime among broad sections of the population. Goebbels adopted a stance of frankness and realism by proclaiming 'total war', demanding the complete mobilisation of Germany's human resources for the war effort, and attempting to elicit a fanaticism to fight to the death against Bolshevism.

During the period 1943–45, Nazi propaganda encouraged the population to believe that Germany was developing secret weapons capable of transforming the military situation. In these final years of the war, the notion of retaliation or revenge by means of these 'miracle' weapons played a crucial role in sustaining morale and was widely seen as a panacea for all of Germany's troubles. However, dejection set in once it became apparent that the new weapons could not fulfil this promise.

In the final year of the war, Goebbels attempted to resurrect the *Führer* cult by depicting Hitler as a latter-day version of the 18th-century Prussian hero Frederick the Great, ultimately triumphant in the face of adversity. In the face of the gathering Russian occupation of Germany, this absurd image represented an alarming flight from reality that no amount of propaganda could sustain. The 'Hitler myth' could not survive the military reverses and was on the verge of extinction—along with the Third Reich.

Propaganda played a central role in the Soviet 'Great Patriotic War', rallying the population to resist the Nazi invasion. The German attack (Operation Barbarossa), trampling over the cynical 1939 Nazi-Soviet Non-Aggression Pact, found Stalin's regime ill-prepared for battle. But after the initial shock, the formidable Soviet propaganda machine hit its stride quickly. Soviet propaganda was supervised by the Directorate of Propaganda and Agitation of the Central Committee under A.S. Shcherbakov and administered by the newly established Soviet Information Bureau. Within two days of the invasion, Commissar for Foreign Affairs Vyacheslav Molotov addressed the nation by radio in defiant tone. Newsreels captured the grim-faced determination of Soviet citizens while listening to his speech, images that were on Soviet cinema screens within a week. And one famous poster reminded the Soviet people: 'Higher vigilance in every unit—always remember the treachery and baseness of the enemy!' Stalin was able to launch his call to arms at the start of July. He addressed his audience as 'brothers and sisters' (eschewing the communist orthodoxy of 'comrades'), and

he called for a defence of the motherland (*rodina*).

The story of US propaganda during the Second World War can be divided into two phases. During the period of neutrality, from September 1939 to December 1941, debate about the war raged among the population at large. President Roosevelt pressured Britain to specify its war aims, which it was slow in doing. But the result, finally, was the Atlantic Charter of August 1941, which prepared the way for the postwar United Nations. The charter played its part in convincing the American people that the war was a noble cause and not just a bid to save the British Empire.

Once in the war, the US government mobilised a major propaganda effort through the Office of War Information (OWI) and the Office of Strategic Services (OSS), the first having responsibility for overt or 'white' propaganda, the second for covert or 'black' propaganda. By 1945 the OWI had a staff of 130,000 and a budget of $110 million per year. The United States used propaganda to orient troops (most famously in the US Army Signal Corps film series *Why We Fight*, directed by Frank Capra) and to motivate its civilian population (*see also* 'The yellow peril and the master race' in Chapter 5). In all phases of war propaganda the commercial media played a key role. At home, campaigns conceived in collaboration with the

60

Сын мой! Ты видишь долю мою...
Громи фашистов в святом бою!

60 A Soviet propaganda poster of 1942, by Fyodor Antonov, its plaintive slogan beginning: 'My son! You see my plight … .' Behind the old woman, who is now reduced to a handful of belongings, are the smouldering remains of the family home. She implores her son to save the country and destroy the fascists.

61 A Japanese 'Save for Victory' cartoon (1942–44). President Roosevelt, depicted as a boxer wearing 'Stars and Stripes' trunks and US-dollar boxing gloves, is dealt a knock-out blow by a Japanese warrior.

61

commercial media included an effort to engage women in heavy-duty war work.

Japanese propaganda operated on three main fronts: domestically; China and Southeast Asia; and the West. Following its attack on the US naval base at Pearl Harbor in December 1941, Japan had to fight on two fronts simultaneously—in China and the Pacific. Official Japanese propaganda asked its people, already under duress since the 1930s, now to endure further economic restrictions, recycle scarce materials, make do with less and live by slogans such as 'luxury is the enemy'. Intense propaganda campaigns directed at Japanese soldiers encouraged suicide over capture.

HOME FRONTS IN THE SECOND WORLD WAR

In 1939–45 civilians were in the frontline as never before. Advances in the technology of war, particularly in aerial bombing, served to transform their experience of war. Other advances meant that radio and cinema were now firmly established as mass media, and governments of all the belligerent states were conscious of the need to gauge the impact of propaganda. During the war, 'feedback' agencies assessed the state of public opinion and the factors affecting public morale.

In Britain, for example, this process involved using the results of the social-research Mass Observation project, while in Germany the weekly reports of the *SS* Security Service (*Sicherheitsdienst der SS*) made it their business to gauge the mood and morale of the people. In the United States, pollsters employed sampling methods both for commercial polls—such as those conducted by Roper and Gallup—and public-interest polls, such as those generated by the Office of Public Opinion Research (OPOR) and the National Opinion Research Center (NORC).

All the belligerents reinforced the central message of the First World War—the importance of citizens contributing to the war effort. In Britain, the theme of 'your country needs you' manifested itself in the notion of a shared 'people's war'—a nation working together (as in the slogan 'Let Us Go Forward Together') and putting aside class, regional and social differences. This strategy was also applied across the British Empire. As the public wanted to be reassured of the nation's capacity to produce armaments and their effective use, artistic compositions of industrial sites and workers produced a new iconography. Office and factories were stages for a shifting social order, adjusted and attuned to wartime needs. Propaganda also stressed the new roles undertaken by women for the war effort—from performing menial tasks with the Auxiliary Territorial Service to complex work in armaments factories. Bearing in mind the un-met promises (the land 'fit for heroes') made during the First World War, British propaganda also emphasised the possibility of postwar change—which, in the end, paved the way for the Labour election victory in 1945.

In the United States, because of acute wartime labour shortages, women were needed in the defence industries, the civil service and the armed forces. Despite the continuing trend for women to enter the work force, propaganda campaigns targeted those women who had never before held jobs. The images that were produced glorified and glamorised the roles of working women, and suggested that a woman's femininity need not be compromised by work. Typists, for example were recruited with such slogans as: 'Victory Waits on Your Fingers—Keep 'Em Flying, Miss U.S.A.' Whether fulfilling their duty in the home, factory, office or military, women were invariably presented as attractive, confident and resolved to do their part to win the war. The artist Norman Rockwell created the character of Rosie the Riveter, a variation of this stereotype, who became the personification of the emancipated American woman in wartime. Rosie had big muscular arms and put her penny loafers on top of a copy of Hitler's *Mein Kampf*.

Rockwell also disseminated President Roosevelt's Four Freedoms, which appealed to the

62 The nanny state? A string of large hoardings (1942) demonstrates how British citizens could not avoid Ministry of Information propaganda campaigns urging them to—among other things—walk, dig for victory, save money, join the forces and save on coal. Women were often the main targets for this advice.

63 One of Norman Rockwell's war-bond posters, encapsulating one of the four key 'freedoms' that the United States was fighting for. An 'ordinary Joe' speaks at a town hall meeting, his right to do so recognised in the rapt attention of the better-dressed men and women around him.

62

nation's resolve by setting out America's freedom of speech and worship, and freedom from fear and from want. In conjunction with the OWI, he produced a series of posters illustrating each of these freedoms in a highly successful war-bond drive.

By the outbreak of war, film had become *the* mass medium. In wartime, going to the cinema remained what it had become in the 1930s, a normal part of everyday life, by far the most popular form of entertainment, particularly for the working class. It was, unsurprisingly, exploited extensively for propaganda purposes by all the belligerents. In Britain, where, by the end of the war, 30 million people were going to the cinema every week, the MOI commissioned morale-boosting films, including documentaries exemplifying British courage or military prowess: *Desert Victory* (1943), about the defeat of Rommel at El Alamein; Humphrey Jennings' exceptional body of work, including *London Can Take It* (1940) about the unfolding German bombing campaign of the 'Blitz'; and Harry Watts' *Target for Tonight* (1941), about an RAF bombing raid on Germany. The commercial film industry, in conjunction with the MOI, portrayed many of the personal experiences of the war. The task was to reconcile individual needs with the necessity of pulling together and to bring out the defining qualities of Britishness such as stoicism and understatement, the 'stiff-upper lip' and the sense of fair play. The result was a series of films about people from different backgrounds and classes successfully welded together for the fight against Nazism, such as *In Which We Serve* (1942), *Millions Like Us* (1943), *The Way Ahead* (1944) and Jennings' *Fires Were Started* (1943).

In Germany, where the cinema was equally popular and wartime cinema audiences were increasing,

Goebbels' strategy (*Filmpolitik*) shrewdly mixed entertainment with propaganda. Documentaries—most famously, Leni Reifenstahl's *Triumph of the Will* (1935)—and the newsreels (*Deutsche Wochenschauen*) provided overt propaganda of Nazi ideology and German military successes, whereas feature films were expected to reflect the ambience of National Socialism rather than loudly proclaiming its ideology. *Soldiers of Tomorrow* (*Soldaten von Morgen*, 1941) took a humorous swipe at the British public-school system and the resultant degeneracy of British youth, comparing it unfavourably with the Hitler Youth (*see also* 'The effete English' in Chapter 5). More generally, feature films were musicals or love stories with a Nazi twist.

While each major belligerent demonstrated, in films and the other media, its own propaganda strategy for its own population, common traits did emerge. Propagandists, whether Allied or Axis, exhorted their citizens to produce more, to eat less, to conserve scarce resources, to keep their lips sealed—and, of course, to keep hating the enemy.

■ The Cold War and beyond

If the two world wars demonstrated the power of propaganda, the post-1945 period witnessed the widespread application of the lessons learnt, in the context of a communications revolution that now embraced television. When the expedient wartime alliances rapidly deteriorated into the opposing blocs of the Cold War, a new type of conflict emerged. This was a war on the mind, a contest of ideologies, a battle of nerves, which over the next forty-odd years was to divide the world into a bipolar competition. It was to be characterised by a

The Cold War nuclear arms race focused much ... propaganda on national security and fear—two incendiary factors, which led to the most extreme forms of xenophobia

64 'You Never Know Who's Listening!': a silk handkerchief designed by 'Fougasse' (Cyril Kenneth Bird) for the Ministry of Information's 'Careless Talk Cost Lives' campaign. In the humorous cartoons, Nazis, including Hitler and Goering, lurk in the most unlikely places, overhearing British conversations.

battle for hearts and minds, but, more sinister, was underpinned by the threat of nuclear annihilation.

The Cold War nuclear arms race focused much of the propaganda on national security and fear—two incendiary factors, which led to the most extreme forms of xenophobia and to claims and counter-claims that gained in momentum. Frequently it was well-nigh impossible for individuals to challenge prevailing assertions for fear of being labelled 'unpatriotic' or, worse, a communist or capitalist spy. In the United States, fear of communist infiltration (whipped up by the

accusations of Senator Joseph McCarthy and his Senate investigating committee), spy mania and the knowledge that the Soviet Union now possessed a nuclear capability led to increased spending on nuclear armaments and intense and prolonged propaganda campaigns to inform the American public of what precautions could be taken in the event of a Soviet nuclear attack. The Federal Civil Defense Administration (FCDA) produced posters, pamphlets and a number of short films for television and movie theatres. The new medium of television proved particularly receptive. The most

65

65 The score for Bert the Turtle's 'Duck and Cover' song, which accompanied the US Civil Defense films of the same name. In this famous propaganda campaign of the Cold War, aimed primarily at children, Bert the Turtle urged children to 'duck and cover' should they see 'the flash'—an atomic explosion.

66 CND protestors on the Aldermaston March (1963), framed by the organisation's powerful and enduring symbol. From 1958 to 1969, large crowds (with attendant media coverage) progressed from Britain's Atomic Weapons Establishment near Aldermaston to London's Trafalgar Square. The iconic symbol representing peace and love dominated proceedings.

66

famous example in this genre was the cartoon series *Duck and Cover,* which featured Bert the Turtle, who informed television and cinema audiences how they should react during an atomic explosion. In the early 1960s the FCDA produced the film series *Home in the Middle,* which was intended to reassure the public that the Defense Department was continuing research in the area of civil defence and to encourage citizens to educate themselves. By continuing to emphasise the dangers of a Soviet nuclear attack, civil-defence propaganda was also used to justify increased defence spending, culminating in President Ronald Reagan's 'Star Wars' (Strategic Defence Initiative) propaganda project in the 1980s.

In Britain the proliferation of nuclear weapons provided the basis for the re-emergence of an official civil-defence organisation, the Civil Defence Corps (CDC), through the provisions of the 1948 Civil Defence Act. The Labour government of Clement Attlee decided to launch a major recruitment campaign, to be coordinated by the Central Office of Information (COI) by means of a nationwide publicity campaign bearing the slogan 'You can't be certain. You can be prepared.' Posters and film were used in the campaign, including a Crown Film Unit production entitled *The Waking Point* (1951), which targeted citizens' social conscience and attempted to expose the global communist threat to democratic life.

However, concern about the proliferation of nuclear arms also led to the establishment, in 1957, of the Campaign for Nuclear Disarmament (CND), which advocated Britain's unilateral disarmament. The new organisation attracted considerable public interest and drew support from a range of parties, including scientists, religious leaders, academics, journalists, writers, actors and musicians. Following in a long tradition of opposition to war, which can be traced to the pacifist movement in the First World War, the CND produced its own distinctive counter-propaganda campaigns calling for the abolition of weapons of mass destruction, in particular chemical and biological weapons, and using a plethora of techniques including leaflets, posters and marches (most notably, the Aldermaston marches from the site of British nuclear weapons research to London). The CND became universally recognised by its iconic symbol, designed in 1958 and now a symbol of peace and opposition to nuclear arms all over the world.

Propagandists on both sides of the Cold War divide used every available medium to sell an ideological view, and their contrasting interpretations of 'freedom' and 'security', to their own citizens and to the world at large. The struggle tended to be represented in American propaganda in simple moral terms as a fight between good and evil. (In the 1980s, President Reagan famously described the Soviet Union as an 'Evil Empire'.) It is important, though, to remember that on the Soviet side the authorities always regarded language as a fundamental aspect of policy to secure Marxist-Leninist 'historical imperatives'. Words as weapons in this ideological battle thus assumed an active and highly potent role in defining concepts such as 'peace', 'security', 'liberation' and 'freedom'.

On two occasions the Cold War developed into major 'hot' wars: in Korea (1950–53) and Vietnam (1965–73), while the Cuban Missile Crisis (1962) almost drew the two superpowers into a nuclear conflict. The Korean War in particular gave a major boost to propaganda efforts on both sides. The US Congress tripled funds for America's propaganda programme (the 'Campaign of Truth'), enabling the administration of President Truman to intensify its efforts at home, and to provide the Voice of America (VOA) with the facilities to broadcast to more than a hundred countries in forty-six languages. The Soviet Union responded by improving its short-wave programming, so that by the end of 1950 it was able to reach more countries, in more languages, than the Americans could. By 1962, Soviet radio was broadcasting 1,200 hours a week, of which only 250 hours were directed at Western Europe. It was true that Radio Moscow now had a rival in Peking Radio, reflecting the fractures in the communist world (the 'Sino–Soviet split'). But this factor was secondary, in US eyes, to the massive increase in communist international propaganda that began, increasingly, to exploit growing Western youth movements in the 1960s. Accordingly, by 1965 the United States Information Agency's budget was substantially increased to counter this threat.

The so-called Truman doctrine—of containing and rolling back communism—proved sufficient for justifying the US presence in Korea, where the United States and its allies were, strictly speaking, fulfilling a United Nations-sanctioned operation to counter the North Korean invasion of the South. But Vietnam proved more problematic from the point of view of propaganda. The US 'domino theory', in which allowing one state to fall to communism might topple others in turn, identified Vietnam as pivotal to the security of Southeast Asia. During the administrations (1961–69) of John F. Kennedy and Lyndon B. Johnson, the US government gradually increased its aid to South Vietnam, with large numbers of troops. They arrived in 1965 to combat the threat posed by the communist North Vietnamese regime (and the 'Viet Cong' insurgents it was sponsoring), which was backed by both the Soviet Union and China. Unlike in Korea, however, US propaganda failed to convince the American people that it was a 'just war' or a war that could be won swiftly. It was the first war fought before a mass television audience, and the impact of this coverage on US (and world) opinion has been regarded by some as decisive. As a result, the Vietnam War became increasingly 'visible', and a credibility gap widened between what the US government and military were claiming had occurred and the events that were seen unfolding on television screens on a nightly basis. Things reached a watershed with the communist Tet Offensive in 1968. Although, militarily, it was a costly failure, when North Vietnamese and Viet Cong troops audaciously stormed the US Embassy in Saigon the images garnered a shocking and powerful propaganda value. Walter Cronkite, the distinguished and respected anchorman of CBS News, summed it up by asking in disbelief: 'What the hell is going on? I thought we were winning the war.' In fact, the American media did not necessarily become *anti-war* after 1968, as many have claimed; they merely became less willing to accept uncritically the official version of events. Crucially, the Americans also underestimated the skill of North Vietnamese

67 **Another, ostensibly grimmer, US Civil Defense poster (by Harold Stevenson, 1951), urging (white, middle-class) citizens to join the Civil Defense Corps. It was run by the Office of Civilian Defense, which organised around 10 million volunteers to fight fires, to decontaminate after chemical attacks and to provide first aid, among other duties.**

propaganda in exploiting massacres of civilians, such as the infamous US attack on the village of My Lai in 1968 and the saturation bombing and defoliation of Vietnam.

The war fostered a powerful anti-war protest movement led largely by American youth, who objected to the draft, to the nature and necessity of the war itself, and to the increasingly horrific images that were emerging. This movement, like the CND, produced its own counter-propaganda calling for peace—a rallying cry that found a resonance among youth movements throughout the

68 Propaganda from the Vietnam War. Hanoi published cartoons in English portraying the United States as both aggressor and as losing the war. Here, President Johnson is depicted sardonically as the dove of peace hovering over Vietnam while carrying a bag of swag as he offloads a furious onslaught of bombs. In the other, Johnson juggles 'peace' bombs in a dangerous circus act, to the accompaniment of a British drum.

Peace dove Johnson!
Ta Luu

10

Dangerous jugglery!
Hoang Lo

11

> The Cold War demanded that policy and propaganda be conducted hand-in-hand. In this sense, the Soviet Union held the initiative …

world. It also inspired a generation of musicians, songwriters, poets and journalists, in Vietnam, the United States and beyond. The band Country Joe and the Fish recorded one of the most popular anti-war anthems in 'I Feel Like I'm Fixing to Die', the singing of which became a symbolic gesture of opposition and resistance to the war ('And it's one, two, three, what are we fighting for? Don't ask me I don't give a damn. Next stop is Vietnam.') The cumulative impact of negative images on television together with the anti-war movements, rather than any decisive military turning point, eventually persuaded the administration of President Nixon to withdraw US forces from Vietnam in 1973, claiming that it was a 'triumph of diplomacy' rather than defeat resulting from North Vietnamese tenacity.

Patriotic propaganda along the 'your country needs you' lines, attempting to mobilise domestic opinion, accompanied subsequent crises and 'low-intensity' conflicts during the Cold War; but the scale of the territorial conflicts were dwarfed by the wider global struggle of two irreconcilable ideologies and ways of life. The Cold War demanded that policy and propaganda be conducted hand-in-hand. In this sense, the Soviet Union held the initiative, because its propaganda was so interwoven with policy. Western democracies had to learn that in order to survive such an ideological battle, they would have to adapt their propaganda and policies accordingly. It was the 19th-century military theorist Carl von Clausewitz who argued that war was the continuation of politics by other means; but, in the Cold War, propaganda became the continuation of politics by other means.

One exception to the rule was the Falklands War (1982), which erupted following the Argentinian invasion of the British-governed Falklands Islands. This conflict was less a Cold War struggle than an old-fashioned territorial and colonial dispute. It provided a new, contemporary take on the theme of 'your country needs you'. At the time, the British government considered it important to get the United Nations—as a forum for world opinion and the international community—to sanction British military action, if the Conservative government of Margaret Thatcher were to be able to claim it was a 'just war'.

The determination not to 'lose' the Falklands on television, in the same way that the Americans had appeared to lose the Vietnam War, created a situation described as the 'worst reported war since the Crimea'. It was striking, therefore, in the late 20th century to witness a territorial conflict unfold primarily through the medium of radio—which was thought to have reached its pinnacle in the Second World War (*see also* 'Black propaganda' in Chapter 1).

The British tabloid press (with exceptions) largely adopted a jingoistic approach, epitomised in the *Sun*'s infamous headline 'GOTCHA', following the torpedoing of the Argentinian cruiser *General Belgrano*. The sinking of the ship, with the loss of 323 lives, was even celebrated in postcards that showed it going down, accompanied by the Union Jack and the heading 'England's Glory'. Drawings—as there were no photographs or television pictures available—of British Marines retaking the Falklands were accompanied by headlines proclaiming (and quoting the prime minister): 'The courage of our boys has given new pride to the country.' As a result of the cheerful mood of despatches from the fleet, combined with the bluntness of tabloid journalists—'Up Yours, Galtieri!' was a suggestion by one *Sun* reporter for the leader of the Argentinian military *junta*—the British public received comparatively little information, though they did get some disinformation about what was happening. For several years after this campaign in the South Atlantic, political and military leaders embroiled in subsequent conflicts referred to the Falklands War as an example of 'good practice'. However, the manner in which the war was reported raised questions about the importance of public opinion and morale and what were the acceptable levels of state censorship and news management in times of war.

The disintegration of the Soviet Bloc, which followed the fall of the Berlin Wall in 1989, brought to an end the Cold War. It was, for a time, accompanied by much promising talk of an 'end of

history', a new world order. But by 1990 a new conflict erupted following the Iraqi invasion of Kuwait, which saw a US-led coalition (including Britain) repel the Iraqi troops. This First Gulf War also saw a heightened propaganda campaign, shown live nightly on global 'rolling news' stations, notably CNN. It was accompanied, in Britain, by a new wave of patriotic propaganda, again led by the tabloid press. The *Sun*, for example, ran a 'crusade' termed 'Our Heroes', which encouraged the public to (among other things) proudly fly posters bearing the Union Jack, which the *Sun* provided: 'Put it in your window, put it on the wall at work—and if anyone moans, tell them you're doing this to show you CARE for our brave boys and girls in the Gulf.' As the 20th century was nearing its end, and in an age increasingly marked by sophisticated 'information wars' and communication superhighways, such emotionally 'primitive' propaganda takes us back to the beginning of the century. *Plus ça change, plus c'est la même chose.*

69

69 The *Sun's* (in)famous front page, 'Gotcha' (4 May 1982), which celebrated news of the torpedoing of the Argentinian cruiser *General Belgrano* during the Falklands War. In language not much different to the demotic strains of the First World War, the story began: 'The Navy had the Argies on their knees last night after a devastating double punch.'

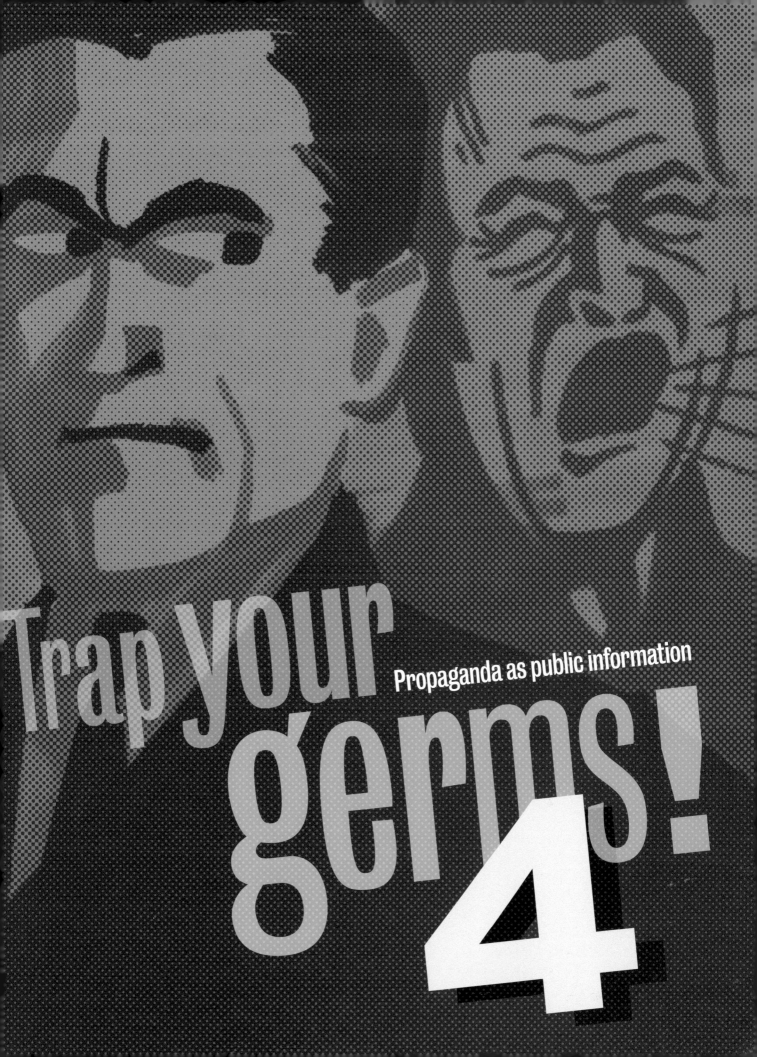

Trap your

Propaganda as public information

germs!

4

I F THE 20TH CENTURY'S wars, both 'hot' and Cold, provided a major spur for propaganda, it was also during this century that we witness governments employing propaganda for very different purposes. While a stress on people's obligations towards their country in the 'your country needs you' spirit was appropriate in times of war, governments were becoming increasingly conscious—partly as a result of the sacrifices made during these wars—of *their* responsibility towards their own citizens. Victorian and Edwardian concepts of *laissez faire* were giving way to new, official concerns about the health and hygiene of a nation. Propaganda came to have an important instructional role in conveying such public information. Today, the promotion of public health has become a staple subject of propaganda, from governmental and non-governmental organisations alike, throughout the world. Public health campaigns are sometimes known as 'soft' propaganda—a gentler way of spreading ideas or customs.

Such campaigns can be traced back to Britain's Public Health Act of 1848, and today they are a global phenomenon. The first public health film, on the 'life drama of the fly', was also made in Britain, in 1910, as part of a national anti-fly campaign. Government-sponsored health campaigns first appeared during the First World War, although at this early stage they were rarely coordinated. But since the end of the First World War, the state has played an increasingly significant role in the management of public health in many countries. The roots and antecedents of this can be found in the state's concern with chronic disease and epidemiology and its mission to promote good health for its citizens. However, a state's desire for a healthy population is not purely an act of altruism: a healthy nation ensures the availability of labour for the economy and recruits for the armed services, as well as reducing the need for state expenditure on welfare and medical treatment. These concerns are heightened during times of conflict, famine or natural disasters.

The interaction, or 'dialogue', between a state and its people is largely conducted through the mass media, by means of major public health campaigns. They may adopt shock tactics, education, persuasion or humour; they may be subtle and embedded in popular press, film, television and radio programmes (and now the internet) or supported by campaigning groups, such as trade unions and health organisations. And the subjects covered stretch from healthy food to safe sex, from the dangers of smoking to the dangers of driving too fast, from the encouragement of vaccination to the discouragement of alcohol consumption—and much more besides.

■ Healthy eating

The relationship between personal health and the health of the nation was a subject of much public debate in the late 19th and early 20th centuries. It was a particular concern of the great imperial powers, anxious to maintain their positions in the world. Some argued that to fundamentally improve the health of a population, intervention was needed at a biological level. Francis Galton's research in the 1860s—what became known as 'eugenics'—

70 **An early British public health poster (c.1920). The point is made in a dramatic but simple way through the outrageously outsize fly, producing an image intended to shock its target audience.**

FLIES AND DISEASE.

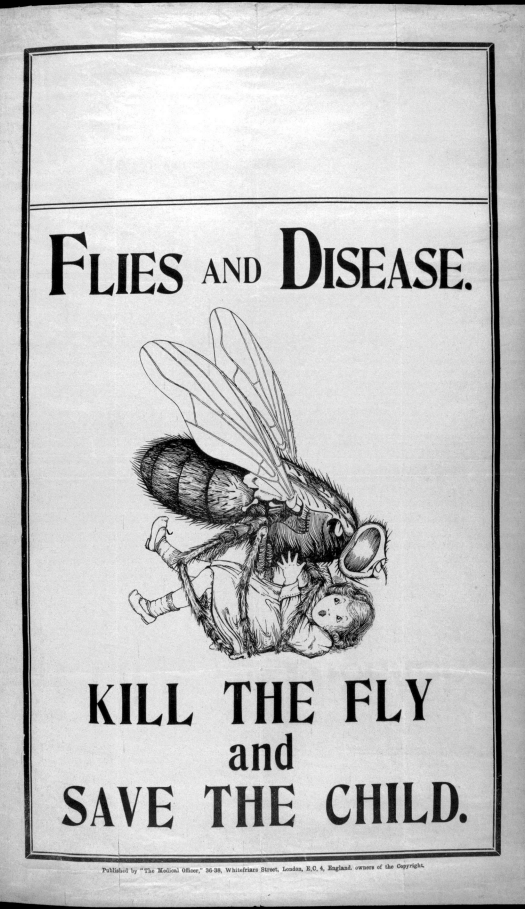

KILL THE FLY
and
SAVE THE CHILD.

Published by "The Medical Officer," 36-38, Whitefriars Street, London, E.C. 4, England, owners of the Copyright.

THERE ARE NO
SILVER SPOONS
FOR CHILDREN BORN INTO
POVERTY

Baby Greg is one minute old. He
should have a bright future. Poverty
has other plans. Poverty is waiting
to rob Greg of hope and spirit and
is likely to lead him to a future of
squalor. We can't end poverty but we
can provide the practical skills that
Greg and thousands of others in the
UK need to stop it predetermining
their lives. Don't let poverty destroy
a future. Call us on 0800 032 7222
or visit www.barnardos.org.uk now.

Barnardo's

GIVING CHILDREN BACK THEIR FUTURE

71 Another disturbing image, in the shape of a poster from the children's charity Barnardo's Child Poverty campaign (2003). Instead of a silver spoon emerging from the child's mouth—the traditional metaphor for a well-to-do background—there is a cockroach, an image that unites childhood poverty with poor health and bad living conditions.

described the application of the emerging scientific understanding of genetics. The aim was to encourage the breeding of those deemed worthy of reproducing and to discourage the perpetuation into a new generation of others deemed 'unfit'—whether because of low intelligence, mental disorders, certain classes of chronic illness and disabilities, or 'criminal proclivities'.

Eugenicists proposed that by controlling human reproduction, humankind could take control of its own future. The eugenics agenda also suggested that much public health legislation encouraged the survival of those normally 'weeded out' by natural selection.

Such attitudes were amplified in times of war. Public health and war have long been close companions, and perhaps strange bedfellows. In the aftermath of the Anglo–Boer War, which ended in 1902, there was considerable gloomy speculation about the likely outcome for the British nation and Empire of the apparent deterioration of the British male population. Between 40 and 60 per cent of recruits for the British Army were turned down as physically unfit for service, and the First World War brought such issues into even greater relief. The advent of industrialised 'total war' drew in much of the adult population, either as combatants or as workers, placing manpower at a premium. Every effort was therefore made to prevent sickness and to restore patients (whether soldiers or workers) to some kind of useful role. Food became a precious resource that would both help secure ultimate victory in war and contribute to restoring the future health of the populations of the belligerent nations.

From 1917, the US Food Administration, for example, urged families to reduce consumption of key staples to aid the war effort. 'Food Will Win the War,' the government proclaimed, and 'Meatless Monday' and 'Wheatless Wednesday' were introduced to encourage Americans to do their part. One poster proclaimed: 'Food will win the war—We observe meatless days, wheatless days, porkless days, and carry out all conservation rules of the U.S. Food Administration'. Herbert Hoover, then head of the Food Administration, spearheaded the implementation of the campaign, and in addition to advertising, his office created and distributed recipe booklets and menus in newspapers, magazines and pamphlets.

The campaign's effect was overwhelming. Some 10 million families, 7,000 hotels and nearly 425,000 food dealers pledged to observe national meatless days. In November 1917, New York City hotels alone saved some 116 tons of meat over the course of just one week. According to a 1929 *Saturday Evening Post* article, 'Americans began to look seriously into the question of what and how much they were eating. Lots of people discovered for the first time that they could eat less and feel no worse—frequently for the better.'

During the war, the earliest illustrated posters were designed to catch the attention of the viewer and communicate messages quickly, most often with limited text and strong graphics. As relatively inexpensive forms of popular media, posters became favourite ways to advocate a cause to a broad public audience. These qualities encouraged public health campaigners, then as now, to use posters as a powerful medium for visually communicating knowledge about disease, identifying health risks and promoting changes in behaviour. By combining innovative imagery and text, posters incorporated the techniques of advertising to sell 'health' as a precious commodity. In the process, poster designers developed a visual vocabulary to help shape and define 'normal' and 'healthy' behaviours and conditions, which has provided the basis for a variety of campaigns against infectious diseases and environmental health hazards. At the same time, posters helped to define (and stigmatise) the abnormal, disabled, unhealthy, or contaminated individual. In the aftermath of the First World War, public health campaigns also made widespread use of the new medium of film to disseminate their messages.

After the war, Britain's Minister of Health, Christopher Addison, concluded that widespread ill health was a 'source of national weakness'. The war had revealed that 15-year-old male children of professional men were on average 2 inches taller and nearly 18 pounds heavier than the 15-year-old sons of artisans. All the major nations recognised the traumatic experience of war and, to varying degrees, were now committed to improving the strength of the future body politic, with the result that public health campaigns proliferated in the interwar years.

72

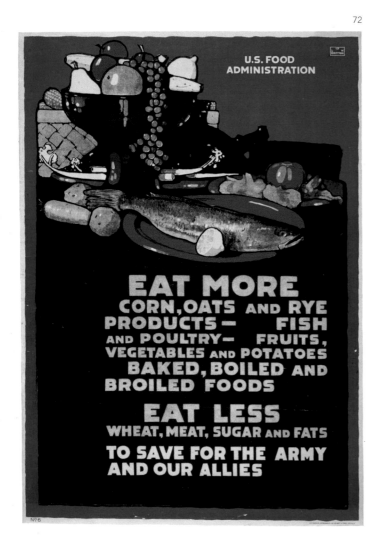

72 A wartime promotional poster (1917) from the US Food Administration. Its instructions on what to eat more/less of were intended to support the troops, by ensuring the US Army and the Allies would then have the food they needed.

73 An emotive French poster (1918) tackling the problem of drink. 'When will we get rid of alcohol?' it asks, as the distressed mother and fearful children confront the dissolute husband/ father.

In Britain, better housing through slum clearance schemes went some way to achieving the wartime promise of 'homes fit for heroes' (and found expression in documentary films such as *Housing Problems*, 1935). Municipal authorities such as Glasgow, and Bermondsey in London, used modern propaganda techniques to publicise the importance of health and hygiene. Glasgow Corporation commissioned films to demonstrate to its citizenry, by means of a judicious propaganda strategy, the possibility of a better and more orderly life. Films such as *Sadness and Gladness* (1928) showed the health benefits of organised holidays for the necessitous children of the city. Bermondsey's Public Health Propaganda Department used mobile cinemas to demonstrate to its inhabitants the facilities it was providing, such as preventative dental care, swimming pools, communal laundries and a solarium for tuberculosis sufferers.

Increasing disquiet was expressed about high levels of ill-health, poverty, maternal and infant mortality rates and poor nutritional standards among large sections of society. Given the alarming discrepancies in health that the First World War had revealed, interwar governments were concerned particularly with improving the diet of the nation. British governments targeted working-class mothers and wives, who, they believed, did not understand the importance of nutrition and a healthy diet. Although official government statements sought to assure the population that 'the State's health defences are effective … the exceptionally good health of the English people continues to be maintained', such complacency was exposed by new research findings, such as John Boyd Orr's *Food, Health and Income* (1936). This showed that up to 50 per cent of the population were badly fed, up to 10 per cent (including 20 per cent of the country's children) were severely undernourished, and that the incidence of tuberculosis, malnutrition, maternal mortality and children's diseases such as rickets was the result of inadequate diet. The study drew on scientific discoveries of vitamins and minerals in certain foods and their importance for an adequate diet. It went on to point out that foods of high nutritional value—such as milk, vegetables and fruit—were precisely those that poor families were least able to afford.

Although the government rejected these claims, the issues were taken up in Edgar Anstey's 'nutrition' film *Enough to Eat* (1936), sponsored by the Gas Light & Coke Company, with a commentary by the evolutionary biologist Julian Huxley. This extraordinary film used arresting visual sequences to bring the material alive. One scene examined the huge disparities in height and weight between boys at a public school with those of the same age in state schools. In another sequence, interviews with women about their family budgets and diet powerfully dispelled the myth that women were purchasing the wrong types of food through ignorance. Their real problem was limited financial resources—they simply could not afford the nourishing foods their families needed. The film also highlighted differentials not only between families in different income groups but also within families. Women often went without in order to provide for their husbands and children,

74 **An interwar poster from the Association of Maternity and Child Welfare Centres London. It advocates an enduring message of the importance of exercise in healthy child development.**

British governments targeted working-class mothers and wives, who, they believed, did not understand the importance of nutrition and a healthy diet.

GROWTH and EXERCISE.

If I'm to walk and run and shout
   I must have room to roll about,
For lungs and muscles stronger grow
   With *use*, as all wise Mothers know.

   Cradle and pram are meant for rest—
     For *exercise* the floor is best;
   Secured from draught, to stretch and squirm
     Will make my limbs well-shaped and firm.

   Of clothing freed, and at my ease,
     I'll scramble soon on hands and knees;
   One effort more—I'm certain quite—
     I'll find the way to stand upright!

M. C. D. WALTERS.

74

GUYAS WILLIAMS

75 A 'Dig for Victory' leaflet, in aid of the wartime Ministry of Food's campaign to promote the home production of fruit and vegetables. Total war meant total effort, and domestic vegetable plots multiplied while allotments flourished. The typography here stresses the urgency of 'DIG … NOW'.

76a&b (overleaf) Potatoes personified. Making ever more versatile use of available foodstuffs was a key concern in the Second World War. In Britain, *Potato Pete's recipe book* focused on the flexibility of the humble spud to offer a surprisingly large range of recipes to satisfy the needs of the day.

and they suffered poor health as a consequence.

In the Second World War health campaigns figured even more prominently in official propaganda. The wartime emergency meant that citizens had to be physically fit in order to fight, work in industry, cope with air raids and endure hardship caused by food and other shortages. In Britain, adequate food supplies were recognised as a key factor in the maintenance of morale. The British government mobilised a number of ministries to explain official policy and to stress the importance of good health for the successful conclusion of the war effort. The Ministry of Food was thus one of the largest spenders on publicity, issuing a constant flow of leaflets and press advertisements, as well as short films explaining the rationing system and providing wartime recipes and ways of making limited supplies last longer.

The Ministry of Agriculture was responsible for increasing the amount of land under cultivation in order to grow more vegetables. One of the most famous slogans of the war was 'Dig for Victory'. Britain's Home Front was encouraged to transform private gardens into mini-allotments. It was believed, quite rightly, that this would not only provide essential crops for families and neighbourhoods, but would help the war effort by freeing up valuable space for war materials (rather than food imports) on the merchant shipping convoys. Over 10 million instructional leaflets were distributed to the British people. *The Kitchen Front* radio broadcasts were also concerned with using food efficiently, as well as with making use of what was readily available to mitigate shortages. In addition to the circulation of familiar Ministry of

Agriculture 'food flashes', literature and poster displays, anthems were also introduced, including one under the slogan 'Dig for Victory':

Dig! Dig! Dig! And your muscles will grow big.
Keep on pushing the spade.
Don't mind the worms.
Just ignore their squirms
And when your back aches laugh with glee.
And keep on diggin'.
Till we give our foes a Wiggin'
Dig! Dig! Dig! to Victory

Carrots were one vegetable in plentiful supply, and as a result widely became a substitute for the more scarce commodities. To improve their blandness, people were encouraged to 'enjoy' the healthy carrot in different ways by the introduction of such characters as 'Doctor Carrot'. The Ministry of Agriculture suggested such culinary delights as curried carrot, carrot jam and a homemade drink called Carrolade (made from the juices of carrots and swede).

Potato Pete was another character introduced to encourage the population to eat home-grown vegetables. As with the Dig for Victory theme, Potato Pete also had his own song amplifying the message. With vocals by Betty Driver (later Betty Williams in the television soap opera *Coronation Street*), the recording was a great success and did a tremendous amount of good in getting the message across:

Potato Pete's recipe book

SCALLOPED POTATOES

1 lb. potatoes   1 tablespoon flour
½ pint milk or half milk
A few breadcrumbs
Half vegetable stock
Salt and pepper to taste
Chopped parsley, sliced spring onion, or
    chopped celery to taste

Method — Scrub and scrape the potatoes, then cut them into fairly thin slices. Arrange the layers in a pie-dish or casserole, sprinkling each layer with seasoned flour. Layer with a little chopped parsley and the minced celery or onion. Pour in the milk, sprinkle the top with breadcrumbs and bake in a moderate oven for about one hour, or cook in a frying pan covered with a plate for ½ to ¾ hour over low heat.

CHAMP

For each pound of potatoes, allow at least ½ lb. vegetables, say a cabbage, or any green vegetables in season, mixed with carrots, peas or beans, etc. Salt and pepper and a few tablespoonfuls of milk. Also a small pat of margarine per person.

Method — Cook a large pan of potatoes, allowing them to steam off and dry in the usual way. Cook the selected vegetable in very little water with the lid on.

Peel and mash the potatoes, beating well, then pour in a little milk, add seasoning of pepper and salt, then the cooked vegetable. Serve piping hot on hot plates, with a small pat of margarine on each portion.

PINK AND GREEN PURÉE

1 lb. freshly cooked potatoes
1 large carrot   1 small bunch watercress
Salt and pepper   Milk
A small piece of fat

Method—Mash the potato while it is hot, add a little milk and a small piece of margarine or dripping if it can be spared. Whip to a purée with a fork. Scrub and grate the carrot. Wash and chop the watercress. Add both to the purée potato, season well, reheat for a few minutes and pile pyramid fashion in a vegetable dish.

POTATO BASKET

1 lb. potatoes   1 lb. carrots
1 oz. oatmeal   1 oz. dripping
½ pint stock or milk   1 egg
Salt, pepper, browned crumbs
Chopped parsley

Method—Scrub the potatoes and boil them gently in a very little water. When they are nearly cooked, drain off the liquid, reserving it for stock. Let them finish cooking in their own steam, covering closely with a folded cloth under the lid and standing at the side of the stove until floury. Remove the skins and mash well. Add the beaten egg and mash again, adding salt and pepper.

A tisket a tasket— I make a lovely basket

Grease a cake tin and coat it with browned breadcrumbs. Press in the mashed potatoes to form a thick lining to the tin. Bake in a hot oven for 10–15 minutes.

Meanwhile dice the carrots, cook them for 15 minutes, and mix them with a sauce made from the fat, oatmeal, and liquid, adding pepper and salt to taste.

When the potato basket is cooked, turn it out and fill it with the carrot mixture. Place it in the oven for a few minutes and serve piping hot, with a sprinkling of finely-chopped parsley.

(5)

Here's the man who ploughs the fields.
Here's the girl who lifts up the yield.
Here's the man who deals with the clamp,
So that millions of jaws can chew and champ.
That's the story and here's the star,
Potato Pete—Eat up, ta ta!

Potato Pete recipe books gave women suggestions and advice on how best to serve potatoes at mealtimes. For example, 'scrubbing instead of peeling' was recommended, thus avoiding unnecessary wastage. Even traditional nursery rhymes were adapted to give a Potato Pete theme.

The propaganda campaign was successful. It was estimated that over 1,400,000 people acquired mini-allotments by turning lawns and flower-beds into vegetable gardens. By 1943, over a million tons of vegetables were being grown in gardens and allotments. People were encouraged to keep chickens, and some kept rabbits and goats. Pigs were especially popular because they could be fed on kitchen waste. As the Minister of Food during this period, Lord Woolton was responsible for explaining the benefits of rationing to the British public and educating it into better eating habits. Later in the war, with plentiful vegetables being produced as a result of the success of the Dig for Victory campaign, some were used as the ingredients for the legendary Woolton Pie, a vegetable pie made from potatoes, parsnips and herbs. Unsurprisingly, it was a dish that never really took off with the British public.

After the United States entered the war in December 1941, a similar propaganda campaign

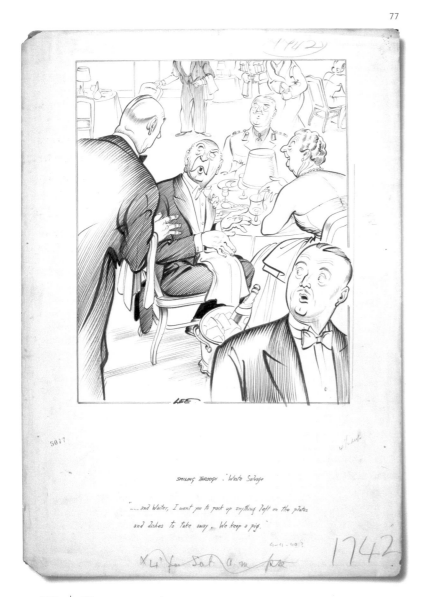

77 'Waste Salvage' (1940), one of Joseph Lee's highly popular wartime 'Smiling Through' cartoons for the *London Evening News*. Its humorous effect is achieved by juxtaposing upper-class society with the officially encouraged trends to keep livestock: (to waiter) 'I want you to pack up anything left on the plates and dishes to take away. We keep a pig.'

78 You are what you eat. A US government chart (1944) sets out the 'basic seven' groups of foods to be eaten on a daily basis, because the 'U.S. needs us strong'. However, Americans were also told that beyond that they could eat what they wanted. It was a long way from the privations of European-style wartime rations.

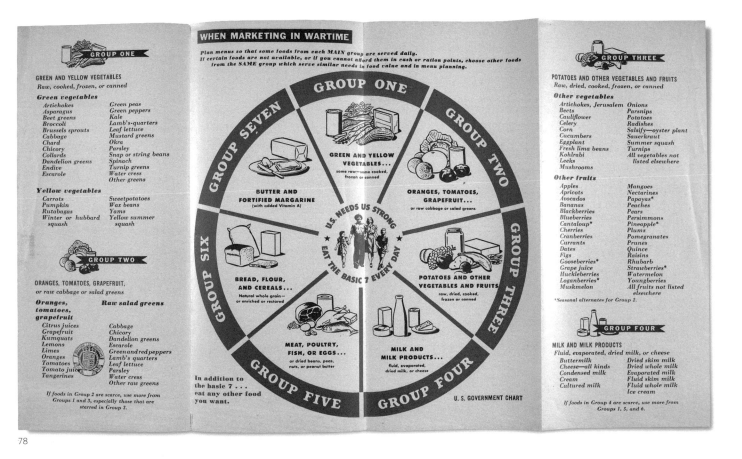

78

was launched there under the slogan 'Your Victory Garden Counts More than Ever!' The US government encouraged people to plant vegetable gardens to help prevent food shortages; and magazines such as *Saturday Evening Post* and *Life* printed articles supporting the campaign, while women's magazines included directions for planting. Because these gardens were regarded as being patriotic, they were termed 'victory gardens', and women were encouraged to tin and preserve food they raised from them. While the US Department of Agriculture provided information, many commercial publishers also issued books on how to plant up the gardens. During the war years, Americans planted 50 million such victory gardens, generating a higher volume of vegetables than the total American commercial production. Much of it was indeed preserved, following the slogan 'Eat what you can, and can what you can't.'

A synergistic relationship between health professionals, politicians and the military flourished during the war. The mobilisation of science and technology on behalf of the war effort famously bore fruit in the development of antibiotics, radar and the atomic bomb. But the war also invigorated and shaped a variety of technological approaches to public health: the development of chemical pesticides to kill mosquitoes and other insect spreaders of disease; the expansion of electronic communication networks for the monitoring of public health; and the production of public health films aimed at mass audiences of military personnel and civilians.

In the immediate postwar period, the provision of public health care and the welfare of citizens became embroiled in the wider political propaganda campaigns associated with the Cold War. In Britain the establishment in 1948 of the National Health Service changed radically the nature of health provision, and between 1946 (when it replaced the wartime Ministry of Information) and 2010 (when it was closed as part of a cost-cutting exercise) the Central Office of Information (COI) was largely responsible for commissioning and disseminating health propaganda campaigns. In 1946, for example, Clement Attlee's Labour government—acting on Orr's findings in the 1930s, which revealed a link between low income,

time for change

If we carry on living as we are, 9 out of 10 kids are set to grow up with dangerous levels of fat in their bodies. This can cause life-threatening diseases like cancer, diabetes and heart disease. Which is why it's really important that we all get together to do something about it today.

So what do we want? CHANGE! And when do we want it? NOW!

Change4Life is a nationwide movement which aims to help us all, but especially our kids, eat well, move more and live longer.

Get involved today!
Search for Change4Life
or call 0300 123 4567*

Eat well   Move more   Live longer

79

79 'Dangerous levels of fat'. From worries over malnutrition to concerns over an obesity 'epidemic', Western nations have travelled a long way in their public health messages over the 20th and early 21st centuries, as this poster from the National Health Service's 'Change4Life' programme (2013) suggests.

malnutrition and under-achievement in schools—introduced the School Milk Act, which guaranteed free school milk to all pupils under the age of eighteen. The Milk Marketing Board had already been established, in 1933, as a government agency to control milk production and distribution. Spurred on by the new Act, from the 1950s there were several memorable advertising campaigns, on which initially the COI and Milk Marketing Board collaborated. Slogans included 'Full of Natural Goodness', 'Is Your Man Getting Enough?', 'Milk's Gotta Lotta Bottle' and 'Drinka Pinta Milka Day'. The decision by the then Education Secretary Margaret Thatcher, in 1971, to end free school milk for the over-sevens generated its own memorable slogan of protest: 'Thatcher, Thatcher, Milk Snatcher'.

In the 21st century, food consumption, eating habits and public health continue to demand attention in the advanced countries of the First World—but for very different reasons than during the wartime period of food rationing. In the two world wars, the problem facing government was educating the nation to eat healthily with scarce resources; but the concern nowadays is with obesity and with its potentially severe impacts, including increasing risks of type-2 diabetes, some cancers, and heart and liver disease. In Britain, for example, the 2010 *Health Survey for England* showed that something approaching two-thirds of adults (aged 16 or over) and almost one-third of children (aged 2–15) were overweight or obese, while over a quarter of all adults and 16 per cent of all children were actually obese. Moreover, it was recently estimated that the direct costs caused to the National Health Service by obesity amounted to £5.1 billion per year.

In response to this modern 'epidemic', the United States and Britain have been in the forefront of major public health campaigns aimed at educating their populations on the dangers of poor eating habits and lack of exercise. The British campaign, spearheaded by the Department of Health, has adopted all the available means of communications—but especially television and the internet. The government set out its approach to tackling obesity through concerted action across society in its 'Healthy Lives, Healthy People: A Call to Action on Obesity in England', which it launched in October 2011, and also through its 'Change4Life' television and internet advertisements.

In the United States the lead was taken by First Lady Michelle Obama, who encouraged Americans to eat more fruits and vegetables in her 'Let's Move!' campaign ('America's Move to Raise a Healthier Generation of Kids'). The US Department of Agriculture's (USDA) obesity prevention and reduction strategy has focused on the 'energy balance', addressing the factors influencing both eating and physical activity. In 2012 the campaign stressed physical activity as well as eating '5 A Day': 3 servings of vegetables plus 2 servings of fruit (the USDA's recommended daily minimum).

■ Health risks and safe behaviours

As more focused and comprehensive approaches to public health were undertaken in the 20th century, they were increasingly accompanied by the idea of personal responsibility. And as personal behaviour and habits can harm others, individuals were expected to care about the health of fellow citizens as well as their own. The improving knowledge about the nature of specific diseases saw the launch of campaigns and the formation of societies aimed at educating the public to adopt healthy and hygienic lifestyles, and central to them was the idea of prevention, targeting human actions and behaviours known to endanger health.

Indeed, the maintenance of good health was a major concern of fascist and communist regimes, although invariably for very different ideological reasons. The Fascist and Nazi regimes of Italy and Germany respectively looked on health in racial and ideological terms, whereas the Soviet Union was more pragmatic: healthy citizens were more desirable, as they were more likely to meet (and surpass) their production targets for Stalin's Five-Year Plans.

DON'T DRINK!

In the Soviet Union, campaigns to combat the chronic problem of alcoholism continued under successive leaders in the Cold War period; indeed, mass alcoholism and the fight against it were integral parts of everyday life in the country throughout its communist history. For much of the 19th century, Russians' per-capita alcohol consumption had been among the lowest in Europe, strictly controlled by rural and urban communities as well as by the intensively working temperance societies. After the beginning of the forced industrialisation introduced under communism, millions of villagers poured into the cities and, liberated from the control of the community and with access to various sources of cheap alcohol, quickly established a culture of permanent drunkenness—drinking that aimed to bring about a rapid unconsciousness.

The Soviet state on the one hand supported this drinking as an instrument for draining off social tensions. In the 1920s Trotsky wrote a famous essay in which he referred to the three 'opiates' of the masses—'vodka, the church and the cinema'—in that order. Stalin wrote in 1930, at the beginning of major industrialisation, to the President of the Council of People's Commissars Molotov demanding 'the greatest expansion of vodka production possible for the sake of a real and serious defence of our country'. At the same time the government was all too aware that it could not renounce the revenues from the alcohol monopoly: as communism was establishing itself in the aftermath of the First World War, taxes on alcohol accounted for no less than a quarter of the state budget; when, much later, this percentage fell substantially during Mikhail Gorbachev's 1985 anti-alcohol campaign (the so-called 'Dry Law'), it contributed significantly to the decline of the Soviet economy.

On the other hand, the state clearly saw that its levels of alcohol consumption would lead to a

Excessive drinking was both socially and politically irresponsible, and ... the anti-alcohol campaigns in the 1920s and 1930s stressed individual and collective responsibility

80

80 Fit for purpose. Agile and athletic Soviet men and women adorn the pages of *USSR in Construction*. In the regimes of both fascist and communist nations, demonstrable good health was regarded as an expression of the ruling party's ideology and goals.

drastic reduction in life expectancy (as it did in post-communist Russia in the 1990s, when average male life expectancy declined dramatically) and that the reduction in the size of, and fragmentation of, families would significantly stunt Russia's birthrate. Since both of these factors risked damaging the Soviet Union's competitiveness in the Cold War environment, from time to time the government tried to reduce consumption with anti-alcohol campaigns, as occurred notably in 1920–25, 1929–30, 1954–58, 1971–72 and 1985–87.

The most spectacular visual manifestation of the Soviet anti-alcohol campaigns was undoubtedly the use of posters. The celebrated 'Rosta Windows', named after the Russian Telegraph Agency that sponsored the theme, consisted of a series of scenes telling a story somewhat in the manner of a child's comic; they were prepared in several hundred copies from cardboard stencils, first of all in Moscow and then in Petrograd, Odessa, Vitebsk and other centres of revolutionary ferment. The anti-alcohol campaigns were launched in tandem with other targets as part of a concerted

're-education' programme for the new, responsible, 'Soviet' citizen. In effect communism also attempted to strike a 'contract' with the people by warning them of the risks of unsociable behaviour. Excessive drinking was both socially and politically irresponsible, and the thrust of the anti-alcohol campaigns in the 1920s and 1930s stressed individual and collective responsibility to the state, the Party and to the family. Education was the key, and therefore the anti-alcohol campaigns went hand-in-hand with other campaigns, such as those intended to raise the literacy rate in Russia: Alexei Radakov's famous poster of 1920 depicted an illiterate person as a blind man, its text stressing that 'He who is illiterate is like a blind man. Failure and misfortune lie in wait for him on all sides.'

In the officially atheist Soviet state, some campaigns also urged citizens to overcome their religious superstitions as part of this collective responsibility. In a coloured lithograph (*image 82*) by Yuri Pimenov, the message read: 'Long Live Industrial and Financial Development! Fulfil the Five-Year Plan in Four years! No Religion!'

82

82 Yuri Pimenov's poster exhorting Soviet workers to 'Fulfil the Five-Year Plan in Four Years!' (1930). Attempting (unconvincingly) to derail the powerful train of progress is an assortment of stereotypes from the Bolshevik gallery of reactionaries and recidivists.

81 A poster from a Soviet anti-alcohol campaign. The sensible construction worker, mindful of his duties to self and the state, attempts to smash the insidious evil that is alcohol, its malevolence reinforced by the presence of a snake.

The main features and themes of the poster designs of the period were pictures of blast furnaces, power stations, technological advance and the people at work. Indeed, the posters of the 1930s provide a panoramic view of Soviet life and record the Soviet obsession with mechanisation, technology and its plans to transform Russia by means of rapid industrialisation. Pimenov's (*image 82*) contains many familiar features of the period. In the top left-hand corner are the factories and blast furnaces from which emerges the thrusting locomotive (symbolically red), a powerful symbol of the new Russia. Spread across the tracks in a doomed attempt to prevent the speeding train from passing are chains representing the past, held together by six stereotypes of the old, discredited, capitalist order (including a priest). The chains—about to be broken—symbolise religious prejudice, wrecking tactics, drunkenness, absenteeism and poor-quality production. Clearly, the Soviet state's fight against alcoholism must be seen as part of this wider political consciousness, which did not distinguish between the public and private lives of citizens in its propaganda.

The concern with alcoholism and absenteeism spread to all of the Soviet satellite states in Eastern Europe. In Czechoslovakia it even featured on matchbox labels, which, during the late 1940s and 1950s, became means to educate the new 'socialist' (communist) citizen. These labels benefited from a consistency of form, distribution, printing technology, size and physical material, ensuring that the propaganda message was adapted to the times and intentions of the propagandist, in this case the Czechoslovak Communist Party.

The Czech state's interest in citizens' health started with the foundation of communist Czechoslovakia in 1947. In accordance with the view that the new communist citizen's private life was also a public concern, excessive drinking was specifically targeted for the benefit of citizen, state and nation. Communist ideology was presented through rational, nationalistic and progressive lifestyle changes. Matchbox labels provided an ideal medium for these messages, as smokers have usually been more likely than non-smokers to drink heavily. One label (*image 83e*) from 1958 expressed the consequences of drinking at work, while

a

b

c

d

e

f

g

h

i

j

k

l

m

n

others appealed to rationalism, offering an array of statistical details such as: 'Drinking alcohol caused, in our land, in 1956 every ninth accident'; '… every tenth divorce' and '… 30 per cent of mental illnesses' (*images 83l–n*). The upside-down exclamation marks, together with the sideways text and the upside-down glasses, give the viewer a sense of dizziness, visually linking alcohol abuse with its ill effects.

Czech children, as the primary collectors of matchbox labels, were key carriers of the state's message into the home; thus they were educated by the state's paternal wisdom while acting as 'agitators' within the family. These children, already fearful of their parents' divorcing (as a result of drink) before their fathers died prematurely of alcoholism, were now given a means of salvation whereby the father (never the mother) could be persuaded to abstain from alcohol and make them as happy and proud as the smiling children depicted on the label.

For young men, a Czech 'beauty' was used to pressure them morally and emotionally into abstention. On one label (*image 83d*), she displayed her *ukazováček* finger (literally, 'pointing' or 'demonstrative' finger) as used traditionally by parents when disciplining children, to tempt and invite the male reader into a suggestive sexual oval, framed with love-hearts and red flowers. For older men, charged with the responsibilities of driving, the anti-alcohol message could be presented in a flow of sequences leading inexorably from drinking, to driving, and ultimately to a jail sentence (*image 83g*).

The intimacy of these simple yet powerful images could not be achieved through posters, reserved for public statements of power, celebration and authority. Matchbox-label propaganda in communist Czechoslovakia (and there were similar campaigns dealing with hygiene and tidiness, sport, recycling, and so on) helped to shape a society where nonconformity and antisocial(ist) actions defined people as the internal enemy. Both educative and evangelical, these labels, together with other forms of propaganda, advocated the levels of conformity that were expected by the state.

DON'T SMOKE!

Health education figured prominently in Nazi propaganda, too, although this was largely in support of its racial and eugenics campaigns. In July 1933 the 'Law for the Prevention of Hereditarily Diseased Offspring' permitted the compulsory sterilisation of people suffering from a number of allegedly hereditary illnesses. Less well known, though, is the world's most aggressive anti-tobacco health campaign, launched by the Nazi government in the 1930s. Nazi policies included bans on smoking in public places, increased tobacco taxes, advertising bans, and research into links between tobacco and lung cancer. A massive anti-smoking propaganda campaign was launched (and maintained) with posters showing smokers being swallowed by cigarettes, bearing the caption: 'You don't smoke it—it smokes you!' The *Führer* was also drafted in to support the programme. The caption beneath one picture of a determined-looking Hitler read: 'Our *Führer* Adolf Hitler drinks no alcohol and does not smoke … His performance at work is incredible.'

Anti-smoking messages were disseminated to people in their workplaces, often with the enthusiastic help of the Hitler Youth, who acted as apostles for a healthy Nazi lifestyle. Well-known health magazines such as the *Gesundes Volk* ('Healthy People'), *Volksgesundheit* ('People's Health') and *Gesundes Leben* ('Healthy Life') published warnings about the health consequences of smoking. The main journal of the anti-tobacco movement was *Reine Luft* ('Clean Air'), which carried dire warnings and pulled no punches in describing and revealing the harmful effects that tobacco had on human organs and tissues. In June 1939, an Office Against the Hazards of Alcohol and Tobacco was formed, and the *Reichsstelle für Rauschgiftbekämpfung* (Reich Office for the Struggle Against Intoxicating Drugs) helped in the anti-tobacco campaign. The Nazis also established ambitious tumour registries, which included the first broad registries of cancer incidence, and not just cancer mortality.

The Nazis' anti-tobacco rhetoric drew on an earlier generation's eugenics rhetoric, and it reflected an ethic of bodily purity and zeal for work. The anti-tobacco campaign must be understood against the backdrop of the Nazi quest for such racial and bodily purity, which also motivated many other public health efforts of the era. In this climate tobacco became, in one description, a 'corrupting force in a rotting civilisation that has become lazy'. By contrast, Hitler once even attributed the success of German fascism to his quitting smoking: the young artist-architect had smoked a couple of packs a day until 1919, when he threw his cigarettes into the Danube and never reached for them again.

The German anti-tobacco policies accelerated incrementally towards the end of the 1930s. The Luftwaffe banned smoking in 1938 and the German Post Office did likewise. Smoking was barred in many workplaces, government offices, hospitals and rest homes. The Nazi Party announced a ban on smoking in its offices in 1939, at which time *SS*

84 'The chain-smoker', a Nazi anti-smoking advertisement (1941). It promises that the smoker will be consumed by his habit: 'He does not devour it … it devours him!' Smoking did not suit Nazi goals of working to perfect the (Aryan) body.

84

> despite government regulations, many women in Germany regularly smoked, including the wives of high-ranking Nazi officials, such as Goebbels' wife Magda.

chief Heinrich Himmler announced a smoking ban for all uniformed police and *SS* officers while on duty. The *Journal of the American Medical Association* that year reported Hermann Goering's decree barring soldiers from smoking on the streets, on marches, and in brief off-duty periods. Sixty of Germany's largest cities banned smoking on street cars in 1941, and smoking was banned in air-raid shelters—though some shelters reserved separate rooms for smokers. During the war years tobacco-rationing coupons were denied to pregnant women (and to all women below the age of 25), while restaurants and cafés were barred from selling cigarettes to female customers. From July 1943 it was illegal for anyone under the age of 18 to smoke in public. Smoking was banned on all German city trains and buses in 1944, the initiative coming from Hitler himself, who was worried about exposure of young female conductors to tobacco smoke. An ordinance on 3 November 1941 raised tobacco taxes to a higher level than they had ever been (80–95 per cent of the retail price). Nazi policies were heralded as marking 'the beginning of the end' of tobacco use in Germany.

Despite all of this, the early anti-smoking campaign was considered a failure; more than this, between 1933 and 1937 there was a rapid *increase* in tobacco consumption in Germany, largely because the cigarette-manufacturing companies were constantly challenging the anti-tobacco campaign. The tobacco industry attempted to hinder the campaign to prevent women from smoking by countering government propaganda with advertisements that showed fashion models, smoking, as 'sexy' and 'liberated'. Indeed, despite government regulations, many women in Germany regularly smoked, including the wives of high-ranking Nazi officials, such as Goebbels' wife Magda.

Similar counter-propaganda was experienced in the United States. Edward Bernays—often referred to as the 'father' of modern propaganda—was engaged by the American Tobacco Company to work out a public relations strategy aimed at encouraging women to smoke. In the late 1920s, for example, they hired a group of young women to march down New York's Fifth Avenue in the Easter Parade, holding their 'torches of freedom'—their cigarettes. Thus, cigarettes were portrayed as symbols of women's emancipation.

By the early years of the Second World War, the rate of tobacco usage in Nazi Germany *had* declined. For example, as a result of the anti-tobacco measures implemented in the German army (*Wehrmacht*), the total tobacco consumption by soldiers decreased between 1939 and 1945. According to a survey conducted in 1944, although the *number* of smokers had increased in the *Wehrmacht* (fewer than 13 per cent were non-smokers), the total *consumption* of tobacco had decreased by just over 14 per cent. More men were smoking, but the average soldier was smoking about a quarter less tobacco than in the immediate pre-war period. The number of very heavy smokers (30 or more cigarettes per day) declined dramatically from fewer than 5 per cent to just 0.3 per cent, and similar declines were recorded for moderately heavy smokers. Rationing may have played a role here, and it should also be remembered that smoking was seen by some Germans as constituting a form of passive social 'resistance' to Nazism in general.

Since those times, anti-smoking campaigns have featured ever more strongly in public health propaganda—especially in the West. In one recent example, Britain's Department of Health launched a hard-hitting £3 million campaign (in January 2013). It looked to capitalise on the British penchant for making health-related New Year resolutions, by way of images designed to shock smokers into quitting. The campaign, embracing television, posters and billboards, and the internet, showed a cigarette mutating into tumours while being smoked. The message was brief and to the point: 'When you smoke, the chemicals you inhale cause mutations in your body … and mutations are how cancer starts. Every 15 cigarettes you smoke will cause a mutation. If you could see the damage you'd stop!'

'CLUNK, CLICK EVERY TRIP'

One highly effective piece of public health legislation in recent years has tackled motor-vehicle safety and the compulsory wearing of seatbelts. The introduction in Britain of this legislation in 1983 led to a 15-per-cent reduction in motor-accident patients brought to hospital, a reduction by a quarter in those requiring admissions to wards, and a similar fall in bed-occupancy. There were fewer patients with severe injuries, and notably a reduction in face, eye, brain and lung injuries. A key task for public health authorities was the education, advocacy and lobbying required in advance of the legislation to ensure its acceptability and subsequent implementation. 'Clunk, Click Every Trip' became the familiar slogan of a series of public information films and posters sponsored by the Royal Society for the Prevention of Accidents. They started in January 1971, featuring BBC disc-jockey Jimmy Savile. (In the United States, a similar campaign used the slogan 'Click it or Ticket'.) The advertisements included graphic sequences of what could happen to an unbelted person in the front of a car during a crash at 30 miles per hour or faster, showing drivers being thrown through the windscreen and an image of a disfigured woman survivor. They helped to lay the groundwork for compulsory seatbelt use in the

85

85 Tufty's tips, on a paper bag. From the 1950s British children were encouraged, via the characters of Tufty and his friends, to learn pedestrian safety, and later Tufty Clubs reinforced the lessons of the Green Cross Code: 'Stop … Look … If all clear ... Quick march!

86 Frightening statistics. A poster issued by the Royal Society for the Prevention of Accidents attempts to shock with numbers, showing an astonishing 1,534 children and teenagers killed on British roads in 1960 (and then breaking down the deaths into categories, in the smaller graphs). Through a combination of factors, including safety campaigns, annual deaths of children and teenagers have diminished very considerably since then.

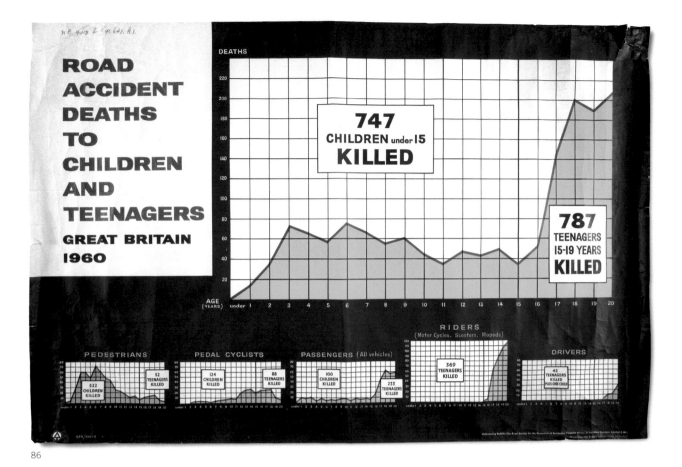

front seat of a vehicle, which came into force on 31 January 1983 (although car manufacturers had been legally obliged to fit front seatbelts in vehicles since 1965.)

An overlapping campaign, designed to promote road safety, encouraged children to observe the short step-by-step road-crossing procedure of the Green Cross Code and to join the 'Tufty Club'. The Green Cross Man is a costumed superhero, created in 1970 as an aid to teaching young children the Green Cross Code and for promoting general road safety. Today, the Code has become a multi-media campaign to enable pedestrians to cross streets safely. It has undergone several changes over the years, but the basic tenets—'Stop, Look, Listen, Think'—have remained more or less the same.

Starting in 1953, a series of puppet-animation public-information films featuring the character Tufty Fluffytail, a red squirrel, were broadcast across the country. The aim was to impart straight-forward and easily understandable safety messages to children, and it used original stories from the Royal Society for the Prevention of Accidents.

It struck a chord, and in 1961, to help disseminate the message, the Tufty Club came into being, targeted at pre-school children (under five years of age). The Club grew to 25,000 branches and an estimated 2 million child members in the early 1970s. Parents were involved too, and the Club issued tens of thousands of road-safety books to families.

Deaths from road traffic injuries have continued to fall in Britain—for example, in the 20 years between 1992 and 2002 down from 4,229 to 3,431. During the same period the number of child pedestrians killed was more than halved, down from 180 to 79. Many factors have played their part, of course, including engineering improvements in vehicles and on highways, the wearing of seat belts, and a raised consciousness of road safety procedures. But part of the mix is the 'propaganda' of the public information campaigns that continue to urge drivers not to 'Drink and Drive', and children to 'Stop, Look, Listen, Think.'

■ Communicable diseases

In 1943 Britain's Minister of Health, Ernest Brown, was responsible for the booklet *How to Keep Well in Wartime*, which offered commonsense advice on a range of health issues. A major concern for the British authorities was the spread of germs, resulting in large-scale absenteeism from work. Among other advice, the booklet urged people to cough or sneeze into a handkerchief and denounced any failure to do so as a 'rude and disgusting habit'. One of the most famous wartime poster slogans read: 'Coughs and Sneezes Spread Diseases'. Popular film stars and celebrities were recruited to add weight to these health campaigns. In 1942, for example, the comedian Arthur Askey appeared in a short film documentary entitled *The Nose Has It!* The propaganda campaign, which was coordinated by the Ministry of Information and spearheaded by a series of eight posters, was designed to show how thoughtlessness helped to spread not only the common cold but also many other diseases. Indeed, the whole 'coughs and sneezes' campaign, which extended beyond

the Second World War, was far more to do with fighting absenteeism than concern about people catching an ordinary cold. According to the Mass Observation research project, the poster campaign proved particularly effective with simple messages such as 'Remember a handkerchief in time saves nine—and helps to keep the nation fighting fit', 'Wanted for Sneezing to the Public Danger—and coughing without due care and attention', and 'The Ministry of Health says: Coughs and Sneezes Spread Diseases. Trap the germs in your handkerchief'. The core slogan endured, and the campaign continues to be used by the National Health Service to this day, for example being extensively exploited to prevent the spread of 'swine flu' in 2009.

'DON'T DIE OF IGNORANCE!'

During both the First and Second world wars, one particular health problem singled out was the need to combat venereal disease (VD). It was assumed that men fighting far away from their home and

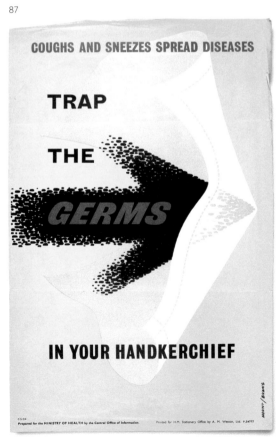

87

87 A 1940s Ministry of Health poster for the 'Coughs and Sneezes Spread Diseases' campaign, combating the evils of sneezing. Handkerchiefs were in the front line of defeating the spread of germs.

88 Another Ministry of Health poster for the 'Coughs and Sneezes Spread Diseases' campaign (*c.* 1940s). The aim of the campaign was to convince people that unprotected sneezing and coughing without covering one's mouth were inherently anti-social.

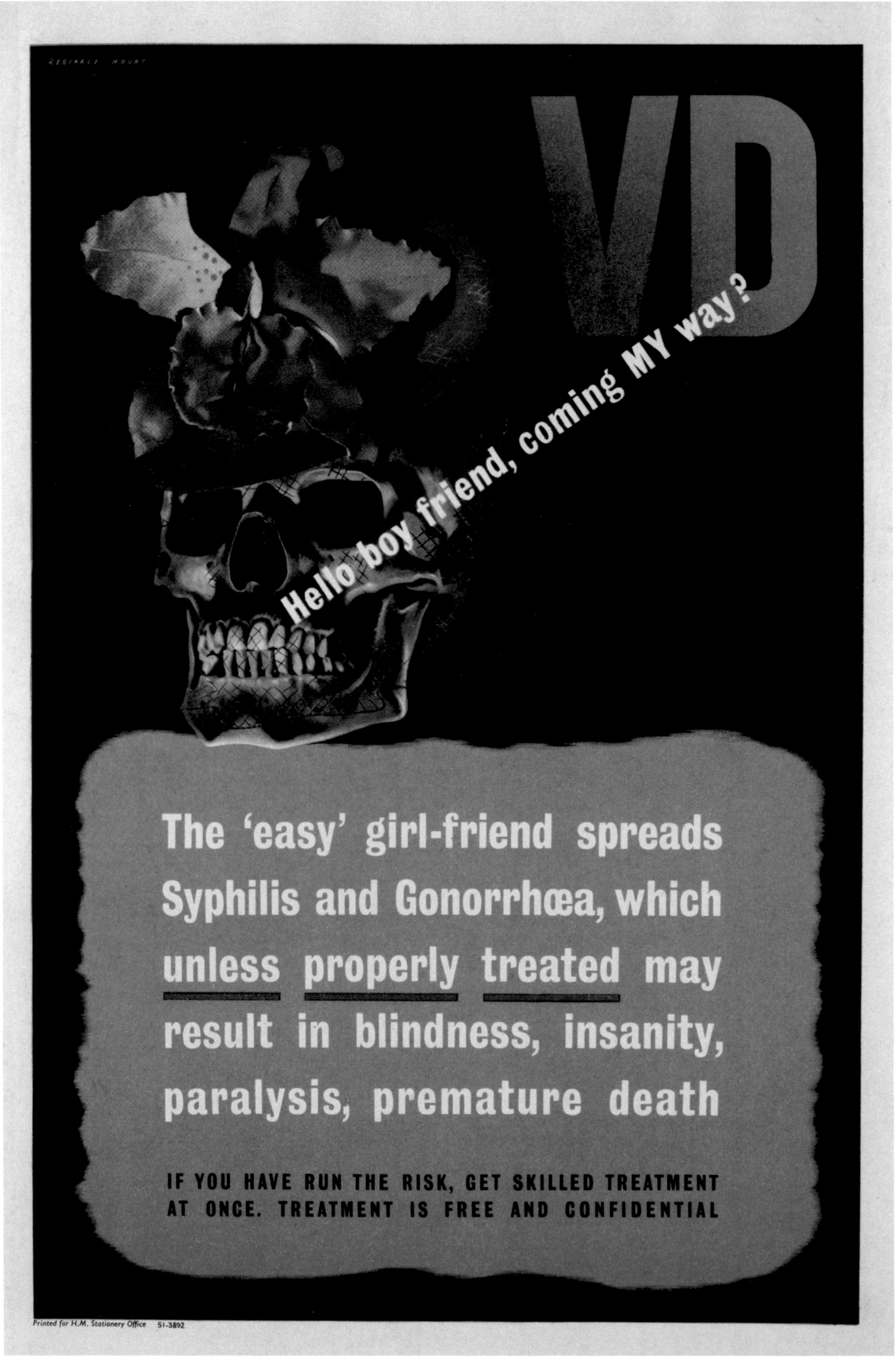
REGINALD MOUNT
VD
Hello boy friend, coming MY way?
The 'easy' girl-friend spreads Syphilis and Gonorrhœa, which unless properly treated may result in blindness, insanity, paralysis, premature death
IF YOU HAVE RUN THE RISK, GET SKILLED TREATMENT AT ONCE. TREATMENT IS FREE AND CONFIDENTIAL
Printed for H.M. Stationery Office 51-3892

89 **Deadly disease. A lurid evocation of the disabling and potentially fatal threats lurking beneath the superficial glamour of the "'easy" girl-friend' is conveyed in this wartime British anti-VD poster (c.1943).**

families would be prone to sexual temptation. During the First World War, for example, sexually transmitted diseases caused the US Army to lose the services of 18,000 servicemen per day. During the Second World War preventative efforts intensified through films, lectures, posters, leaflets and the greater availability of condoms. US propaganda posters targeted at soldiers and sailors appealed to their patriotism in urging them to protect themselves, with such slogans as 'You can't beat the Axis if you get VD.' Images of women were used to catch the eye on many VD posters, combined with a message that had to be unequivocal: 'She may look clean—But … Pick Ups, 'Good Time' Girls, Prostitutes—Spread Syphilis and Gonorrhoea.' (Such efforts were not confined to the United States, of course. For example, in the Soviet Union the great film-maker Alexander Medvedkin was producing films for the Red Army, including the hygiene film *Watch Your Health*, 1927.)

Infection rates remained stubbornly high, but treatment times were drastically reduced with the arrival of penicillin. Cases of venereal disease even gained priority access to drugs if that meant a faster return to the frontline. By 1944 the number of men lost to service had been reduced thirty-fold (though there were still around 600 servicemen incapacitated every day). This drop in numbers was partly because of the US Army's effort to raise awareness about the dangers faced by servicemen through poor sexual hygiene, and the War Department supplied each recruit, on enlistment, with a 16-page leaflet entitled *Sex Hygiene and Venereal Diseases*. The other important factor lay in the medical advances. In late 1943 a case of gonorrhoea

required a hospital treatment of 30 days, and curing syphilis remained a 6-month ordeal; by mid-1944, the average case of gonorrhoea was reduced to a treatment of 5 days, and in many cases the patient remained on duty status while being treated.

All combatant nations in the war designed their own campaigns to warn military and civilian personnel of the dangers of sexually transmitted diseases. A colourful 1943 VD poster produced in Britain by Reginald Mount depicted a skull wearing a bright pink bonnet, its ironically tempting text inviting the reader: 'Hello boy friend, coming MY way?' (*image 89*).

In December 1942, Mass Observation questioned British people on press advertisements about sexually transmitted diseases. Half of them still seemed ignorant about the subject, and about 10 per cent were embarrassed by it, with some men worried about their womenfolk viewing the subject in the newspapers. Few understood what the different venereal diseases were, although 'the pox' and 'the clap' were mentioned in responses—and in one case the 'venerable' disease.

Forty years later, in the 1980s, a new global threat posed by the AIDS epidemic persuaded many governments around the world to launch campaigns (mainly through television and advertising posters), warning of the dangers of unprotected sexual intercourse. Many of these campaigns broke new ground in terms of their explicit references to sexual practices and their honesty about the scale of the epidemic.

In 1987 the British government launched a major campaign with the slogan 'AIDS: Don't Die of Ignorance'. The spearhead of the campaign, which was intended to shock the nation into action, was a stark television advertisement sponsored by the Central Office of Information for the Department of Health. In it, against the background of an ominous sky, a volcano erupted. Amid the smoke and the tumbling rocks a tombstone became visible, in the act of being chiselled. Actor John Hurt's deep voiceover warned: 'There is now a danger that has become a threat to us all. It is a deadly disease and there is no known cure.' Then the viewers saw the word etched into the blackened granite: 'AIDS'. The slogan rounding it off was: 'Don't die of ignorance.'

With its unambiguous warnings and stark message, the advertisement (and an equally strong one featuring icebergs) shocked viewers and gave rise to accusations of panic-mongering. Some thought it was completely inappropriate for television and might scare children. Indeed, some critics argued that such approaches were counterproductive because the message was *so* bleak that it scared people, who 'turned off' or chose not to listen (echoing similar concerns expressed about the wartime VD campaigns). Yet the campaign—the world's first major government-sponsored national AIDS awareness drive—would later be hailed as the most successful. In addition to the tombstone advertisement, a leaflet was sent to every household in the country, with the advice that 'Anyone can get it, gay or straight, male or female. Already 30,000 people are infected', and a week of educational programming was scheduled at peak time on all four British terrestrial television channels then in existence. The scale of the campaign was unprecedented in the sphere of public health. It and other active work in the field of HIV prevention among intravenous drug users have helped to keep British rates of infection in this group relatively low compared to a number of other European countries. The campaign's tactics were then copied around the world. But such success was in stark contrast to the scale of the disease in sub-Saharan Africa, where two-thirds of the world's estimated HIV-infected population of over 34 million people live. Eradication campaigns are the most ambitious and technically complex of global health programmes. In July 2012, UNAIDS (Joint United Nations Programme on HIV/AIDS) launched its latest report and propaganda campaign entitled: 'Together We Will End Aids'.

A MARCH OF DIMES

One of the most successful 20th-century propaganda campaigns was that launched against polio in the United States. Although it was initiated by a US president, Franklin D. Roosevelt, it was not sponsored by the government, nor indeed by any governmental agency. In 1921, at the age of 39, Roosevelt contracted polio and became paralysed from the waist down. For the rest of his life he was committed to finding a way to rehabilitate himself as well as others afflicted with the infantile paralysis that had been dubbed 'the crippler'. In 1934, he began using the occasion of his birthday each year to encourage Americans to throw 'birthday balls' to help raise funds for his Georgia Warm Springs Foundation, which he had established in 1927 to facilitate polio rehabilitation. In 1938 Roosevelt created the National Foundation for Infantile Paralysis (NFIP) to support the centre and also to

radio personality Eddie Cantor took to the airwaves and urged Americans to send their loose change to President Roosevelt

90 **A leaflet warning about the threat of AIDS, as distributed throughout Britain in 1987. Its simple and stark message was emphasised through the sombre, funereal, granite-like visuals.**

aid the victims of polio throughout the country. To increase awareness of the foundation's campaign, radio personality Eddie Cantor took to the airwaves and urged Americans to send their loose change to President Roosevelt in 'a march of dimes to reach all the way to the White House'. The name 'March of Dimes' was later tagged onto the National Foundation's own title, effectively revitalising that organisation.

The first 'March' brought in over 2.5 million dimes. The NFIP immediately began issuing research grants, giving scholarships to doctors and nurses, and providing equipment for laboratories and hospitals. The non-profit foundation was desperately needed, because there was little government funding for medical research, no public health insurance, and little private health insurance. It bought iron lungs, crutches and laboratory equipment as well as trucks to transport it all in, so all that was needed could be moved quickly to regions in the midst of an outbreak. The NFIP established a network of local chapters that could raise money and deliver aid, boosted by endorsements from Hollywood stars and personal appeals. But the local chapters effectively raised money without star power. The March of Dimes called on ordinary people to contribute just a little money. One tactic was to go to cinemas, stop the film in the middle, turn up the lights and pass out a collection can. March of Dimes collection cans were placed on store counters, and people filled them with change, while children mailed in dimes on special cards. The March of Dimes effectively changed the way it approached fund-raising. Rather than soliciting large contributions from a few wealthy individuals, the March sought small donations from millions of individuals. Its hugely successful fundraising campaigns collected hundreds of millions of dollars—more than all of the US charities at the time combined, with the exception of the Red Cross.

Little was still known about polio during this period. But the scientific committees established by the NFIP to fund virus research began to investigate diseases affecting those in uniform in the Second World War, and thus, in 1943, the NFIP awarded a grant to the US Army Neurotropic Virus Commission to study polio in North Africa; Albert Sabin (who would later develop the oral polio vaccine) conducted parts of this study.

After his death Roosevelt was memorialised on the US dime in 1946, which assured the remembrance of his connection to the March of Dimes. By the end of the war, millions of dimes had flooded the White House. In 1945, the annual March of Dimes campaign raised $18.9 million for the NFIP and indeed March of Dimes-funded medical research accelerated as the patient aid programme was tested to its limits, particularly in the huge polio epidemic of 1949 (the 1944 epidemic has been memorably captured in the Philip Roth novel *Nemesis*). In the early 1950s, 3,100 chapters of the NFIP were operated almost completely by volunteers, although well-known stars of film and music continued to support the campaign. In support of the 1954 March of Dimes campaign all of the major Walt Disney characters (Mickey, Donald, Pluto) marched to an adapted version of the Seven Dwarfs' song ('Hi Ho, Hi Ho, we'll lick ol' polio. With dimes, quarters and our dollars … Hi Ho, Hi Ho.')

By 1955 the March of Dimes had invested $25.5 million in research, most importantly the research and development of a polio vaccine by Jonas Salk.

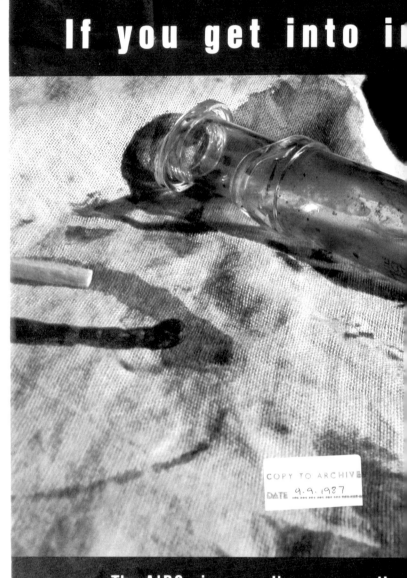

91 'Don't Inject AIDS'. A British poster (1987; archive copy) targets the vulnerable community of intravenous drug users as part of the battle against HIV infection. The emphasis was less on giving up drug use, and more on precautionary hygiene, such as avoidance of dirty needles. It achieved some notable success.

ing, what's going to get into you?

quipment. Never share, not even once. DON'T INJECT AIDS.

In 1954, the drug was tested in a trial involving 1.8 million schoolchildren known as 'polio pioneers'. On 12 April 1955, the vaccine was announced to the news media as 'safe, effective, and potent'. Polio declined rapidly from tens of thousands of new cases per year to a mere handful; by 1961, only 161 cases were recorded in the United States. Arguably, without the massive propaganda effort and the accompanying fundraising, the breakthrough with the polio vaccine may have come much later.

VACCINATION AND COUNTER-PROPAGANDA

As the example of polio demonstrates, the emergence of vaccines created new dreams and hopes of a world in which a range of diseases could be prevented, perhaps once and for all. By promising drastic, immediate and mass protection against disease, vaccines became one of the main medical tools during armed conflict, particularly during the First and the Second world wars and the more recent Gulf wars. At the beginning of the 21st century some funding organisations, such as the Bill Gates Foundation, have returned to the

Pasteurian dream by channelling vast resources into high-profile and media-attracting research for a malaria or HIV vaccine, for example—though these developments have side-effects in diverting and sometimes reducing the availability of expertise and resources in the global effort to eradicate poverty and disease.

Mass-media campaigns, including those described above, have shaped the debate about the maintenance of good health and the relationship between the state and citizenship, and have implied a 'contract' of sorts, not unlike that between a doctor and his patient: while the state has provided scientific information and advocated behavioural change, the citizen has been expected to follow that advice uncritically. Vaccines have both reinforced and tested this relationship; they have provided state authorities, both in developed and developing countries, as well as international organisations and charities, with a scientific rationale and legitimacy for greater intervention. However, in promoting and maintaining good health can the state continue to expect an 'acquiescent' public? Vaccines and

92

92 **Propaganda against polio. Marilyn Monroe was one of the many high-profile American personalities who lent their lustrous names and images to the battle against polio. Here she accompanies the March of Dimes' poster twins, six-year-old Lindy and Sandy Sue Solomon, at its annual fashion show at New York's Waldorf-Astoria Hotel (1958).**

> in other countries the 'contract' between the citizen and the state is less formal and this has enabled counter-propaganda campaigns to challenge the advice provided by the state

vaccine research have raised serious ethical dilemmas in the past, in production and clinical experiments, and have led to public protest and sometimes resistance against medicine. In some countries, such as France and Germany, children are expected to furnish proof of vaccination before they can attend school; in other countries the 'contract' between the citizen and the state is less formal and this has enabled counter-propaganda campaigns to challenge the advice provided by the state. Recent examples in the UK have concerned the MMR, cervical cancer and swine flu campaigns.

The MMR controversy is an interesting case study. The MMR vaccine is a combined immunisation against measles, mumps and rubella and was first developed in the late 1960s. It is generally administered to children around the age of one year, with a second dose before starting school. It is widely used around the world, and since its introduction in the 1970s over 500 million doses have been administered in over 60 countries. As with all vaccinations, long-term effects and efficacy are subject to continuing study. Before the use of a vaccine against measles, its incidence was so high that infection with measles was felt to be as inevitable as, in the well-known saying, 'death and taxes'. Today, the incidence of measles has fallen to less than 1 per cent of people under the age of 30 in countries with routine childhood vaccination. During 1999–2004, a strategy led by the World Health Organization and UNICEF resulted in improvements in measles vaccination coverage that (it was estimated) averted an estimated 1.4 million measles deaths worldwide. The combined MMR

vaccine was introduced to avoid the necessity of three separate injections.

In Britain, however, the MMR vaccine was the subject of controversy in 1998, following the publication of a study of 12 children who had bowel symptoms along with autism or other disorders; the parents of some of these children attributed the onset of autism to the MMR vaccine. These findings were subsequently refuted by both the General Medical Council and the medical journal *The Lancet*; nevertheless, they prompted a vociferous counter-campaign, conducted largely over the internet, which encouraged parents to reject the MMR vaccination and to seek separate injections or alternative therapies. Health experts credited the media reporting of the MMR–autism controversy and the online campaign with triggering a decline in vaccination rates. Before publication of the discredited findings, the British inoculation rate for MMR was 92 per cent, but after publication it dropped to below 80 per cent. By November 2012, the vaccine had recovered to reach its highest level for 14 years. Nevertheless, it was still short of the 95 per cent that health experts believed was required to stop the spread of measles.

■ Propaganda: on the side of the angels?

Sometimes, then, health and hygiene propaganda can provoke a backlash. In the case of MMR it was fear of unintended consequences for small children. At other times it can simply be a form of resistance to authority. During the American occupation of the Italian island of Lampedusa towards the end of the Second World War, some inhabitants took exception to new rules and exhortations against defecating in public, as published in the US Army's propaganda newspaper. A group of Lampedusa's men protested by gathering on the main piazza, and 'with one accord they struck a blow for freedom'.

But the whole subject of public health, which has been defined as 'the science and art of preventing disease, prolonging life and preventing disability through the organised efforts of society', amply demonstrates the scale of propaganda campaigns in times of peace, not just in war. Governments have a responsibility for their citizens, and the media are the obvious means of conveying public health information. The methods can vary enormously as we have seen, from shock tactics to humour, and the vehicles may be many, from matchboxes to music. Sometimes a state's motivations are more complex, darker, than the mooted health benefits suggest, as we have seen in the Soviet and Nazi contexts; and sometimes groups of citizens and pressure groups, especially in the age of the internet and social networking, band together to resist the orthodoxies of public information. But by and large it could be said that when it comes to public health, propaganda's pejorative associations *tend* to slip away—it is generally seen in a much more favourable light.

'Know
your enemy'

Case studies in negative propaganda

5

PERHAPS AT the opposite pole of propaganda's moral compass—the obverse to helpful public information—is the propaganda that attempts to create or exploit difference. 'The cult of hatred and xenophobia is the cheapest and surest method of obtaining from the masses the ignorant and savage patriotism which puts the blame for every political folly or social misfortune upon the hand of the foreigner.' So said the publisher Leonard Woolf in his *Principia Politica: A Study of Communal Knowledge* (1953). Certainly, in terms of propaganda, the use of contrasts has proved one of the most identifiable stylistic devices. Not only do strong contrasts contain a greater emotional intensity than more subtle nuances, but they also guide the audience's sympathies with more certainty.

Propaganda based on contrasts is full of confrontations between good and evil, beauty and 'the beast', order and chaos; in each case the contrast serves to force the individual into a desired, established commitment to a particular view. In this ultimate purpose, propaganda is aided by our psychological need for value judgements in simple black-and-white terms. This is particularly so if a country is in a state of crisis or war, when there is an increasing need for a *simplification* of the issues. At such times, the 'other side' becomes totally

malevolent, one's own cause indisputably just, and everyone gathers around the symbols of unity.

Political propaganda therefore thrives in times of uncertainty, and fuelling hatred is generally its most fruitful aid. In any society a people cannot be kept too long at a pitch of sacrifice and conviction in aid of a cause. Even in regimes that have demanded a relentless fanaticism, such as the Third Reich or during periods in the Soviet Union, some form of diversion was needed. Hatred of an enemy can be manipulated to fulfil such a need. The very immediate, spontaneous nature of hatred, a simple and sometimes violent emotion, can be aroused through the most elementary of means. In essence, it consists in attributing one's own misfortunes to an outsider. A frustrated people needs to hate, because hatred—when shared with others—is the most potent of all unifying emotions; or, as Heinrich Heine put it in the 19th century, 'What Christian love cannot achieve is affected by a common hatred.' Whether the object of hatred is the Bolshevik, the Jew, the Muslim or the Anglo-Saxon, such propaganda has its best chance of success when it clearly designates a target as the source of all misery or suffering, providing the target it chooses is not *too* powerful. The aim of propaganda is to identify the object of this hatred in order to solidify the feelings of hatred.

93 Demonising the enemy. In this White Russian poster issued by the Southern armies during the Russian Civil War (1918–21), leading Bolsheviks—including Lenin, Trotsky, Zinoviev and others—are driven into Hell (and its array of tortures) by White Guardsmen and an avenging angel.

the Duke of Wellington once proudly remarked that: 'We have been, we are, and I trust we always will be, detested by the French.'

Clearly, identifying an object to hate means exploiting *stereotypes*—conventional figures that come to be regarded as representative of particular classes, races, nations, and so on. Indeed, this is one of the most striking means by which different propaganda media such as the cinema and television have influenced social attitudes, changing or reinforcing opinions. The American social scientist Walter Lippmann developed the term 'stereotype' to describe the knowledge people *thought* they possessed—that is, knowledge based on myths or dreams. He believed in the power of the myth, or stereotype, to arouse popular enthusiasm, and he argued that abstract ideas and concepts such as national pride were more real to the masses than actual realities. In this context, propaganda gives individuals the stereotypes they no longer take the trouble to work out for themselves; it furnishes stereotypes in the form of slogans or labels. The recognition of stereotypes is therefore an important part of understanding the use of anti-symbols and the portrayal of the enemy in propaganda (and notably in film propaganda). Not only does it provide a target that can be attacked, but it also offers a scapegoat, the easiest means of diverting public attentions from genuine social and political problems at home.

Stereotypes invariably come ready made, having evolved, whether consciously or subconsciously, over a considerable period of time. They frequently attach themselves to myths associated with other nations, races or groups—one only has to think about anti-Jewish motifs in Nazi propaganda or anti-Soviet motifs in US propaganda during the Cold War to illustrate the point. In propaganda

terminology there are two kinds of images of the enemy that emerge: the enemy from 'within', and the enemy from 'without'. Propaganda is usually concerned with the latter—particularly in times of war—but not exclusively, as the following case studies will show.

■ The 'avaricious' French

When France and Britain put recent colonial disputes to one side at the turn of the 19th century, this signalled a rapprochement overturning years of mutual suspicion, sometimes hatred. In 1904 this new era was expressed in the signing of a historic agreement, and the *Entente Cordiale* was born. In earlier times, when not clashing on the battlefield, they were trading insults and name-calling, with the French transformed into 'frogs' and the English into 'rosbifs'. Britain's last military engagement on the continent had been with the French at Waterloo, and the Duke of Wellington once proudly remarked that: 'We have been, we are, and I trust we always will be, detested by the French.'

A recently translated 12th-century poem, *Roman des Franceis*, reveals just how deep-rooted in history the rivalry and name-calling is. The 396-line poem is dated to between 1180 and 1194. Just over a century earlier, in 1066, Duke William of Normandy had added the English crown to his titles, and his successors as kings of England now ruled Normandy and other parts of what today is modern France. The poem's author, Andrew de Coutances, was an Anglo-Norman cleric who refers

94 The *Entente Cordiale* under a little 21st-century strain, in a cartoon by Chris Riddell, published in the *Observer* (12 June 2005). Anglo-French love–hate propaganda has absorbed many themes over the years. In this case, Tony Blair and Jacques Chirac hug in amity as they attack each other's presumed economic stance—and stab each other in the back.

to the French as godless, arrogant and cowardly—as lazy dogs, heretics and rapists. It is no surprise that the poem also coincided with conflicts between the English and French kingdoms not long before the French conquered Normandy in 1204. The poem is arguably one of the earliest examples of anti-French propaganda, in which racial rhetoric plays an important role in creating support for the war.

When the poem was written, Philip II of France was launching repeated attacks on Normandy, taking advantage of infighting among England's royal family. While rivalry between the English and their Gallic neighbours now only tends to surface at sporting occasions and European summits, the poem recalls battles between them and describes the vices of the French in detail.

It is worth remembering that during this period 'intellectuals' were deployed to compose diatribes against the enemy. This particular poem was poisonously undermining the French and their

national legend while promoting the legend of King Arthur. Andrew de Coutances refutes criticisms of Arthur and celebrates a legendary victory over Frollo, the French ruler, who is portrayed as lazy and incompetent: 'Lying flat out without stirring himself / Frollo got the French to equip him / For that is the way of the French / Getting their shoes on while lying down,' he writes. Having described at length the cowardly nature of the French, de Coutances even claims, wrongly, that Paris loosely derived its name from the word *partir*, meaning 'to flee'. He also calls the French 'serfs' and 'peasants' in an attempt to suggest that they are a race without nobility, adding: 'People remind them often enough about this source of shame, but they may as well have not bothered; for they take neither offence nor account, as they know no shame.'

Several passages are worth recalling to appreciate the range of insult. On King Arthur leading the English against France:

94

Arthur besieged Paris, doubt it not at all!
He had a large force of
Well trained and equipped knights,
So he fiercely attacked the city.
The English went on the attack,
And the French defended like cowards,
They gave up at the first onset
And shamefully ran away.
It was from this flight [*partir*] that
Paris got its name, there is no concealing it,
Originally the place was called Thermes
And was indeed very famous.

On France's humiliation:

Arthur took homage from the French
And he established as a release-payment
A four-pence charge for being a peasant
To be paid as their poll tax.
People remind them often enough about
This source of shame, but they may as well not
    have bothered;
For they take neither offence nor account,
As they know no shame.

Such a Frenchman as does value virtue and honour
Will not like it of course,
But so far as he is the more ashamed
He will boast twice as much
So know that, wherever you go,
Believe a Frenchman not at all;
Seek indeed and you shall find
But you find no prowess if there's none to be had.

On French culinary habits:

A man who dines with the French
Should grab whatever he may
As either he will end up with nuts
Or will just carry off the shallots
A Frenchman would need to own the world
To live as well as he would like.

Because that is something that cannot happen
The French know to hold what provisions they have.
That's the way they are in their own land
But when they're abroad they're even more greedy
And shamefully gorge themselves at every table
Whenever they get near one.

And whenever hosts have them in their homes
They realise the French are such men
So greedy and so avaricious
That they ought to drive them off with kicks.

De Coutances's assertions, that the French 'live more vilely than a dog' and are 'rascals' and 'mockers', almost seem to presage the vivid insults uttered by the French knights in the 1975 comedy film *Monty Python and the Holy Grail*. The 12th-century poem provides early evidence that today's usually convivial Anglo-French relations were preceded by centuries of robust invective and negative propaganda: less an *entente cordiale*, and more a love–hate relationship, with the hate in evidence for much of the time.

95 **One of the many woodcuts from John Foxe's *Actes and Monuments* (*Book of Martyrs*), 1583 edition, showing the sufferings of Protestants for their faith. In this case, Cuthbert Simpson undergoes the rack in the Tower of London during Mary I's reign. Foxe's *magnum opus* in many ways amounted to an early example of atrocity propaganda.**

■ Muslims and martyrs

In the Western tradition, it is the early Crusades that witness the first examples of 'atrocity propaganda' in wartime. In 1095 Pope Urban II, in a sermon given at Clermont, justified war against Islam by claiming that the enemy had ravaged the churches of God in the Eastern provinces, circumcised Christian men, violated women and carried out the most unspeakable torture before killing them. Urban's sermon, when disseminated, succeeded in mobilising popular enthusiasm for

what became known as the People's Crusade.

Centuries later, powerful representations of martyrdom can be found in the engravings in John Foxe's *Actes and Monuments* (better known as *Book of Martyrs*), its first edition printed in England appearing in 1563. The suffering of English Protestants, especially during the reign (1553–58) of the Catholic Mary I, and the sensational manner in which they were represented by Foxe captured the bitter religious divisions during the

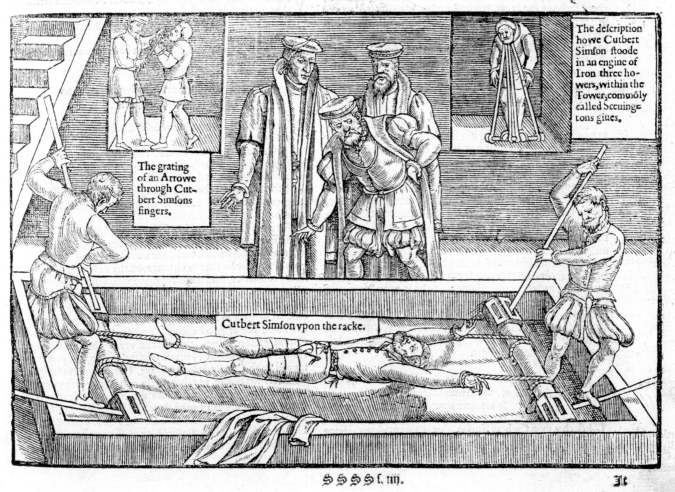

English Reformation. The book was produced and illustrated with more than sixty distinctive woodcut impressions and was, at that time, the largest publishing project ever undertaken in England. In 1571 the Convocation of Canterbury decreed that the book was to be placed, together with the English-language Bishop's Bible of 1568, in the house of every bishop, dean and archdeacon. In the preface to the first edition Foxe claimed that he wished to reach 'every man' and the 'simple people'. Foxe's vast work, expensive as it was, proved massively popular.

In many ways the horrifically graphic portrayals of torture and burnings can be seen as the forerunner to the type of atrocity propaganda more familiar in the 20th century. As religious propaganda, the messages sent out by the text and engravings influenced anti-Catholic sentiment for generations and helped to stoke an atmosphere of fear and suspicion against Europe's Catholic powers and a view of Catholics at home as potential traitors.

In our own recent past, following the recognition of the full dimensions of the Holocaust, atrocity propaganda has continued to figure prominently in all major modern wars, from Korea to Kosovo. Regimes and combatants who commit atrocities risk yielding a powerful propaganda tool to their opponents, especially in an age where international law has defined 'war crimes'. In the First Gulf War, for example, Western journalists were able to exploit the earlier *Anfal*—the extermination by Saddam Hussein's regime of ethnic Kurds in the north of the country. Ethnic cleansing, as well as the atrocities that occur as a result of such policies, were strongly featured in the reporting of

the Kosovo conflict too, where both Albanians and Serbs employed atrocity stories to stir nationalist identity and mutual hatred.

Arguably, the modern history of atrocity propaganda began with 'the Hun' in 1914.

■ The Hun and the Prussian bully

It was during the First World War that the German enemy came to be derogatorily called the 'Hun'. The original Huns were actually Mongols from Central Asia, who spread into Europe in the 4th century AD, and who became popularly linked with ideas of barbarian invasion and destruction. But by 1914, British soldiers and civilians alike were familiar with the destructive associations of 'the Hun' in a more immediate context, an association fuelled by a relentless and potent propaganda campaign that was able to exploit the fact that the Germans had laid waste places of cultural significance such as Louvain (in Belgium) and Rheims (in France). The association of 'the Hun' with contemporary Germans persisted throughout the war, with Kaiser Wilhelm II sometimes portrayed as Attila the Hun.

While British public opinion about Germany was transformed by propaganda during the war, the negative stereotype had been in construction since the late 19th century. Much of British propaganda was built on the premise that Germany was the unprovoked aggressor in the war and that Britain was taking up arms, reluctantly, for deeply held principles. The demonisation of Germany was, however, a relatively recent phenomenon. After all, the traditional enemy had been France, which, as we have seen, often reciprocated with a bitter contempt for 'perfidious Albion'.

The German invasion of neutral Belgium was the pretext for an anti-German campaign that rapidly mobilised widespread support among all sections of the British population. Belgium was depicted as a defenceless child or woman ravaged by a brutal 'Prussian militarism' (in fact a term that had only been applied since the turn of the century). One of the most famous cartoons of the First World War, 'Bravo Belgium!' by F.H. Townsend, was published by *Punch* on 12 August 1914, when the comparatively tiny forces of the Belgians appeared to be resisting the German advance. It conjures up a David-versus-Goliath struggle ('The Prussian bully invades an inoffensive neutral country'), with a little shepherd boy representing the brave and 'inoffensive' Belgium dwarfed by the threatening and overbearing Prussian bully, whose shadow is already spreading into neutral territory ('No Thoroughfare'). The contrast between the huge raised club wielded by the German and the small lowered stick held by 'Belgium' could not be more

96

96 'Bravo, Belgium!', from the pages of *Punch* (12 August 1914, cartoon by F.H. Townsend). A valiant Belgian boy stands firm against the advancing Prussian bully, who is replete with sausages to reinforce the stereotype. A violated Belgian neutrality played a large role in the British rationale for war.

PUNCH, OR THE LONDON CHARIVARI.—August 12, 1914.

NO THOROUGHFARE

F.H Townsend Aug. 1914

BRAVO, BELGIUM!

obvious, and was playing on a traditional British feeling of support for an underdog. Germany proved to be the perfect enemy, and whenever enthusiasm for the war began to flag there was an endless stream of German atrocities (both real and imagined) to strengthen national resolve.

As already mentioned, the 1914–18 conflict witnessed governments taking their first tentative initiatives in using film propaganda to depict their enemies. Although the Russian tsar had famously dismissed cinema as 'complete rubbish', when war came others took a different view and seized on the opportunities that this new medium offered, and soon the cinema was widely used by all the belligerents to make the enemy as villainous as possible. In Britain, the government could rely on both official and commercial film-makers to depict Germany unflatteringly. The theme of the Prussian bully was taken up by Lancelot Speed and his animated cartoons (known as 'lightning sketches'), which sought to ridicule the Kaiser and German military might. They proved to be a great success with British audiences, and Speed's cinematic cartoons contained many topical references. In 'The Prussian Bully' (1915) the audience were shown the German shelling of Rheims cathedral—thought at the time to be the height of German barbarism. In the film, Speed draws a picture of Rheims cathedral and across the sketch writes: 'The World's Greatest Gothic Work'. He then draws a large artillery weapon similar to the 'Big Bertha' howitzer that destroyed the cathedral, carrying the title: 'The Work of the World's greatest GOTH!' The Kaiser appears with a devil emerging from his Prussian helmet to exclaim: 'Do

I hear any Cheers?' In an interview in 1914, Speed revealed that an exaggerated drawing of Lord Kitchener's drooping moustache had provided the inspiration behind the image of the British bulldog, which would remain the implacable guardian of the British Empire and could always be relied upon to eat the German *Bratwurst*—a shorthand for German barbarism.

Vilification of the Kaiser and his *Weltpolitik* (often referred to 'kaiserism') and accusations of German brutality remained hallmarks of British propaganda throughout the war. The German policy of *Schrecklichkeit* (literally 'frightfulness' or 'terror', based on the idea that ruthlessness shortens war) continued during the German advances into Belgium and was widely reported in the British (and foreign) press. The popular press needed no encouragement from the government to publish such stories of German atrocities and as a result public opinion, suitably whipped up, could periodically tip into hysteria.

Adrian Gregory, writing about the British press in the early stages of the war, attributes the proliferation of atrocity reports to the recruiting panic after the Battle of Mons in August 1914, but more significantly to the sacking of the Belgian university town of Louvain also in that month. As he has noted, 'Louvain was an undoubted cultural jewel, a perfect site for proposing a powerful thesis that the German army was a real enemy of civilisation.' Gregory points out that Louvain provided a unique opportunity for the verification of atrocity stories, since it was briefly recaptured and photographs were taken. While 248 citizens were killed and one-sixth of the town's buildings destroyed, it was a far

97 'The Prussian Butcher', a wartime cartoon by Edmund Sullivan (1915). It is Mercy who is on the chopping block, about to be dismembered by the bestial Hun, signified by the traditional spiked helmet, the *Pickelhaube*. German atrocities in Belgium, real and imagined, helped to fuel the more lurid depictions of Germans as sub-human beasts.

73

THE PRUSSIAN BUTCHER

cry from 'Louvain has ceased to exist' as the *Times* proclaimed at the time.

British propaganda, and in particular the press, disseminated many tales of brutalised Belgian refugees, violated nuns, babies with hands cut off, corpses boiled to make soap, priests used as clappers in church bells, and so forth. Edmund Sullivan's horrific cartoons were in a similar style to those of the Dutch cartoonist, Louis Raemaekers. Sullivan's wartime images caricatured Germans as bloated, half-human militaristic monsters and dramatised their alleged atrocities. 'The Prussian Butcher' became an ape-like figure and the 'Gentle German' bayoneted the angel of mercy.

Film propaganda continued to identify German atrocities in *In the Clutches of the Hun* and *Under the German Yoke*. Similarly, in September 1914 *The War Illustrated* took up this theme by including a graphic illustration of how 'Belgian Miners Formed a Living Shield for Germans' ('This may be Teutonic cunning, but who can imagine the Allies adopting such barbarous methods?') and also a drawing of the 'Latest German Invention—The Red Cross Machine Gun', revealing the Kaiser as the driver of the vehicle. In depicting the enemy's brutality there were a number of constant themes of virginal women, innocent children and defenceless old people—all being violated and tortured. 'There are only two divisions in the world today,' Rudyard Kipling wrote, 'human beings and Germans.'

With an eye on the propaganda war, the government was also swift to exploit alleged German atrocities in occupied Belgium for enlistment purposes. In October 1914, Percy Illingworth, the chief government whip, addressed a recruiting meeting and assured his audience that the terrible atrocities in Belgium were being investigated

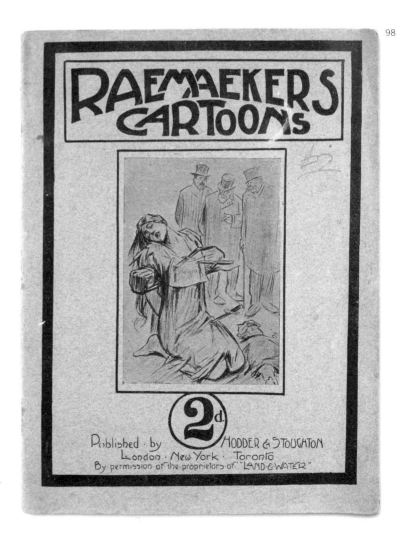

98 More alleged Hunnish brutalities, illustrating an edition of Dutch cartoonist Louis Raemaeker's drawings (*c.* 1916). Again, it is the allegorical figure of Mercy who is the victim, this time crucified. The sardonic caption read: 'Why couldn't she submit? She would have been well paid.'

99 A British postcard (1915) portraying the execution of Nurse Edith Cavell as the ultimate barbaric act of a debased German culture (*Kultur*), in which the land of Bach and Beethoven gives way to the music of death. Cavell's fate prompted a deluge of such images in British newspapers, cartoons, postage stamps and posters.

THE MURDER OF MISS CAVELL INSPIRES GERMAN "KULTUR.,

99

and, when they were revealed, 'all mankind would stand aghast'. A few months later, Prime Minister Asquith appointed Lord Bryce, the former Ambassador to the United States, to investigate the allegations. The Bryce Report (more formally, the *Committee on Alleged German Outrages*) published its findings in 30 languages in May 1915 and concluded that German troops had committed atrocities against Belgian civilians as part of a conscious strategy of terror. Taken alongside the Zeppelin raids over Britain, the use of poison gas on the Western Front, the sinking of the passenger liner *Lusitania* in May 1915 and the execution in Brussels, in October 1915, of the British nurse Edith Cavell, the Bryce Report (its contents widely believed at the time) provided a powerful and influential indictment of German war crimes and helped the government's recruitment drive.

It was following the sinking of the *Lusitania* by a German U-boat, and the loss of 128 US citizens aboard, that one of the most evocative (and effective) anti-German posters distributed in the United States appeared. It was published in 1915 by the Boston Committee of Public Safety, precisely when Germany was conducting a fierce counter-propaganda campaign aimed at keeping the country neutral. The murder of innocent women and children (particularly American) was

seen, at the time, as an act of German barbarism and Fred Spear's poster focused on the victims rather than the perpetrators, recalling an American mother and her baby sinking to the bottom of the sea. In fact, the *Lusitania* sinking was widely used for propaganda by *both* sides. A German medallion was struck commemorating the events, correctly asserting that the ship contained munitions. The British produced a counterfeit of the medallion, which was widely circulated. The British public interpreted the sinking as a premeditated attack on women and children that confirmed the wider atrocity stories of German barbarism, as extensively documented in the Bryce Report.

Both the British stereotype of the Hun and the French image of Germans as the *Boche* provided a platform for Allied propaganda to launch a moral offensive against a society portrayed as being founded on militaristic values, thereby bringing home to its own populations the unimaginable consequences of defeat. Atrocity propaganda therefore played a major role in the wave of patriotism that enveloped Europe in the early stages of the war. The image of the enemy and the epithet 'Hun' were crucial components of British propaganda and served many objectives: to justify the war, encourage enlistment, help raise war loans, strengthen the fighting spirit of the armed forces, and bolster civilian morale throughout the conflict. The receptiveness of the British public to atrocity stories and rumours deprived wartime society of much of its sense of perspective on events. It became capable of believing almost anything. It is quite extraordinary that the majority of the British people ended the war as they had begun it—their determination to defeat 'the Hun' possibly more passionate, even more implacable than it had been in August 1914. Furthermore, the idea of Teutonic brutality and ruthless inhumanity as encapsulated in the phrase 'Prussian militarism' played a significant role in shaping opinions *vis-à-vis* Germany in the immediate postwar years.

Once the United States entered the war in 1917, Hollywood cinema became a vehicle for patriotism and hatred towards the Germans. Film stars such as Charlie Chaplin and Lillian Gish offered their services in the war effort. A typical film is *The*

Bond (1918), a short film starring Chaplin. In it, German military might in the form of a stereotypical Prussian bully is literally flattened by Chaplin wielding a huge mallet, in an effort to encourage Americans to support the war effort by investing in Liberty Bonds. Often German treachery was equated with sexual depravity. In *The Little American* (1917), directed by Cecil B. DeMille, an innocent Mary Pickford faces a fate worse than death at the hands of a Prussian colonel, who scornfully proclaims: 'My men are in need of a little relaxation.'

The discrediting of wartime propaganda in the interwar years and the revelations that few of the atrocity stories had been true led to a widespread disinclination on the part of the British and American public during the Second World War to believe real stories about extermination camps when they began to emerge from Nazi Germany.

100 **'Enlist' (1915),** Fred Spear's dramatic poster of mother and baby sinking to a watery death. It recalled the sinking of the *Lusitania*, at a time when the United States had yet to enter into the war. Both Britain and Germany were waging their own propaganda war to win over neutral US opinion.

> Kulaks as a class were depicted as the enemy within, together with other traditional 'counter-revolutionaries' such as capitalists and priests.

■ The greedy kulaks

If 'the Hun' provided a good example of denunciation of an enemy without, the derogatory Russian term 'kulak' denoted a very distinct type of enemy within, engaged in 'wrecking' the Marxist-Leninist project. Kulaks were former peasants, who owned medium-sized farms as a result of the reforms introduced by the tsarist prime minister, Peter Stolypin, in 1906. But Soviet propaganda painted these farmers as greedy and standing in the way of the 'utopian' collectivisation, because it would take away their land, livestock and produce. The Bolsheviks declared them 'enemies of the people' and kulaks were left homeless and even without a single possession as everything was taken from them, including their pots and pans. It was also forbidden by law for anyone to aid dispossessed kulak families.

During the so-called War Communism period (1918–21), the Soviet government undermined the kulaks' position by organising committees of poor peasants to administer the villages and to supervise the requisitioning of grain from the richer peasants. But the introduction in 1921 of the New Economic Policy (NEP) favoured the kulaks. Although the Soviet government considered the kulaks to be capitalists and, therefore, enemies of socialism, it adopted various incentives to encourage peasants to increase agricultural production and enrich themselves. The most successful peasants (less than 4 per cent) became kulaks and assumed traditional roles in the village social structure, often rivalling the authority of the new Soviet officials in village affairs.

In 1927 the Soviet government began to shift its peasant policy by increasing the kulaks' taxes and restricting their right to lease land; in 1929 it began a drive for rapid collectivisation of agriculture. The kulaks vigorously opposed the efforts to force the peasants to give up their small privately owned farms and join large cooperative agricultural establishments. At the end of 1929 a campaign to 'liquidate the kulaks as a class' ('dekulakisation') was launched by the government. By 1934, when approximately 75 per cent of the farms in the Soviet Union had been collectivised, most kulaks— as well as millions of other peasants who had opposed collectivisation—had been deported to remote regions of the Soviet Union or arrested and their land and property confiscated.

The rationale behind forced collectivisation was that peasant smallholdings should merge to form large collective farms (*kolkhoz*). To achieve this, Stalin believed he had to obliterate the kulak class, some of whom responded to the changes by destroying crops, livestock and property rather than allow the state to take them. In order therefore to liquidate the kulaks Stalin sought the support of the poorer peasants. He embarked on a concerted propaganda campaign that targeted the kulaks and blackened them as bourgeois small capitalists who should be eliminated to allow the collectivisation of agriculture. Kulaks as a class were depicted as the enemy within, together with other traditional 'counter-revolutionaries' such as capitalists and priests.

The propaganda demonised kulaks by portraying them as hostile to the workers' movement; a famous slogan of 1930 proclaimed: 'We will keep out kulaks from the Collective Farms.' Film-maker Sergei Eisenstein idealised the village cooperative

ХУДОЖЕСТВЕННОЕ ИЗДАТЕЛЬСКОЕ АКЦ. О-ВО АХр, Москва 6, Цветной бульвар, 25.

КУЛАКИ САМЫЕ ЗВЕРСКИЕ, САМЫЕ ГРУБЫЕ, САМЫЕ ДИКИЕ, ЭКСПЛОАТАТОРЫ, НЕ РАЗ ВОССТАНАВЛИВАВШИЕ В ИСТОРИИ ДРУГИХ СТРАН ВЛАСТЬ ПОМЕЩИКОВ, ЦАРЕЙ, ПОПОВ И КАПИТАЛИСТОВ. *ЛЕНИН.*

101 **A fat (and implicitly greedy, selfish) kulak is forced from the collective farm in this unambiguously hostile poster from the Soviet campaign against kulaks. The text reads: 'Down with the kulaks; kick the kulaks out of the *kolkhoz* [collective farm]'. To the** right of the large fist is a quotation attributed to Lenin: 'The kulaks are most bestial, brutal and savage exploiters, who in the history of other countries have time and again restored the power of the landlords, tsars, priests and capitalists.'

101

and by association vilified the kulaks in his film *The Old and the New* (1929). He had begun making the film about agriculture, with the working title *The General Line*, when he was called upon to make *October* (1927) for the tenth anniversary of the October Revolution. By the time he returned to the original project the 'general line' of the Party had changed. Parts of the film had to be amended and the title changed to *The Old and the New*. Eisenstein now embarked upon a contemporary film by identifying a scapegoat for the ills afflicting Soviet society. The kulaks fitted Soviet negative stereotypes. Some, like the priest (witness Eisenstein's depiction of the cunning priest in his film *Battleship Potemkin*, 1925) or the bourgeois, were perceived to be inherently hostile to the Revolution for ideological reasons. Others, such as the kulak, were seen as emerging only as a threat after the Revolution. But all were collectively denounced as 'enemies of the people'.

The negative stereotypes had certain common characteristics, be they kulak, priest or spy. In Soviet films as in Soviet posters, they lived off the fat of the land, and off the honest toil of the workers, peasants and soldiers. Alexander Dovzhenko's film *Earth* (1930) focused on the hostility of the kulaks to collectivisation, and Alexander Medvedkin's *Happiness* (1934) shows how a lazy peasant is eventually shown the way to happiness by his wife, who embraces the life of the farm by mastering the machines and techniques necessary to make the system work. These stereotypes were represented as fat, heartless, cold and cruel, and—in contrast to the heroes of the Revolution—they lived a parasitic existence.

The negative image of the grasping kulak was juxtaposed with the 'heroes' of the Revolution. Stalinist propaganda focused on the ethic of industrial productivity and the selling of the Five-Year Plans, and factory and agricultural targets. Most notable in this context was the eponymous standard-bearer Aleksei Stakhanov, who fronted the work-ethic propaganda campaigns. Numerous films, posters, paintings and leaflets were produced to turn this role model into a folk hero and a motivational tool for the regime. Artists like Aleksandr Gerasimov were reduced to producing bland paintings promoting the merits of the collective farm and the promotion of tractor outputs and grain yields. Moreover, in the late 1920s and for most of the 1930s the cult of personality surrounding Stalin served as a unifying focus for public political activity, a rallying point against 'saboteurs and wreckers' and other 'enemies of the people'. It facilitated, and indeed attempted to justify, the enormous sacrifices made by the Soviet population during the twin campaigns of rapid industrialisation and forced collectivisation

that characterised the first Five-Year Plan of 1928–32, and later the other sacrifices made during the Great Terror, with its mass deportations and incarcerations and widespread deployment of forced labour.

A new wave of persecution against 'ex-kulaks' began in 1937. It was part of the Great Purge, conducted by Nikolai Yezhov and the NKVD (secret police). Those deemed to be former kulaks were either executed or sent to labour camps. With few rich or middle-class peasants left to arrest, in order to satisfy the conviction quotas demanded by Stalin and Yezhov the NKVD terrorised the rest of the peasantry to induce more denunciations. In the wave of round-ups that followed, the term 'kulak' lost its previous distinction and became a general accusation, which could be levelled at anyone whom the regime wished to convict. During the Great Purge, hundreds of thousands of peasants were falsely accused of being ex-kulaks and sent to the Gulag labour camps or executed on the basis of circumstantial evidence, forged evidence or even none at all.

102*a*

102*b*

■ The Teutonic Nazis

102*a*&*b* Nazis through a 13th-century prism, in scenes from Eisenstein's epic *Alexander Nevsky* (1938). The film's real aim was to strengthen the resolve of the Soviet people in their contemporary struggle with Germany. The Teutonic knights' intimidating helmets (*a*) evoke the *Wehrmacht* of the 1930s and 40s, while, in one of the film's most shocking scenes (*b*), knights and priests cast innocent Russian children onto the fire.

During the Second World War, enemies from within the Soviet state became suddenly of secondary importance as the authorities hastily constructed a different stereotype depicting the enemy without—the invading Nazis.

In 1938, when Nazi foreign policy was increasingly expansionist, Eisenstein produced the historical film epic *Alexander Nevsky*. The film was an allegory, a projection of present events onto the past, an appeal to the example offered by Russian history. The story of this Prince of Novgorod's legendary victory in 1242 over the Teutonic Knights, who were rampaging through what was now Russian territory (today in Estonia), clearly implied that Germans could not be relied upon to uphold peace treaties. The film was intended to arouse patriotic sentiment against the Nazi threat by emphasising the despicable nature of the enemy, and Nevsky symbolised the spirit of Russia and its historical resistance to foreign invaders. When Soviet policy changed abruptly in 1939, with the Nazi-Soviet Non-Aggression Pact, Stalin banned the film; but it was re-released in 1941 after the Nazi invasion.

In *Alexander Nevsky*, the conventional meanings of light and dark are inverted. Eisenstein consciously allowed the lighter shades to represent the enemy and the darker ones the heroes. The cunning high priest of the Teutonic order sports an emblem similar to a swastika on his collar and helmet. The Germans are depicted as ruthless and heartless, and they commit numerous atrocities. In an extraordinarily brutal scene, the Teutonic Knights, in full military regalia with their

monstrous helmets, murder innocent children by callously throwing them into a fire. The Germans are faceless, often hooded and frequently shot in profile, with cruel, animal-like features. One scene, following the sacking of the city of Pskov, shows fleeing refugees and wounded soldiers calling for vengeance. Tension mounts as stories of the German atrocities are recounted:

> *Soldier*: If they catch you with a sword, they beat you for having it! If they catch you with bread, they beat you for the bread! They've tortured mothers and wives for their sons and husbands.
> *Crowd*: The German is a beast! We know the Germans!

The Russian victory is ultimately confirmed by a one-to-one struggle between Alexander Nevsky and the Master of the Teutonic Order. The German forces gather around their war horn, and the ice covering Lake Peipus, on which the battle took place, cracks beneath them. Like the forces of Napoleon and, in due course, those of Hitler, they fall victim to the Russian winter. At the end of the film Alexander addresses his army and his people with the warning: 'Let people come to us as guests without fear. But he who comes with sword shall perish … Arise people of Russia. To glorious battle, mortal battle! Arise, men of freedom. For our fair land!'

So powerful was the role the film played in strengthening the Soviet resistance that Stalin instituted a new battle honour: the Order of Alexander Nevsky.

■ The beastly Germans

Lancelot Speed's 'lightning sketches' (described above) contained rare examples of humour in British propaganda during the First World War, which, as in American films, tended to be dominated by stories of German treachery and atrocities. In the years immediately following the First World War, various investigations, particularly in France and Britain, suggested that much atrocity propaganda had been either false or exaggerated. As a result, atrocity propaganda diminished in scale during the Second World War (the British took the view that Nazism itself was, in essence, an atrocity), though literature detailing Nazi atrocities and human rights violations did go on to form the staple content of MOI posters, leaflets and pamphlets. Much of British propaganda in the Second World War, however, was to be characterised by the use of humour to deflate the enemy.

However, no protracted war can be fought without attempting to rouse the people against the enemy. In 1939 there was less need than in

1914 to justify Britain's declaration of war against Germany. Initially, the Ministry of Information pointed out that Britain had done its utmost to avoid war and that it was wholly the fault of aggression by Germany's Nazi rulers. As the war escalated in the spring of 1940, the Ministry accepted there should be no separation in the official propaganda between the German people and Nazism and launched its 'anger' campaign designed to draw public attention to the brutality of the Nazi regime and its policies.

Germany's dramatic military successes in Western Europe in 1940, leading to the Allied evacuation from Dunkirk and the fall of France, had to be explained. This gave rise to the belief that a Fifth Column had been operating as an advance guard for the German army. This notion of the 'enemy within' was behind the Ministry of Information's 'Careless Talk Costs Lives' campaign, and it was pursued in numerous films, such as *Miss Grant Goes to the Door* (1940), *The*

103

103 *Struwwelhitler*, by 'Doktor Schrecklichkeit' (Dr Horror), a 1941 parody of *Struwwelpeter* or 'Shockheaded Peter', the German children's book by Heinrich Hoffmann. His original comprised ten illustrated and rhymed stories, each with a clear moral demonstrating the disastrous consequences of misbehaviour in an exaggerated way. In the anti-Nazi version stories include 'The Story of Cruel Adolf' and 'The Story of Little Gobby [Goebbels] Poison Pen'. It was published by *The Daily Sketch* for the War Relief Fund.

The BATTLE for CIVILISATION

104 Nazis versus civilisation, in this Ministry of Information leaflet (1942). The First World War had provided the template of the German beast destroying civilised values, ready to be revived and applied to the Nazi regime. *Blitzkrieg* warfare delivered a suitable accompaniment of a war machine trampling over Europe.

104

Next of Kin (1941) and *Went the Day Well* (1942). Films about Nazi spies were ideal for propaganda purposes. They were also useful in demonising the Germans as the 'same old Hun'.

In a series of broadcasts made on the BBC's overseas service in 1940, Lord Vansittart, former Permanent Under Secretary at the Foreign Office, was able to play on the 'Hun' theme and portrayed Germans as violent and aggressive, with Nazism being merely the latest manifestation of this national characteristic. The broadcasts proved extremely popular, as did the pamphlet that

followed: *Black Record: German Past and Present*. 'Vansittartism', as the phenomenon became known, suited well the MOI's Anger Campaign in which it was pointed out that 'The Hun is at the gate. He will rage and destroy. He will slaughter women and children.' In the face of a stream of pamphlets explaining the historical roots and antecedents of German barbarity—largely written by political refugees—some politicians expressed concern about the sheer vindictiveness of this propaganda, not least because it would make a settlement with Germany after the war all the more

105 Pages from a British Ministry of Information booklet, *Chansons de BBC*, dropped over France in 1943. It contains the sheet music of songs in French that make fun of the Germans and Italians by anticipating their impending defeat.

difficult. Noël Coward parodied those critics in his patriotic song 'Don't Let's Be Beastly to the Germans':

> Don't let's be beastly to the Germans
>   When our victory is ultimately won,
> It was just those nasty Nazis who persuaded them
>   to fight
> And their Beethoven and Bach are really far worse
>   than their bite
> Let's be meek to them
> And turn the other cheek to them
> And try to bring out their latent sense of fun.
> Let's give them full air parity
> And treat the rats with charity,
> But don't let's be beastly to the Hun.

In June 1941, in a radio broadcast to the nation after the Nazi invasion of the Soviet Union, Prime Minister Winston Churchill pledged aid to Russia and emphasised once again that Britain was fighting against:

> …the Nazi war machine, with its clanking, heel-clicking dandified Prussian officers, its crafty expert agents fresh from the cowing and tying down of a dozen countries. I see also the dull, drilled, docile, brutish masses of the Hun soldiery plodding on like a swarm of crawling locusts.

In the same year the film-maker Charles Ridley cleverly re-edited actuality film for the MOI of goose-stepping Nazi soldiers at Nuremberg (taken from Leni Riefenstahl's *Triumph of the Will*) to

the popular tune of 'The Lambeth Walk'. At the beginning of the film, which was entitled *Germany Calling* (and also shown as a newsreel), the narrator exclaims: 'I'm going to show you a showman that we all hate … and it's going to be in the form of a ballet—a *Panzer* ballet. It's entitled "Retreat from Moscow" and it's going to be done to the Lambeth Walk.' Ridley chose this music because members of the Nazi Party had called the tune 'Jewish mischief and animalistic hopping'. By speeding up the film, the incipient threat of the SS was diluted and their formations—directed by a preposterous-looking Hitler—rendered comically, in a silent-film tradition.

The reduction of a frightening enemy to the level of visibility and ridicule, as in this lampooning of Hitler and his forces, is, in psychological terms, a means of achieving power over him. The British used a similar technique to undermine and humiliate Mussolini; for example, Alberto Cavalcanti's 1940 documentary film *Yellow Caesar* was a highly effective piece of propaganda, which reinforced the impression of Mussolini as a clown.

■ The yellow peril and the master race

During the Second World War the United States also employed humour, notably through the Walt Disney studios and its popular animated icons such as Donald Duck, in order to symbolise true American values. *Der Fuehrer's Face* (1943), for example, depicted in simplistic terms what life was like for someone living in the Third Reich: namely, swastika wallpaper, even swastika-shaped trees, substitute coffee and regimentalised work without holidays for the glorification of the *Führer*. Its opening song, played by a strutting Nazi 'oompah' band (though also with a Japanese bandsman, for good measure), slyly mixes subservience with insult: 'When der Führer says, "We ist der master race" / We Heil! Heil! Right in der Führer's Face. / Not to love the Führer is a great disgrace ….' Fortunately, the oppression of life under Nazi rule is just a nightmarish dream. In the final scene Donald awakes to see a shadow on his bedroom wall that turns out to be a replica of the Statue of Liberty—revealing in symbolic terms why the American people are fighting the war. The film ends with a custard pie being thrown in the *Führer's* face in typical vaudeville tradition. *Der Fuehrer's Face* emphasises stark contrasts throughout. In the language of director Frank Capra's 1942 propaganda film *Prelude to War*, 'this is a fight between a Free World and a Slave World' (a theme that would endure during the Cold War).

Prelude to War was the first of Capra's series of seven documentary films (1942–45) in the *Why We Fight* series, produced for the American armed forces. They were supplemented by the *Know Your Ally* and *Know Your Enemy* series, and later shown to the US public too, to persuade them to support American involvement in the war. The Office of War Information at first concentrated on the civilian Front, but given the years of US political isolationism there was a need to target those Americans who had joined the armed forces, and to this end the US War Department spent more than $50 million annually on film production, with the aim of providing soldiers with a cause for which to fight.

Prelude to War has been described as the 'greatest gangster film ever made'. It charts the rise of Fascism, Nazism and Japanese militarism between 1931 and 1939. The 'Free World' is exemplified by religious figures, such as Moses, Mohammed, Confucius and Jesus Christ, and by political liberators such as George Washington, Abraham Lincoln, Giuseppe Garibaldi and the Marquis de Lafayette. By contrast, in the world of the Axis powers, 'people surrendered their liberties and worshipped their leaders'. Germans, Italians and Japanese are represented as people inclined towards regimentation and willing to sacrifice their freedoms. Germany is represented as an anti-Christian and philistine society, for example through images of destroyed churches and synagogues, and by the replacement of the crucifix with the swastika. Fascist leaders are presented as objects of fanatical worship by the masses. In depicting the 'slave' world, the utterances of Hitler, Mussolini (always presented as Hitler's stooge) and Emperor Hirohito figure largely. In one scene a stained-glass window is shattered by several

Whereas the enemy in Europe was depicted by the United States as an evil regime, the enemy in Asia was depicted as an entire race.

106

106 Images of the
enemy: a still from Frank
Capra's *Prelude to War*
(1942), the first film in
the *Why We Fight* series,
which identified the
rise of Italian Fascism,
German Nazism and
Japanese militarism
between 1931 and
1938. Hirohito, Hitler
and Mussolini embodied
the 'slave world' they
collectively administered.

bricks to reveal a 'Heil Hitler!' poster behind; for
additional emphasis, to play up Hitler as an Anti-
christ figure, a class of German schoolchildren is
shown singing:

Adolf Hitler is our Saviour, our hero
He is the noblest being in the whole wide world.
For Hitler we live, For Hitler we die.
Our Hitler is our Lord
Who rules a brave new world.

The US Army used *Prelude to War* as a training
film for indoctrinating soldiers. Prior to the men's
deployment, it was compulsory for all US soldiers
to have seen it (and eventually the entire series).
President Roosevelt was so delighted with the way
the film addressed residual isolationist sentiment
that he ordered the series to be released commercially to the American public, and three of the films
were shown publicly. Churchill filmed a special
Introduction for their British release, and Stalin
allowed *The Battle of Russia* to be shown in the
Soviet Union. *Prelude to War* was so well received
by the American public that it won the Academy
Award for Best Documentary for 1942. At least 54
million Americans had seen the series by the end of
the war, and studies were undertaken to gauge the
impact of the films. The findings, however, were
inconclusive.

Prelude to War pointed to the Japanese invasion
of Manchuria in 1931 as the start of the Second
World War: 'Remember that date: September 18,
1931, a date you should remember as well as
December 7, 1941. For on that date in 1931 the
war we are now fighting began.' The Japanese

surprise attack on Pearl Harbor provided the
rallying cry for war, even more than the sinking
of the *Lusitania* in 1915 had crystallised anti-
German attitudes. Whereas the enemy in Europe
was depicted by the United States as an evil
regime, the enemy in Asia was depicted as an
entire race. In Europe, the United States fought
to defend its allies against a Nazi expansionist
regime motivated by a racist utopian ideology.
In the Pacific War, Japanese expansion was also
accompanied by a belief of racial superiority, but
American propaganda was itself driven by hatred
of the 'sub-human Jap'. (The Australian government's Department of Information launched a
similar 'Know Your Enemy' campaign, which was
characterised by highly emotional appeals and
crude racial stereotypes that demonised the Japanese.) Such feelings seemed to stem from much
more than simply vengeance for Pearl Harbor.
They often reflected a pre-existing racism, which
had been reinforced by the Japanese attack. The
animosity was demonstrated in the hysterical
and unconstitutional deportation of Japanese
Americans from their homes on the Pacific Coast
to internment camps, which demonstrated that
the Japanese were viewed as an enemy within *and*
without.

Interestingly, the OWI generally sought to
restrain, rather than generate, the more extreme
attitudes, partly because it was concerned about
the negative effects of racially based propaganda
on African Americans' support for the war and
also because it feared, with good reason, that such
blatant evidence of white American racism would

be exploited by Japanese propaganda. Nevertheless, 'yellow' terminology was the branding of choice when referring to the Japanese, along with depictions of them as animals. They were the 'yellow peril' and 'yellow monkeys'. US war-bond posters variously pictured the Japanese as rat-like or simian monsters, and snakes also figured. Films and cartoons took up the theme without official prompting, with the result that the fanatical Japanese soldier became a familiar and enduring stereotype. In several posters and editorial cartoons (notably Arthur Szyk's savage portrayal of the Japanese as inhuman beasts), the Japanese were drawn as monkeys hanging from trees or lumbering around like big gorillas. The image of a subhuman primate was key to devaluing the humanity of the enemy.

Hollywood produced a series of films that dramatised the 'yellow peril': *Wake Island* (1942), *Guadalcanal Diary* (1943), *Bataan* (1943), *Corregidor* (1943) and *Destination Tokyo* (1943). In 1944 Bugs Bunny featured in an episode of Warner Brothers' *Merrie Melodies* entitled 'Bugs Bunny Nips the Nips', where the enemy were referred to as 'monkey face', 'slant eyes' and 'bow legs'. Accessories and paraphernalia with a propaganda theme abounded: patriotic buttons carried slogans such as 'Slap that Jap. Fight for Four Freedoms'; ashtrays were sold with pictures of a Japanese soldier in a rat's body and the slogan 'Jam your cigarette butts on this Rat'; matchbox labels urged 'Hang One—on Nippon', showing a US Marine beating a Japanese soldier; and in 1945 a number of 'atomic bombs games' were even produced, the object being to tilt the game in order to simultaneously manoeuvre the bomb into two holes labelled Hiroshima and Nagasaki.

Throughout the war, Japan used historical accounts of the United States' racist past to cite the many racial injustices of the country, which were juxtaposed against their own innate belief in Japan's spiritual and racial superiority. Thus, both sides indulged in race-based propaganda, helping fuel a war of mutual extermination on the bitterly fought-over island battlefields of the Pacific. Arguably, the vehemence of such propaganda laid the foundation for the US use of the atomic bomb against the Japanese in August 1945.

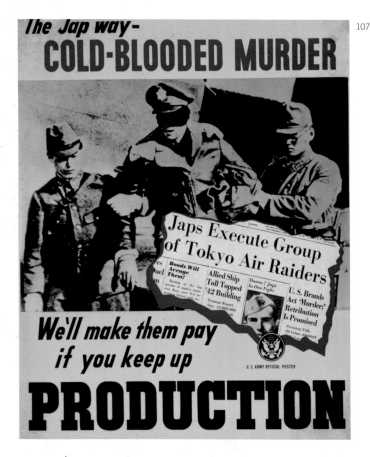

107

107 **Images of the enemy: 'Cold-Blooded Murder'.** By claiming that the Japanese had executed captured US servicemen, it played on the pervasive caricatures of the Japanese as rats, apes and menacing monsters. The message to American citizen-soldiers was to work harder and avoid absenteeism to help the military defeat of an unfeeling and cruel enemy.

108 **Images of the enemy: The Tokio Kid.** As part of the effort by the US Douglas Aircraft Company to improve its workers' efficiency and avoid waste, the short-sighted and bucktoothed Tokio Kid fronted a poster campaign. The grotesque racial stereotype combined the comic-book absurd with a sense of threat and danger, visible here in the bloodstained dagger. The message here is that workers who rush to finish their shifts are, implicitly, a boon to the enemy.

TOKIO KID Say-
WASH UP EARLY
RUSH OUT DOOR
GIVE JAP TIME
FOR WIN WAR
JACK CAMPBELL

108

109 **A Nazi postcard showing a beleaguered Churchill-like admiral aboard the ship of Britain, surrounded by mines and about to swallow a German bomb. The text is a play on words, but translates as: 'For you things are going to get really rotten … We're going to use a *Stuka* to shut your big mouth!' This card was sent from Kassel in 1942, a city that, ironically, would be largely destroyed by Allied bombs.**

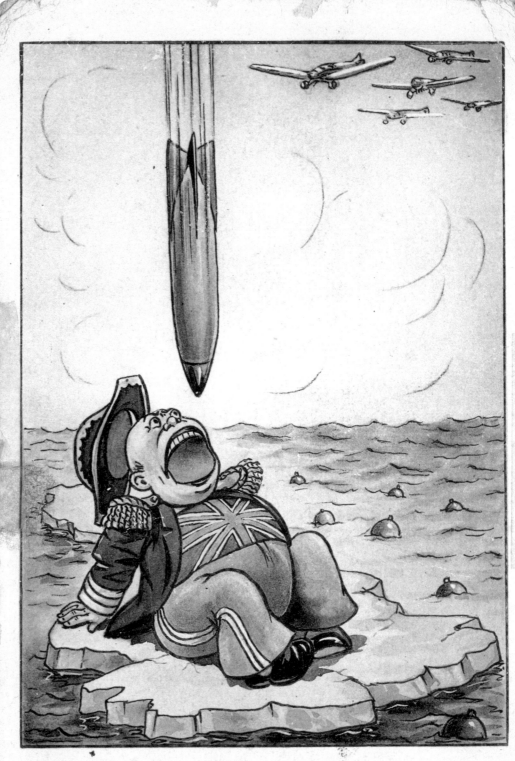

■ The effete English

Anti-Jewish and anti-Bolshevik motifs were central to the Nazi *Weltanschauung* ('worldview'). The Nazi movement had developed and finally emerged from a struggle in which communists together with the Jews formed the main target of Nazi violence and invective. Indeed, by claiming a Marxist-inspired Jewish-Bolshevik conspiracy, Nazi propaganda was able, at times, to fuse these two enemies into one. However, for a brief period following the defeat of France in 1940, German propagandists switched to targeting the British. Once Britain had declared war on Germany in September 1939, it became a distinctive enemy and object of hatred in Nazi propaganda. Throughout the early part of the summer of 1940, as the struggle for control of the skies above Britain took place, anti-British propaganda reached a new crescendo, claiming that it was only a matter of time before Britain's fate was sealed. Propaganda emphasised British hypocrisy and 'plutocracy'. Churchill in particular was targeted and mercilessly lampooned. One famous poster depicted him as an American-style gangster ('The Sniper'), brandishing a machine gun. The SD Reports (of the *Sicherheitsdienst* secret police) suggested that German hatred of Britain, incited by incessant propaganda, was now widespread.

It is surprising, though, to discover that the Nazis used humour—albeit rarely—to undermine their enemies. In 1941, they released the anti-British documentary film *Soldaten von Morgen* ('Soldiers of Tomorrow'). It was a film made *by* the Hitler Youth *for* the Hitler Youth, but it was also shown widely in the Third Reich. The film takes the form of a Hitler Youth theatrical skit on the English public-school system and the resultant

effete degeneracy supposed to result from such an education. Leading British political figures such as Churchill, and both the former and current foreign secretaries, Lord Halifax and Anthony Eden, are cited as examples. British youth is ridiculed quite savagely. The film ends with dishevelled British troops being captured at Dunkirk. The morale of the story is clear: effete young English schoolboys turn into easily captured British troops. The second half of the film offers an unfavourable comparison with the virile qualities and athletic activities of German youth, who are seen fencing, gliding, parachute jumping, horse-riding, and participating in 'mock' battles along with a final parade.

Soldaten von Morgen reflects the euphoric nature of Nazi propaganda in general during this period. Goebbels referred to the British as the 'Jews among the Aryans'—a decaying society dominated by Jews. Despite the propaganda, the Battle of Britain turned out to be a failure not only for the Luftwaffe, but also for Nazi propaganda, which was not prepared to admit a British defensive victory in the air. Goebbels' anti-British propaganda suffered a further setback in May 1941, when the leading Nazi Rudolf Hess flew to Scotland in a desperate attempt to bring the British to their senses—only to end up in ignominious captivity.

■ The Jewish rats

While the British represented a clear enemy without—one whom the Germans were actually fighting in a conventional war—Nazi ideology had simultaneously identified Jews as the enemy within. Anti-Semitism was not only the core of Nazi ideology, but the Jewish stereotype that developed from it provided the focal point for the feelings of aggression inherent in the ideology. Before 1939, anti-Semitism was propagated chiefly through the German educational system and the press. Three major campaigns were waged: the boycott of Jewish shops in 1933, the anti-Semitic Nuremberg Laws in 1935 and the destruction of Jewish-owned property in the *Reichskristallnacht* of 1938.

An important function of Nazi propaganda was therefore to disseminate Nazi racial ideology. Press directives had ensured that racial issues would figure prominently in the daily newspapers. Goebbels had even suggested that not one week should pass without a discussion of racial-political questions. Emphasis would often be placed on aspects of Jewish 'criminality' against German interests. Before the proclamation of the Nuremberg Laws, for example, a 'public enlightenment' programme had been instigated to demonstrate the history of Jewish 'crimes' and 'conspiracies'. A similar campaign followed the *Kristallnacht*, when synagogues were torched and vandalised.

Nothing illustrates the campaign more clearly than the Nazi use of film. In coordination with propaganda campaigns in other media, a number of films were prepared, in an attempt to make the German people aware of the 'dangers' posed by Jewry and also to rationalise any measures that were, or might be, taken by the regime, either publicly or in secret.

In 1940, three major anti-Semitic films were released—*Die Rothschilds* ('The Rothschilds'), *Jud Süss* ('Jew Süss') and *Der ewige Jude* ('The Eternal—or Wandering—Jew') to justify Nazi measures to convince the people that a Jewish Question did exist, which needed to be 'solved'. The most notorious and virulent of all anti-Semitic films is *Der ewige Jude*, which ran the gamut of Nazi allegations against Jews and was intended to prepare the German people for the genocide of the Final Solution. The film begins with scenes from the Warsaw Ghetto, designed to show the reluctance of Jews to undertake creative labour, and it continues by depicting the migration of Jews and their attempts to assimilate with European peoples. Animated maps show how the Jews, starting from Palestine ('the spiritual centre for international Jewry'), diffused across the world; furthermore, the 19th century 'with its vague ideas of human equality and freedom, gave the Jew a powerful impetus', according to the film's narration. This diffusion is illustrated as a dense network over the map, resembling festering sores. The film then cuts

110

110 **Visitors at Germany's 'The Eternal Jew' exhibition, which opened in Munich in November 1937 and ran until 31 January 1938. It attracted 412,300 visitors – over 5,000 per day. Reports from the Nazi Security Service (*Sicherheitsdienst*) claimed that the exhibition helped to promote a sharp rise in anti-Semitic feelings, and in some cases violence against the Jewish community.**

111 **Poster for the film *Der ewige Jude* (1940), a piece of dedicated anti-Semitism that claimed to be 'a documentary about world Judaism'. Racial stereotypes abound in the poster's depictions of Jewish physiognomy.**

111

to a sequence of rats devouring grain and scurrying in packs, filling the screen, in an analogy between rats and Jews that Hitler had first used in *Mein Kampf*. The commentary continues:

> Comparable with the Jewish wanderings through history are the mass migrations of an equally restless animal, the rat… Wherever rats appear they bring ruin, they ravage human property and foodstuffs. In this way they spread disease: plague, leprosy, typhoid, cholera, dysentery, etc. They are cunning, cowardly, and cruel and are found mostly in packs. In the animal world they represent the element of craftiness and subterranean destruction—no different from the Jews among mankind!

By contrasting Jewish individualism and 'self-seeking' with the National Socialist ideal of a 'people's community' (*Volksgemeinschaft*), and by claiming that Jews were only motivated by money, it was possible to demonstrate that Judaism was the total antithesis of the cherished values of the German cultural tradition as interpreted by Nazi ideology. But more importantly, the constant analogy made with rats and parasites suggested that the Jew differed from the Aryan not only in body but, more significantly, in soul, for the Jew had no soul. The implication was that here was a menace that had to be 'resisted'. Thus, the conclusion to be drawn from watching such films was that the killing of Jews was not a crime but a necessity: Jews, after all, were not human beings but pests, which had to be exterminated. *Der ewige Jude* represents a form of National Socialist 'realism' depicting not so much what was, but what ought to have been, in accordance with the pre-conceived notion of Nazi racial ideology. Having previewed the film before its release, Goebbels recorded in his diary the 'scenes so horrific and brutal in their explicitness that one's blood runs cold. One shudders at such barbarism. This Jewry must be eliminated.'

Despite such attempts at whipping up anti-Semitism, the regime encountered problems. At precisely the time that Jewish persecution was being intensified and the details of the Final Solution were falling into place, during the summer and autumn of 1941, the SD Reports were noting either boredom with, or massive indifference to, the 'Jewish Question' among the population. Ironically, such indifference proved fatal for the Jews. Interest in the fate of Jews had, in fact, rapidly evaporated after the *Reichskristallnacht*. Historian Ian Kershaw has written that the 'road to Auschwitz was built by hate, but paved with indifference'. It was no longer necessary after 1941 to publicise the 'threats' posed by Jews, and as a result the Jewish Question became of no more than marginal importance in the formation of popular opinion within the Third Reich. Propaganda had helped to create such apathy and indifference by persuading people that they could retreat into the safety of their private lives and leave the solutions to such 'problems' to others. Tragically, the moral ambiguity that characterised the public's response to the well-publicised plans to exterminate Jews and other 'inferior' races encouraged the regime to realise the unthinkable.

According to George Mosse, 'a myth is the strongest belief held by the group, and its adherents feel themselves to be an army of truth fighting an army of evil'. Goebbels maintained that the purpose of propaganda was to persuade the audience to believe in the viewpoint expressed by the propagandist. But if propaganda is to be effective it must, in a sense, always preach to those who are already partially converted. The Nazi attitude to the Jews is an excellent example of this facet of propaganda. It cannot be argued rationally that anti-Semitism was a result of National Socialism or that Goebbels' propaganda made Germans anti-Semitic; but the fact remains that the Third Reich was responsible for attempting a genocide of unparalleled scope and brutality. This situation may be attributed partly to the effects of propaganda itself and partly also to the closed political environment within which that propaganda was necessarily working. Thus, when Hitler came to power he needed the Jews as a permanent scapegoat on which those in the movement could work off their resentment; the Jew was manipulated to fulfil a psychological need. Nazi propaganda simply used the historical predisposition of the audience towards an anti-Semitic explanation for Germany's cultural, economic and political grievances. The appeal of *Völkisch* thought was very much linked to its projection of stereotypes—of its own image and the image it created of those who opposed its doctrine or did not correspond to its racial dogma. The importance of the image of the Jew was defined in antithesis to Nazi ideology. The Jewish stereotype thus provided the focal point for the feelings of aggression inherent in the ideology.

The whole purpose of anti-Semitic propaganda was to reinforce such beliefs and prejudices, and to unify the people into the desired thoughts and actions. The Jew provided an escape valve from serious social and political problems. The 'image' of the Jew as portrayed in the mass media was outside the range of rational intellectual analysis, and that was its strength. In this way anti-Semitic propaganda was able to overcome any doubts that may have existed, while at the same time providing the emotional basis for a totalitarian solution to the country's problems.

■ Tutsi traitors

Genocide (or attempted genocide) such as the Holocaust is invariably a product of intense hatred of a people perceived as an enemy, and is invariably fuelled by propaganda. In 1994 the phenomenon struck Africa in the shape of the mass slaughter in Rwanda. It was the culmination of ethnic tensions between the minority Tutsi people, who had exercised a longstanding hold on power, and the majority Hutu peoples, who had come to power relatively recently in the rebellion of 1962. In 1990 Tutsi refugees calling themselves the Rwandan Patriotic Front (RPF) invaded northern Rwanda to defeat the Hutu-led government, thus triggering a bitter civil war in which the Hutus clearly identified the Tutsi as the threatening enemy within.

A genocide was planned by members of the Hutu power group known as the *Akuza*, many of whom occupied positions at top levels of government; it was supported and coordinated by the national government as well as by local military and civil officials and mass media. Indeed, the news media played a crucial role in the genocide; local print and radio media fuelled the killings, while the international media either ignored or seriously misconstrued events on the ground. A campaign of hate was launched first of all by the print media, and this was later taken up and intensified by radio stations. Due to high rates of illiteracy at the time of the genocide, radio was an important way for the government to deliver its messages. Two radio stations that were key to inciting violence before and during the genocide were *Radio Rwanda* and *Radio Télévision Libre Mille Collines* (RTLM). From October 1993, the RTLM repeatedly broadcast on themes that had been disseminated by the press and in leaflets suggesting the inherent differences between Hutu and Tutsi, the foreign origins of the Tutsi, the disproportionate share of wealth and power owned by the Tutsi, and the horrors of past Tutsi rule. These broadcasts also claimed that all Tutsi were supporters of the RPF force fighting against the elected government. Women in particular were targets of the anti-Tutsi propaganda. For example, the 'Hutu Ten Commandments' (which had been published in 1990 in *Kangura*, the anti-Tutsi language newspaper) included four commandments that portrayed Tutsi women as tools of the Tutsi people, and as sexual weapons to weaken and ultimately destroy the Hutu men. Gender-based propaganda also included cartoons printed in newspapers depicting Tutsi women as sex objects. Examples of gender-based hate propaganda used to incite war rape included statements by perpetrators, such as 'You Tutsi women think that you are too good for us', and 'Let us see what a Tutsi woman tastes like.'

■ Irish 'men of violence'

As the civil war was escalating in Rwanda, Northern Ireland's thirty years of 'Troubles' were entering a new phase. While the roots of the conflict could be traced to the early 20th century and the partition of Ireland, the propaganda war presented the British government with a challenge not entirely dissimilar to that facing the United States in Vietnam: could a democratic state, which deployed its troops in the full glare of the modern media, succeed in achieving its military objectives?

The Troubles, of course, represented a different type of struggle to that in Vietnam—both from the military/security perspective and from the point of view of the propaganda war. Not only were British troops being deployed on what was officially home soil, in lower intensity security operations, but their opponents were also dressed as civilians. British propaganda sought to explain the military presence in terms of protecting Northern Ireland from itself (that is, from the two warring sectarian factions, Nationalists and Loyalists), and emphasised the association of 'terrorism' with the activities of the IRA. However, the government underestimated the effectiveness of IRA counter-propaganda; the sight of heavily armed British troops confronting stone-throwing children in the streets of Belfast, night after night on news bulletins throughout the world, was a public-relations disaster—especially in the American cities with large expatriate Irish populations.

The British government sought initially to treat the Troubles as a domestic problem, which concerned no-one else. But the situation came to

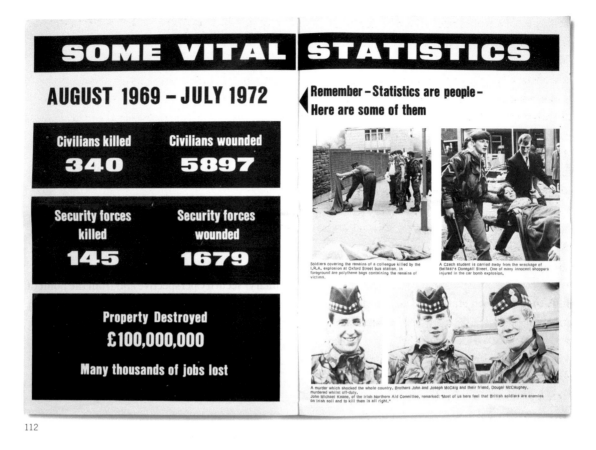

112 A pro-Unionist leaflet from the early years of Northern Ireland's 'Troubles' attempts to shock through 'some vital statistics' while also individualising and humanising some of those numbers.

be viewed by many critics as a cancer that eroded freedoms and exposed the hollowness of British claims to be championing democracy. The introduction of internment and trial without jury in 1973 (under the Emergency Powers Act) only served to reinforce such views (both in Britain and around the world). The long-running conflict in Northern Ireland served to demonstrate a principle that is now well established; namely that democracies cannot fight terrorism on their *own* terms. The terrorist bomber invariably holds the advantage and, in the age of the mass media, thrives on publicity.

In attempts to combat the so-called 'men of violence', the British military was clearly circumscribed by the circumstances of fighting a domestic war, and so resorted to a wide range of measures and strategies through the secret services, other intelligence-gathering activities, the law (for example, the Prevention of Terrorism Act) and, in the 1980s, efforts to starve terrorists of the 'oxygen of publicity' via a broadcasting ban. The Army and the Northern Ireland Office (NIO) continued to focus on propaganda campaigns designed to

isolate the 'men of violence' and win the hearts and minds of the Ulster community. To this end they adopted a policy of identifying all terrorists as the enemy within. However, the IRA in particular developed its own highly sophisticated use of black propaganda and rapidly learned how to control the media, operating invariably at an emotional rather than an intellectual level. This was exemplified in the portrayal of jailed IRA hunger-strikers as Christ-like martyrs—suffering, instead of inflicting suffering—and in the high-profile funeral of one of them, Bobby Sands, in 1981.

The Army's response was generally more low key and less emotional. When the Provisional IRA started its bombing campaign, the security forces attempted to drive a wedge between the Catholic community and the IRA (invariably referred to as 'terrorists'). A poster and handbill campaign encouraged citizens to use the Confidential Telephone line and inform on illegal and violent activity. This campaign was extended to include bus and train tickets. One of the first posters showed two images of violence (including a hooded gunman—an image frequently employed) and a telephone with the heading: 'All of us together could stop it! Use the confidential telephone.' More dramatic was a poster targeting Belfast: 'Your finger on the dial can take the finger off the trigger.' One of the most emotional and explicit images (issued by the Royal Ulster Constabulary, after the La Mon House Hotel attack in 1978) showed the charred remains of a body and the accusation of 'Murder', repeated 12 times: 'This is what the bombers did to a human being.' Details on the back of the handbill provided background information and a call to 'Help us stop the slaughter now.' The security forces also used posters offering rewards for any information given ('£50,000 reward is offered for information leading to the conviction of any person or persons found guilty of murder or explosions ...'). Invariably, however, propaganda focused on IRA criminality and the senseless violence destroying the fabric of community ('One of the best shops in Rosslea ... So the Provos blew it up! This is the Provos' contribution to your Community. Mace!') . The problem was that many Catholics no longer saw themselves as 'stakeholders' in the community.

In fact there was little that propaganda could do to change this perception—especially in the face of sustained IRA accusations (and intimidation). Ironically, a contemporary IRA counterpropaganda poster reminded the Catholic community that 'Loose talk costs lives', recycling the familiar British slogan from the Second World War ('Whatever you say—say nothing'). It is interesting to note that the Army rarely mentioned its original peacekeeping role in Northern Ireland. The message became difficult, in any case, after the

Army shootings of unarmed protesters on 'Bloody Sunday' (30 January 1972), as it had lost the moral and political high ground. Indeed, images of the British Army and its role largely disappeared at this point from official propaganda.

The propaganda dynamic was reversed, however, in the early 1990s, largely due to changing political and economic circumstances. A battle-fatigued province now looked enviously at the growing political confidence and economic prosperity in the Irish Republic. In 1985, an Anglo-Irish Accord sought to lay the groundwork for talks between Northern Ireland and the Republic of Ireland. Dublin agreed not to contest Northern Ireland's allegiance to Great Britain in exchange for British acknowledgment of the Republic's interest in how Northern Ireland should be run. A 1993 Anglo-Irish Declaration offered to open negotiations to all parties willing to renounce violence, and in 1994 the IRA and, later, Protestant paramilitary groups declared a ceasefire. A resumption of violence in 1996 by the IRA (a bombing in Manchester) threatened to derail the peace process, but some years later negotiations to seek a political settlement went ahead nonetheless, a landmark being reached with the Good Friday Agreement of 1998.

During the early 1990s a series of television advertisements was commissioned by the Northern Ireland Office in support of the Confidential Telephone campaign. They were produced by the advertising company McCann-Erickson, and they attracted a considerable amount of interest within the advertising industry—although to this day they remain largely unseen on the British mainland. Employing sophisticated techniques, the television commercials supplanted the old poster campaign and raised the techniques of persuasion to new levels. They were based on the conviction that the people of Northern Ireland wanted peace and therefore were receptive to new initiatives, so the commercials urged the community: 'Don't suffer it—Change it … Anything You Know Can Help.'

These were slick productions employing subliminal techniques and popular music. Individual productions such as 'Lady', 'I wanna be like you' and 'Carwash' targeted specific groups and individuals. 'Lady', for example, told the story of two women, two traditions and two tragedies within Ulster: 'One married to the victim of violence, one married to the prisoner of violence. Both scarred, both suffering, both desperately wanting to stop it.' The commercials pulled no punches, by depicting in graphic detail the senseless violence brought about by sectarian paramilitarism but also affirming the message that the time was right for change. Interestingly enough the military and security forces rarely appeared in these commercials and when they did, it was only fleetingly (in 'Carwash' for example, it is the RUC not the Army who turn up to prevent a senseless killing). The advertisements represent an interesting attempt by the British political and military authorities to cut through the sectarian divide by identifying 'the men of violence' as the enemy, and to shock the population into the desired action.

113

113 **A pro-Republican leaflet (c. 1984) from Northern Ireland, issued by Sinn Fein. The emphasis here is on oppression of the vulnerable (babies, mothers), while also asserting the legitimacy of an armed struggle through the reference to prisoners as 'POWs'.**

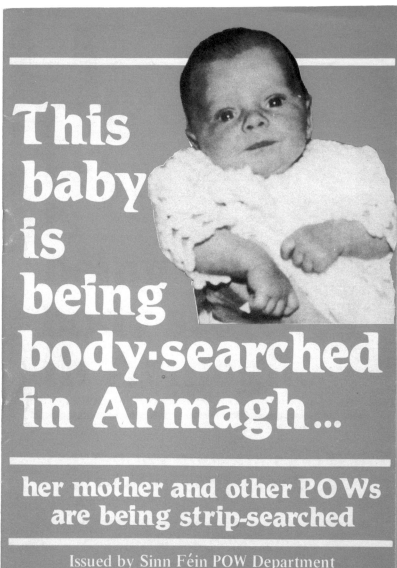

This baby is being body-searched in Armagh…

her mother and other POWs are being strip-searched

Issued by Sinn Féin POW Department

■ Them and us

Images of the enemy clearly come in many shapes and forms. Some are humorous in order to deflate the enemy's presumed power and authority; some are brutal to elicit feelings of hatred. Different techniques are used by the propagandist to construct an identikit picture that corresponds to stereotypes and myths that have often developed over a considerable period of time. The propaganda image of the enemy must, however, remain of stylised simplicity. The message must be expressed in a way that does not invite discussion. Its appeal is intrinsically emotional and excludes all alternatives. Such propaganda also reinforces one's own sense of national or racial / ethnic identity and strengthens commonly held symbols of unity.

It is important to remember that the images of the enemy we have seen were not constructed in isolation. The film, the poster, the leaflet, the cartoon, the radio or the television broadcast (and now the internet footage) would not have been viewed in a vacuum—they each formed only one aspect of a wider and concerted propaganda drive, in which all the available means of communication were generally employed. The case studies chosen are 'historical', and, for the most part, the stereotypes are of their time and have since withered, if not necessarily died. Today, many people may wonder how audiences in the past could be so gullible in accepting and acting on such propaganda. But the principle is timeless, and the construction of 'enemies', both real and imagined, is perennial; many of its incarnations have been employed on both sides in what, since 2001, the West has called the 'war on terror'. A human tendency to think of 'them' and 'us' is always liable to be exploited by those with the means and the power to do so.

114

114 **Symbols and counter-symbols.** This Soviet poster subverts the traditional symbolism of the Statue of Liberty. In a probable reference to the 'police riot' at Chicago's Democratic Party Convention (1968), the eyes become policemen, and a truncheon becomes a falling tear, in lament for what the caption describes as 'Freedom American-style'.

СВОБОДА ПО-АМЕРИКАНСКИ

'We are all Americans now'?

Propaganda in the 21st century

6

THUS FAR, we have looked at four principal propaganda themes, largely in the context of the 20th century: the importance of nationhood and leadership; the ways in which states have attempted to promote and maintain a healthy population; and ways by which wars have been justified, and enemies defined and targeted in order to mobilise mass support. The examples and case studies represent, in the main, propaganda campaigns that could be described as 'successful' in their historical contexts, from the point of view of the propagandist. But a new century has brought with it new questions, propelled not least by astonishing technological developments, and these have reshaped the relationship between politics, propaganda and public opinion.

In the 20th century, the advent of 'total war' changed forever the relationship between the media, old-style diplomacy and the need for secrecy; the new media had the power to shape public opinion, a power that gave politicians reason to fear them. Later on, the changing nature of international crises—when the Cold War gave way to a post-Cold War environment—together with rapidly changing technology transformed the nature of warfare and its reportage. The colossal impact of 9/11, in which a handful of dedicated zealots found means to inflict such damage on a superpower, highlighted a new term in the vocabulary of conflict: 'asymmetrical warfare'. Defined as the means by which a weaker nation or group attempts to offset deficiencies in the quality and quantity of military resources by resorting to resilience and terror tactics, 'asymmetry' has exerted a profound hold on early 21st-century thinking.

■ 'Old' news versus 'new' news

The Vietnam War was arguably a watershed, particularly in the way it was covered by television. The BBC broadcaster Robin Day observed in this context that: 'The full brutality of the combat will be there in close-up and in colour, and blood looks red on the colour television screen.' At the end of the 1980s, as the Cold War was coming to an end, the term 'information warfare' started to gain currency. In subsequent 'limited' and 'asymmetric' wars and in the 'war on terror', discussion shifted to the importance of 'soft power' (information operations), 'psychological operations' ('psyops'), 'public diplomacy' and the appropriation by the military of public-relations and strategic-communications approaches as part of the repertoire of war-fighting.

But the road was not linear. Partly as a result of the United States' defeat in Vietnam, military psychological warfare entered a period of decline and discredit. It was President Reagan who was responsible for revitalising US 'psyops' in the 1980s. At a strategic level this involved flooding the Soviet Bloc with Western propaganda, especially after the arrival of satellite television and new communication technologies such as video-cassettes, fax machines and mobile phones. Following Iraq's invasion of Kuwait in August 1990, President George H.W. Bush was persuaded to incorporate psyops as an integral part of the First Gulf War (Operation Desert Storm) in 1990–91. As a result, psyops came of age. Operation Desert Storm became associated with modern media technology—a 'media war'. However, one of the oldest forms of propaganda devices, the humble leaflet, was also extensively employed by psyops. More than 29 million of them (weighing approximately 29 tons) were disseminated between 30 December 1990 and 28 February 1991. During the war 69,000 Iraqis surrendered or deserted (many more than were actually killed), and they invariably carried the 'safe conduct' passes that had been a feature of leaflet propaganda and psychological warfare in the two world wars. In the ostensibly high-tech environment of the Gulf War, the leaflets were crude and no more sophisticated than those employed during the First World War.

Revealingly, the Iraq War (sometimes called the Second Gulf War) in 2003 continued where Operation Desert Storm left off in terms of psyops. US and British 'Coalition' forces intensified the use of psychological operations. The United States employed its long tradition of radio psyops, which could be traced back to Vietnam. Broadcasts were used in Afghanistan after 9/11 to persuade citizens to reveal Taliban and al-Qaeda factions. In the Iraq War, the United States engaged in a comprehensive airwaves campaign to soften its enemy and

115*a*

115*a&b* 'YOU ARE UNARMED!!', a propaganda leaflet dropped over Iraqi troops by US psyops units during Operation Desert Storm. It continues: 'Your supply lines have been cut off and you will not be receiving any more. Saddam does not care about your end and he has deserted you. Put down your arms and join your other Arab friends in the love of peace!!!'

115*b*

soothe its population at home. Spearheading the electronic propaganda campaign were converted C-130 US cargo planes from the Commando Solo fleet, transmitting a mixture of Arabic and Western music and spoken announcements to the troops and citizens of Iraq, urging them not to fight and explaining how to surrender. The planes were the Coalition's weapons of mass persuasion. An intense leaflet-dropping campaign reinforced the radio transmissions once again: over 17 million leaflets were dispersed in the first week of the war, offering detailed information on how to signal surrender to advancing Coalition troops. Warnings on the leaflets included: 'Attacking Coalition aircraft invites your destruction. Do not risk your life and the lives of your comrades. Leave now and go home. Watch your children learn, grow and prosper.' Force was backed by persuasion.

If the war in Kosovo (1998–99) had marked the decline of the 'old' news—of network television,

broadsheet newspapers and current affairs journals—in favour of the 'new' news of satellite and cable television, tabloid newspapers and television and radio chat shows, the military itself became increasingly concerned about image management and 'information control'. Professional military communicators have recognised that technology has not only freed the media from the physical constraints under which war correspondents used to labour, but also that with 24-hour rolling news and the proliferation of international news agencies, such as (the once Arabic, and now multilingual) al-Jazeera, the world's media are going to be present in large numbers and must therefore be factored into their own strategic thinking. Recent years have witnessed a more volatile news environment, with a profound effect on the conduct of foreign affairs, journalism—and propaganda.

The Iraq War produced a number of technological shifts in the reporting of war, notably

116 Saddam Hussein, the Ace of Spades. During the 2003 Iraq War, the US military created playing cards to depict the most-wanted members of the Iraqi regime, a hierarchy naturally topped by Saddam himself. The cards entered the public domain and were also produced commercially, this set credited to the 'Intelligence Agency of United States of America'. It indicates which of the wanted have been captured.

117a&b 'We can see everything.' A US psyops leaflet from the 2003 Iraq War warns the enemy against using nuclear, chemical or biological weapons, and that the Coalition forces' all-seeing satellites will hold unit commanders 'accountable for non-compliance'.

117a

117b

> 9/11 represented an extraordinary 'David-versus-Goliath' propaganda coup for al-Qaeda and its supporters, a textbook operation of asymmetric warfare.

the decision to embed reporters and television journalists as actual members of the invasion forces. The multitude of news channels beaming constant images attracted two different types of criticism. Some critics suggested that the 24-hour news channels amounted to little more than purveyors of 'war porn' for the manner in which they broadcast relentless images without context or explanation. Other critics feared that too much reality could have serious effects on morale. To put such fears in historical context, we might wonder how long the governments of Asquith and Lloyd George could have maintained the British war effort had the public been able to see live coverage of the Somme in 1916 or Passchendaele in 1917? In the subsequent war, would it have been possible to evacuate 300,000 troops from Dunkirk under the scrutiny of 24-hour rolling news?

In today's conflicts, governments have attempted to influence the media through what, in the United States, the Pentagon has termed 'perception management'—a euphemism for propaganda. In terms of military–media relations, one of the consequences of the increasing sophistication of the military's media operations in the aftermath of the Vietnam War is the accusation of 'spin' or manipulation. The rise of professional military communicators from 2001 created a situation whereby the media were seen by the military as part of the problem rather than the solution. At the time of the Gulf War in 1991, the military were firmly in control of the media, but by 2003 and the invasion of Iraq, power had shifted to politicians who were now in control of state–media relations and the information environment. The

ten years of fruitless war in Afghanistan together with the contested history of the Iraq War have resulted in an unprecedented concentration of 'communication power' within political elites. Furthermore, the sense of an ever-present 'war on terror' steered domestic public and political perceptions towards a chronic sense of insecurity.

■ The age of asymmetry

In international affairs, the 21st century—for the United States in particular—has been dominated by that one phrase: 'war on terror'. It was a term with serious, and not always expected or helpful, implications. Following the 9/11 attacks, the US administration of George W. Bush justified its military response by announcing the 'Global War on Terror' (GWOT), arguing that it had the right and ability to pursue al-Qaeda and any state or group that harboured them and their leader Osama bin Laden. By declaring a global *war* on terror, the West invoked Article 51 of the UN Charter (the right to self-defence) and in the process empowered the terrorists with the status of 'warriors', lending them an aura of legitimacy—something that groups such as al-Qaeda went on to shrewdly exploit in their own counter-propaganda against the West.

More than a military confrontation, GWOT became a long information war of ideas, a global struggle for hearts and minds and a battle of indefinite durability—although it took the West a long time to recognise it as such. Its starting point, 9/11, represented an extraordinary 'David-versus-

Goliath' propaganda coup for al-Qaeda and its supporters, a textbook operation of asymmetric warfare. After that, terms such as 'Operation Infinite Justice' and 'Operation Enduring Freedom' framed the immediate responses in Afghanistan and Iraq. The term 'Islamofascism' came, in the United States, to define a dangerous, militant ideology on the march worldwide, preying on the disadvantaged and deluded: a picture not unlike that presented of communism in the Cold War.

The decision to extend the war from Afghanistan to Iraq represented a major propaganda error (leaving aside the moral and strategic arguments) on the part of the Bush administration. Following the 9/11 attacks, the United States had an opportunity to tap into the groundswell of supportive world opinion as exemplified by *Le Monde*'s famous front page: 'We are all Americans now.' But the erroneous claims that Saddam Hussein possessed weapons of mass destruction and had links with jihadist groups, followed by the American-led invasion, offered support to the al-Qaeda narrative of Western aims: not liberators intent on bringing democracy, but invaders intent on occupying and destroying the Muslim world. The invasion therefore represented a wonderful opportunity for al-Qaeda propaganda. Bin Laden declared

Baghdad to be the centre for the new Caliphate that would restore Islamic purity to the Middle East, and foreign Muslim fighters responded. The Global War on Terror now had a new battlefront and at the same time it emboldened the Taliban in Afghanistan.

Part of the problem lay in a widespread absence, in the United States, of serious debate about the war and the reasons for war. In the post 9/11 atmosphere, the public was generally under-informed about the circumstances of Iraq, and the media did not initiate debate—there was a sense in which it was deemed unpatriotic to question or scrutinise. The cudgel of patriotism prevented the healthy dynamism needed in a democracy between political leaders and the public. The great failing of US media coverage of the Iraq War was, accordingly, its complicity. (By contrast, the build-up to war incited strong and divided feelings in Britain and in much of Europe.)

As US forces took hold of Baghdad, the toppling of the statue of Saddam Hussein was intended to be a symbolic act that represented the swift conclusion to a campaign of 'shock and awe' (a phrase at odds with the slogan 'enduring freedom'). It mimicked those famous symbolic moments of victory from the Second World War—the Stars and Stripes

118

118 Osama bin Laden, calling for *jihad* (3 November 2001). Video allowed al-Qaeda's leader to disseminate his public pronouncements, often released as 'exclusives' to the new Arabic-language channel al-Jazeera, which challenged the West's domination of the media.

planted on Iwo Jima, and the Red Flag unfolded from the smouldering Reichstag in Berlin. It was depicted in the Western media as widely celebrated by frenzied Iraqis, beating the statue with their shoes to show their contempt for Saddam; yet, in retrospect, we know that it was largely constructed and editorialised by the US military. In total, the images and the accompanying rhetoric suggested that a short war was over, whereas the truth was that a long war was only just beginning.

The 'Saddam statue' coverage pointed to the way that the need to service 24-hour rolling news channels has become a form of tyranny—'the tyranny of time'—witnessing editorial interference from a distance, greater visual gimmicks and less interest in the wider context. This has led to charges that current war journalism (often referred to as 'infotainment') produces less detailed and analytical information than in the past.

It is also true that fundamental changes in the nature of warfare have affected both the ability to cover wars and the style of reporting. While some geopolitical strategists worry about the rise of China, including militarily, it is likely that

119

119 **Spontaneous celebration or media distortion? The toppling of this statue of Saddam Hussein in Baghdad's Firdos Square, in April 2003, was broadcast live around the world.** Viewers saw jubilant Iraqis venting their hatred of Saddam and cheering on the Americans. But the spontaneity, size and significance of the incident were later questioned.

asymmetric warfare is going to be the dominant form of conflict in the modern age, simply because of the lack of enemies capable of contemplating a conventional war against the United States and the major industrial powers. In the face of conventional firepower, the weaker state or organisation adopts different weaponry. In the 21st century, al-Qaeda has shown itself to be the first guerrilla movement to migrate from physical space to cyberspace, to marshal followers globally.

Terrorism, simply defined, is the weapon of the weak adopted by aggrieved groups who want to destroy the *status quo* but who feel unable to do so by conventional war. Unconstrained by the international laws of warfare supposed to operate among states, such groups pinpoint symbolic targets with a view to creating maximum impact. The aim is literally to terrorise, to generate sufficient fear to persuade leaders—or to persuade public opinion to press its leaders—to accede to their demands. In the 21st century, small groups, operating without overt state sponsorship, are able to exploit the vulnerability of 'open' societies. Groups such as al-Qaeda and those it has inspired represent a new and profoundly dangerous type of organisation, a 'virtual state', borderless but potentially global in scope. And access to the means of communications through the internet (and other social networks) changes the dynamics of the propaganda war. The internet has provided terrorists with a vast ethereal recruitment arena. Internet chat rooms are supplementing and replacing mosques, community centres and coffee shops. Al-Qaeda's main propaganda outlet is as-Sahab ('The Clouds'), which has the overriding aim of promoting global *jihad*. Distributed through Arab television networks (such as al-Jazeera, al-Arabia and local Pakistani television stations), as-Sahab uploads its propaganda of 'martyrdom videos' onto YouTube—a format favoured by younger audiences. The numbers of these videos have increased and the quality has improved since 2005. In short, cyberspace is now a major battlefield and the 'war' is one of ideas.

Since early 2009, the phrase 'war on terror' has been downplayed in official documents in both the United States and Britain, as it was recognised that—through the amplification of the global media channels—it was fuelling the terrorists' rhetoric of a Western 'crusade' against Islam. In March 2009 the US Defense Department officially changed the name of operations from 'Global War on Terror' to 'Overseas Contingency Operation,' and President Obama rarely used the term 'war on terror' in speeches during his first term in office. The killing of bin Laden in May 2011 by US Special Forces represented a major propaganda coup for Obama. This was timely, as for some time the West had been losing the propaganda war. Bin Laden's death, together with the outpourings of all types of long-suppressed popular feeling evidenced in the Arab Spring weakened (at least in the short term) al-Qaeda's fundamentalist appeal to sections of the Muslim world. The events after December 2010 in Tunisia, Egypt and Libya, involving the toppling of deeply entrenched dictators, illustrated the power of the new social media (including blogs, real-time news and community conversations) to 'liberate' citizens from state interference and to facilitate the mobilisation of spontaneous popular protest.

■ Are we all propagandists now?

In the past, governments could largely control the coverage and shape the narrative. But the 21st century's new media have brought a host of new questions. How is propaganda changing in a world populated by the internet, social media, advertising and the press? Have the new media freed citizens from the tyranny of oppressive governments? Can propaganda still be *identified* as such, given the preponderance of communication methods and the sophistication of the originators? In the age of Facebook and Twitter, is everyone a propagandist? What is the role of state propaganda in the 21st century and where does it go next? Is democracy moving into cyberspace and will the values of the internet prevail? We have seen in recent times that virtual campaigns on Facebook and Twitter have resulted in a number of witch-hunts, which at times appear to be above the law. Does this mean they amount to a global megaphone for gossip? Edges are now dangerously blurred between what happens online (the lawless place we call the internet) and what occurs in the mainstream media.

In the White House and other organs of governments, there now exist teams whose sole responsibility is to monitor the world according to social media. Thus, the traditional flow of information from news providers to the reading/listening/viewing public has been inverted. So is *real* power shifting from a judicious mainstream to the texting 'mob'? In some ways there is purity in such a 'virtual democracy'; it reflects the public mood in real time, it is difficult to rig, and sometimes 'truth' is flushed out. However, politics by Facebook rarely adds up to considered, rational debate. It is a visceral communal response, and governments are becoming extremely scared by it. Old-fashioned focus groups in a room appear irrelevant against thousands of tweeters suddenly getting angry about something. With politics conducted on social media sites and with no judicial rules appearing to operate, it is almost inevitable that standards and values that underpin 'civilised' behaviour in the real world do not always apply. It is now possible to 'google' any accusations made against individuals, governments and companies without the need to verify the facts.

There is plenty here to worry about. We have, on the other hand, also witnessed the positive aspects of the new media. In the Arab Spring the new media (particularly the mobile phone) are credited with facilitating the growing citizen discontent with the region's regimes. The former dictators were simply unable to control the speed and flow of information. Similarly, in the fields of health or the provision of aid to counter natural disasters, non-state players and individuals may contest government decisions, or criticise the lack of resolve at state level. Social media can therefore generate a spontaneity that may lead to direct action. Equally (as we saw in Chapter 4), the internet and social networks have allowed individuals and groups to challenge medical orthodoxy and provide 'alternative' advice and treatments. Generally speaking, these can only be positive developments, in that they provide different layers of information. The problem arises from the sheer

120

121

120 Capturing the moment. A youth in Cairo's Tahrir Square films the aftermath of a police tear-gas volley on protestors (23 November 2011). In the 21st century the once routine forms of state oppression, reinforced by official media, can less often go unwitnessed.

121 Recording the Arab Spring. Young Egyptians use their mobile phones to film celebrations after the resignation of the authoritarian President Mubarak (12 February 2011). The sheer ubiquity of the mobile phone, from the First to the Third World, gives everyone a tool to disseminate a message—or a counter-message.

plurality of sources and the volume of information in cyberspace. How can one navigate such a vast reservoir of information and verify its authenticity? Professional and ethical concerns may still largely deter the mainstream from resorting to social media practices, but how long will that resistance last? If a plurality of cacophonous voices is inevitable as democracy completes its journey into cyberspace, what kind of democracy will we be left with?

■ Hearts and minds—the enduring goals

In this Information Age it is not unreasonable to expect governments and other groups to conduct propaganda and censorship—both in times of war and in times of peace. (For example, the Bush administration's ban on photographing coffins returning to the United States, containing the bodies of soldiers killed in action in Afghanistan and Iraq, was arguably justifiable.) Equally, citizens and consumers should be able to hold the global elite media to account by demanding viewpoints and perspectives from across the spectrum of public opinion, disseminated by open and diverse channels of communications.

Arguably, propaganda is most effective when it is less noticeable. In a totalitarian regime—indeed in any closed society—propaganda is more obvious and visible and largely tolerated for fear of the consequences. In a so-called open society propaganda is much more problematic when it is hidden and integrated into the political culture. Once it is exposed, people can feel duped and betrayed, and this serves only to reinforce the pejorative associations with the practice of propaganda, deemed to be at odds with that open society. Too often, *effective* propaganda is associated with the control of the flow of information and with duplicity and falsehood. But propaganda has the potential to serve a constructive purpose.

Writing in 1928, Edward Bernays, who did so much to frame the nature of modern advertising, argued that: 'Propaganda will never die out. Intelligent men must realise that propaganda is the modern instrument by which they can fight for productive ends and help to bring order out of chaos.' It is perfectly possible to argue that in democracies politics has nothing to fear from propaganda. Propaganda is merely a process of persuasion that forms a normal part of the political dynamic and as such it could be argued that we need more propaganda, not less.

So there you have it! Propaganda is ethically neutral—it can be good or bad. Citizens have to be more informed and arm themselves with a greater understanding of the nature and processes of the Information Age.

Perhaps the key here, though, is the multiplicity of voices. An editorial in the *New York Times* on 1 September 1937 observed: 'What is truly vicious is not propaganda but a monopoly of it.' Perhaps more focus should be placed on the intention behind the propaganda and not exclusively on the propaganda itself. Understanding the 'message' also requires a widening access to information in order that *informed* opinion can be shaped.

Whatever definition of propaganda we choose to use—or, indeed, whether we need more or less propaganda—we have been living through *the* age of propaganda. The relationship between politics, propaganda and public opinion is both complex and controversial. It is a relationship that has changed in the light of new technology and different types of warfare. But throughout, propaganda, power and persuasion are all about winning hearts and minds, and that remains as relevant today as it always was.

Before 1918

❛A propagandist presents many ideas to one or a few persons; an agitator presents only one or a few ideas, but he presents them to a mass of people.' (p. 409)

Georgi Plekhanov
'What is to Be Done?' (1902), quoted in V.I. Lenin, *Collected Works*, Vol. 5, London: Lawrence and Wishart, 1961.

1920s

❛Propaganda, conducted by the means which advertisers have found successful, is now one of the recognized methods of government in all advanced countries, and is especially the method by which democratic opinion is created ... There are two quite different evils about propaganda as now practised. On the one hand, its appeal is generally to irrational causes of belief rather than to serious argument; on the other hand, it gives an unfair advantage to those who can obtain most publicity, whether through wealth or through power.' (p. 35)

Bertrand Russell
'Free Thought and Official Propaganda' (1922 Conway Memorial Lecture), in his *Let the People Think: A Selection of Essays*, London: Watts, 1941.

❛The task of propaganda is to attract followers; the task of organization is to win members. A follower of the movement is one who finds himself in agreement with its aims; a member is one who fights for it.' (p. 163)

❛The receptivity of the great masses is very limited, their intelligence is small, but their power of forgetting is enormous. In consequence, all effective propaganda must be limited to a few points and must harp on these in slogans until the last member of the public understands what you want him to understand by your slogan.' (p. 165)

Adolf Hitler
Mein Kampf (1925), translated by Ralph Manheim, Boston: Houghton Mifflin, 1943.

❛Propaganda may be defined as a *technique* of social control, or as a species of social *movement*. As technique, it is the manipulation of collective attitudes by the use of significant symbols (words, pictures, tunes) rather than violence, bribery or boycott. Propaganda differs from the technique of pedagogy in that propaganda is concerned with attitudes of love and hate, while pedagogy is devoted to the transmission of skill ... The spread of controversial attitudes is propaganda, the spread of accepted attitudes and skills is education.' (p. 189)

Harold D. Lasswell
'The Person: Subject and Object of Propaganda', in *Annals of the American Academy of Political and Social Science* (1935), Vol. 179.

❛Propaganda is the executive arm of the invisible government.' (p. 20).
❛Propaganda will never die out. Intelligent men must realize that propaganda is the modern instrument by which they can fight for productive ends and help to bring order out of chaos.' (p. 159)

Edward L. Bernays
Propaganda, New York: Liveright, 1928.

1930s

'Propaganda is not education, it strives for the closed mind rather than the open mind. It is not concerned about the development of mature individuals. Its aim is immediate action. The propagandist merely wishes you to think as he does. The educator is more modest, he is so delighted if you think at all that he is willing to let you do so in your own way.' (p. 29)

Everett Dean Martin

The Conflict of the Individual and the Mass, New York: Henry Holt, 1932.

'Propaganda is promotion which is veiled in one way or another as to (1) its origin or sources, (2) the interests involved, (3) the methods employed, (4) the content spread, and (5) the results accruing to the victims – any one, any two, any three, any four, or all five.' (p. 44)

Frederick E. Lumley

The Propaganda Menace, New York: Century, 1933.

'May the bright flame of our enthusiasm never be extinguished. It alone gives light and warmth to the creative art of a modern political propaganda … It may be a good thing to possess power that rests on arms. But it is better and more lasting to win the heart of a people and to keep it.' (p. 25)

Joseph Goebbels

at the 1934 Nuremberg rally, quoted in David Welch, *The Third Reich: Politics and Propaganda*, London: Routledge, 2002.

'If individuals are controlled through the use of suggestion … then the process may be called propaganda, regardless of whether or not the propagandist intends to exercise the control. On the other hand if individuals are affected in such a way that the same result would be obtained with or without the aid of suggestion, then this process may be called education, regardless of the intention of the educator.' (p. 80)

Leonard W. Doob

Propaganda: Its Psychology and Technique, New York: Henry Holt, 1935.

'Propaganda gives force and direction to the successive movements of popular feeling and desire; but it does not do much to create those movements. The propagandist is a man who analyses an already existing stream. In a land where there is no water, he digs in vain.' (p. 39)

Aldous Huxley

'Notes on Propaganda', in *Harper's*, Vol. 174, December 1936.

'There are two kinds of propaganda—rational propaganda in favor of action that is consonant with the enlightened self-interest of those who make it and those to whom it is addressed, and non-rational propaganda that is not consonant with anybody's enlightened self-interest, but is dictated by, and appeals to passion.' (Ch. 4)

Aldous Huxley

'Propaganda in a Democratic Society', in *Brave New World Revisited*, London: Chatto & Windus, 1959.

'Propaganda is an attempt, either unconsciously or as part of a systematic campaign by an individual or group holding certain beliefs or desiring certain ends, to influence others to adopt identical attitudes.' (p. 35)

A.J. Mackenzie,

Propaganda Boom, London: John Gifford, 1938.

'We shall here limit propaganda to intentional special pleading.' (p. 285)
'There is deliberate distortion by selection … The objective of the propagandist is to achieve public acceptance of conclusions, not to stimulate the logical analysis of the merits of the case.' (p. 286)
'Propaganda is a special term referring to the intentional dissemination of conclusions from concealed sources by interested individuals and groups.' (p. 287)
'Propaganda is essential to the development of unanimity in modern states. It was incidental to the development of tribes or simple folk peoples.' (p. 296)
'Propaganda is pervasive in our time. There has always been some propaganda, but in the modern age it is organized, intentional and relatively more effective. However, modern propaganda emphasizes distortion and derationalizes the public opinion process. It usually does not help the individual to come to a rational understanding of public issues but rather attempts to induce him to follow non-rational emotional drives.' (p. 309)

William Albig

Public Opinion, New York: McGraw-Hill, 1939.

1940s

❛ It is a part of the regular method of propaganda to use the symbol, which stirs the sentiment, always in an atmosphere of stress, strain or crisis. Thus the generalisations which fit the sentiments will be met by that enthusiastic sweeping away of criticism which fits the emotion.' (p. 65)

Sir Frederic C. Bartlett
Political Propaganda, Cambridge: Cambridge University Press, 1940.

❛ Propaganda in itself has no fundamental method. It has only purpose—the conquest of the masses.' (p. 66)

Joseph Goebbels
(quoted), ibid.

❛ The power of propaganda, as of all other weapons, must depend very largely upon the time when it is used. In the early stages of war its weight is not so great as in the last stages, when it can prove decisive. There is no dispute about the fact that propaganda against victory in arms is powerful, but when victory in arms is on your side, propaganda can press the results of victory miles further. Then propaganda can shorten the period required for the achievement of victory by months, possibly by years, and it is therefore in these early days that we should gradually perfect the machinery of propaganda, in order that when the time comes we may be ready to strike.' (col. 1622)

Alfred Duff Cooper
(British Minister of Information), House of Commons speech, *Hansard*, 3 July 1941.

1950s

❛ Propaganda in the broadest sense is the technique of influencing human action by the manipulation of representations. These representations may take spoken, written, pictorial or musical form.' (pp. 521–2)

Harold D. Lasswell
'Propaganda', in *International Encyclopedia of the Social Sciences*, Vol. 12, New York: Macmillan, 1950.

❛ Toute est propagande.' (p.18)

Jacques Driencort
La Propagande: Nouvelle Force politique, Paris: Colin, 1950.

❛ Propaganda in the sense of diffusion of conclusion while discouraging the subjects from examining the reasons for the positions which they are asked to accept, has existed throughout the history of human society. Leaders and institutional representatives are always desirous of furthering their objectives without argument. They wish to win converts and to reproduce (*Propagare*) the conclusions, the essential statements and values of their ideology.' (p. 293)

William Albig
Modern Public Opinion, New York: McGraw-Hill, 1956.

❛ Propaganda may be defined as the activity, or the art, of inducing others to behave in a way in which they would not behave in its absence.' (p. 1)
❛ The central element in propagandist inducements, as opposed to compulsion on one side and payment, or bribery, on the other, is that they depend on 'communication' rather than concrete penalties or rewards. To affect a donkey's behavior by whipping is not propaganda, nor is plying it with carrots. But if its owner shouts at it in a threatening manner, or tries to coax it with winning words or noises then the word begins to become appropriate.' (p. 3)
❛ Perhaps a better metaphor is to call it a burning glass which collects and focuses the diffused warmth of popular emotions, concentrating them upon a specific issue on which the warmth becomes heat and may reach the firing-point of revivals, risings, revolts, revolutions.' (pp. 196–7).

Lindley Fraser
Propaganda, Oxford: Oxford University Press, 1957.

❛ Statements of policy or facts, usually of a political nature, the real purpose of which is different from their apparent purpose … a statement by a government or political party which is believed to be insincere or untrue, and designed to impress the public at large rather than to reach the truth or to bring about a genuine understanding between opposing governments or parties.'

Florence Elliott & Michael Summerskill
Definition of 'Propaganda', in *The Penguin Dictionary of Politics*, London: Penguin, 1957.

1960s

❝ Propaganda is thus defined as the deliberate attempt by some individual or group to form, control, or alter the attitudes of other groups by the use of the instruments of communication, with the intention that in any given situation the reaction of those so influenced will be that desired by the propagandist. The propagandist is the individual or group who makes any such attempt.' (p. 27)

Terrence H. Qualter,

Propaganda and Psychological Warfare, New York: Random House, 1965.

❝ Propaganda is the relatively deliberate manipulation, by means of symbols (words, gestures, flags, images, monuments, music, etc.), of other people's thoughts or actions with respect to beliefs, values, and behaviors which these people ('reactors') regard as controversial.' (p. 579)

Bruce L. Smith

'Propaganda', in *International Encyclopedia of the Social Sciences*, Vol. 12, New York: Macmillan, 1968.

❝ Propaganda is made, first of all, because of a will to action, for the purpose of effectively arming policy and giving irresistible power to its decisions … Ineffective propaganda is no propaganda.' (p. x)

❝ Propaganda is the expression of opinions or actions carried out deliberately by individuals or groups for predetermined ends and through psychological manipulations.' (p. xii)

❝ The propagandist uses a keyboard and composes a symphony.' (Quoting Lasswell) (p. 10)

❝ The aim of modern propaganda is no longer to modify ideas but to provoke action. It is no longer to change adherence to a doctrine, but to make the individual cling irrationally to a process of action. It is no longer to lead to a choice but to loosen the reflexes. It is no longer to transform an opinion, but to arouse an active and mythical belief.' (p. 25)

❝ Propaganda is a set of methods employed by an organized group that wants to bring about the active or passive participation in its actions of a mass of individuals, psychologically unified through psychological manipulations and incorporated into an organization.' (p. 61)

Jacques Ellul

Propaganda: The Formation of Men's Attitudes, New York: Knopf, 1965.

1980s

❝ [Propaganda is] the systematic propagation of information or ideas by an interested party, especially in a tendentious way in order to encourage or instil a particular attitude or response.' (p. 124)

Terrence H. Qualter

Opinion Control in the Democracies, London: Macmillan, 1985.

❝ Biased information'

Definition of 'Propaganda'

in the *Pocket Oxford Dictionary*, Oxford and New York: Oxford University Press, 1984.

'The systematic propagation of a doctrine or cause or of information reflecting the views and interests of those people advocating such a doctrine or cause.'

Definition of 'Propaganda'

in the *American Heritage Dictionary of the English Language*, 3rd edition, Boston: Houghton Mifflin, 1992.

'Propaganda is the deliberate, systematic attempt to shape perceptions, manipulate cognitions, and direct behavior to achieve a response that furthers the desired intent of the propagandist.' (p. 4)

Garth Jowett & Victoria O'Donnell

Propaganda and Persuasion, Santa Barbara, CA: Sage, 1992.

'The *deliberate* attempt to persuade people to think and behave *in a desired way*.' (p. 6)

Philip Taylor

Munitions of the Mind: A History of Propaganda from the Ancient World to the Present Day, Manchester: Manchester University Press, 1995.

'Propaganda is neutrally defined as a systematic form of purposeful persuasion that attempts to influence the emotions, attitudes, opinions, and actions of specified target audiences for ideological, political or commercial purposes through the controlled transmission of one-sided messages (which may or may not be factual) via mass and direct media channels. A propaganda organization employs propagandists who engage in propagandism – the applied creation and distribution of such forms of persuasion.' (pp. 232–3)

Richard Alan Nelson

A Chronology and Glossary of Propaganda in the United States, New York: Greenwood Press, 1996.

'Modern political propaganda can be defined as the deliberate attempt to influence the opinions of an audience through the transmission of ideas and values for the specific persuasive purpose, consciously designed to serve the interest of the propagandists and their political masters, either directly or indirectly.' (p. 26)

David Welch

'Powers of Persuasion' in *History Today*, Vol. 49 (August 1999).

'Propaganda is a deliberate attempt to persuade people to think and then behave in a manner desired by the source; public relations, a branch of propaganda, is a related process intended to enhance the relationship between the organization and the public. Both in turn are related to *advertising*. Bill Backer, in *The Care and Feeding of Ideas* (1993), suggests that advertising and propaganda are half brothers. An advertisement connects something with human desires; propaganda shapes the infinite into concrete images.' (pp. 571–2)

David Culbert

'Government, Propaganda and Public Relations', in John Whiteclay Chambers II (ed.), *Oxford Companion to American Military History*, New York and Oxford: Oxford University Press, 1999.

'Propaganda is to a democracy what the bludgeon is to a totalitarian state.' (pp. 20–1)

Noam Chomsky

Media Control, 2nd edition, New York: Seven Stories Press, 2002.

'Information, especially of a biased or misleading nature, used to promote a political cause or point of view.'

Definition of 'Propaganda'

in *Oxford Dictionaries*, oxforddictionaries.com (accessed February 2013).

Further reading

JAMES AULICH, *War Posters: Weapons of Mass Communication*, London: Thames & Hudson, 2007.

N.I. BABURINA, *The Soviet Political Poster 1917–1980, from the USSR Lenin Library Collection*, London: Penguin, 1984.

SUSAN A. BREWER, *Why America Fights: Patriotism and War Propaganda from the Philippines to Iraq*, Oxford and New York: Oxford University Press, 2009.

JAMES CHAPMAN, *The British at War: Cinema, State and Politics 1939–45*, London: I.B. Tauris, 1998.

NOAM CHOMSKY, *Media Control: The Spectacular Achievements of Propaganda*, New York: Seven Stories Press, 1991; 2nd edition, 2002.

MARK CONNELLY and DAVID WELCH (eds), *War and the Media: Reportage and Propaganda 1900–2003*, London: I.B. Tauris, 2005.

NICHOLAS J. CULL, *The Cold War and the United States Information Agency: American Propaganda and Public Diplomacy, 1945–1989*, Cambridge and New York: Cambridge University Press, 2008.

NICHOLAS J. CULL, DAVID CULBERT and DAVID WELCH, *Propaganda and Mass Persuasion: A Historical Encyclopedia, 1500 to the Present*, Santa Barbara, CA: ABC-Clio, 2003.

JACQUES ELLUL, *Propaganda: The Formation of Men's Attitudes*, translated into English, New York: Knopf, 1965.

JEREMY HAWTHORN (ed.), *Propaganda, Persuasion and Polemic*, London: Edward Arnold, 1987.

EDWARD S. HERMAN, *Beyond Hypocrisy: Decoding the News in an Age of Propaganda; including the DoubleSpeak Dictionary*, Boston: South End Press, 1992.

EDWARD S. HERMAN and NOAM CHOMSKY, *Manufacturing Consent: The Political Economy of the Mass Media*, New York: Pantheon, 1988.

GERD HORTEN, *Radio Goes to War: The Cultural Politics of Propaganda During World War II*, Berkeley, CA: University of California Press, 2002.

GARTH JOWETT and VICTORIA O'DONNELL, *Propaganda and Persuasion*, Santa Barbara, CA: Sage, 1992; 5th edition, 2012

PETER KENEZ, *The Birth of the Propaganda State: Soviet Methods of Mass Mobilization 1917–1929*, Cambridge and New York: Cambridge University Press, 1985.

DAVID KING, *Russian Revolutionary Posters: From Civil War to Socialist Realism, from Bolshevism to the End of Stalinism*, London: Tate Publishing, 2012.

RANDAL MARLIN, *Propaganda and the Ethics of Persuasion*, Peterborough, Ontario: Broadview Press, 2002.

PETER PARET, BETH IRWIN LEWIS and PAUL PARET, *Persuasive Images: Posters of War and Revolution*, Princeton, NJ: Princeton University Press, 1992.

ANTHONY PRATKAVIS and ELLIOT ARONSON, *Age of Propaganda: The Everyday Use and Abuse of Persuasion*, New York: Henry Holt, 1991; revised edition, 2004.

ANTHONY RHODES, *Propaganda, the Art of Persuasion: World War II*, New York: Chelsea House, 1975; London: Angus and Robertson, 1975.

CHARLES ROETTER, *The Art of Psychological Warfare 1914–1945*, n.p.: Stein and Day, 1974.

K.R.M. SHORT (ed.), *Film and Radio Propaganda in World War II*, London: Croom Helm, 1983.

NANCY SNOW, *Information War: American Propaganda, Free Speech and Opinion Control Since 9-11*, New York: Seven Stories Press, and London: Turnaround, 2003.

PHILIP M. TAYLOR, *Munitions of the Mind: A History of Propaganda from the Ancient World to the Present Day*, Manchester: Manchester University Press, 1995; 3rd edition, 2003.

OLIVER THOMSON, *Easily Led: A History of Propaganda*, Stroud, Gloucestershire: Sutton, 1999.

DAVID WELCH, *The Third Reich: Politics and Propaganda*, London: Routledge, 1993; 2nd edition, 2002.

DAVID WELCH, *Germany, Propaganda and Total War, 1914–1918: The Sins of Omission*, London: Athlone, 2000.

STEPHEN WHITE, *The Bolshevik Poster*, New Haven, CT and London: Yale University Press, 1988.

MARION YASS, *This is Your War: Home Front Propaganda in the Second World War*, London: HMSO, 1983.

Index

Page numbers in *italics*
denote illustrations

Cuba 40
Cuban Missile Crisis (1962) 107–8
cult of personality 5, 66–74; *see also*
    Hitler; Kim; Mussolini; Stalin
Czech propaganda 133, *134*, 135

D *Daily Mail* 80
Daladier, Édouard 16
Day, Robin 190
de Coutances, Andrew 154–6
Defence of the Realm Act (DORA) 26, 84
Department of Agitation and Propaganda
    (Agitprop) 23, *94*
Department of Health 129, 138
Desert Victory (film) 104
Dig for Victory campaign *122*, 123, 126
disease prevention campaigns 140–9; *see
    also* public health campaigns
Duck and Cover (cartoons) *106*, 107

E *Earth* (film) 167
eating *see* healthy eating campaigns
Egypt, Ancient 5, 50
Eiffel Tower 52, 59
Eikon Basilike 8
Eisenhower, Dwight D. 40
Eisenstein, Sergei 165, 167, 169
Elizabeth II, Queen 74
Ellul, Jacques 28, 33
embedded reporters 24, 194
Empire Marketing Board 59
Empire Stadium 56
'Ems telegram' 25
Enemy Propaganda Department 86
Enough to Eat (film) 120
Entente Cordiale 154, *155*
eugenics 114, 117
Ewige Jude, Der (film) 180–2, *181*
exhibitions *see* world fairs

F Facebook 198
Faivre, Jules Abel *89*
Falklands, Battle of (1914) *30*
Falklands War (1982) 27, 35, 111–12, *112*
Federal Civil Defense Administration
    (FCDA) 106, *106*, 107
Ferdonnet, Paul 34
Festival of Empire (1911) 56
film 15–16, *18*, 19–20, 27, 104, 160, 164,
    168, 169, 175, 176, 180–2, *181*
First Gulf War *see* Gulf War (1991)
First World War 5, 15–16, *15*, 31, 25–7,
    33, 37, 38–9, 78, 80–93, *81, 83, 86, 87,
    88, 89, 90, 91, 92, 93*, 117–18, *118*, 143,
    158–64, *159, 161, 162, 163, 164*
flag, national 42, 46–8, *47, 48*
food campaigns *see* healthy eating
Foxe, John: *Book of Martyrs* 157–8, *157*
France / French propaganda 11–12, *11*,
    13, *15*, 16, 19, *43, 44*, 45, 59–60, *88, 119*;
    anti-French propaganda 34, 154–6, *155*
Franco-Prussian War 25

French Revolution 11, 45
Fuehrer's Face, Der (film) 174

G Gagarin, Yuri *57*
Galton, Francis 114, 117
Gandhi, Mahatma 46
Gellner, Ernst 42
General Belgrano (cruiser) 111, *112*
George III, King 11
George V, King 56
Gerasimov, Aleksandr 168
Germany / German propaganda 12, *15*,
    16, 25–6, 31, 33, 45, 82, 84, 89, 94, *98,
    99*, 104; *see also* Nazis; anti-German
    propaganda *see* First World War;
    Second World War
Germany Calling (film) 173
Ghana: first stamp of postcolonial *46*
Glasgow Corporation 120
Global War on Terror (GWOT) 24, 35,
    194–5, 197
Goebbels, Joseph 2–3, 30, 31, 33, 34, 36,
    68, 95, 99, 104, 180, 182
Goering, Hermann 137
Gorbachev, Mikhail 130
Great Exhibition (1851) 56
Green Cross Code 139
Greene, Hugh Carleton 36
Gregory, Adrian 160
Gregory XIII, Pope 6
Gregory XV, Pope 6
Grenada: US invasion of (1983) 27
grey propaganda 37–8
Guernica: bombing of (1937) 20, 62
Gulf War (1991) 24, 112, 158, 190–1, *191*,
    194

H Halifax, Lord 19
Happiness (film) 167
Haydn, Franz Joseph 45
Hays Code 27
health *see* public health campaigns
Health Survey for England 129
healthy eating campaigns 114–29, *118, 122*
Heine, Heinrich 152
Himmler, Heinrich 136–7
Hindenburg, Paul 39
Hindenburg Programme 89–90
Hirohito, Emperor *175*
Hitler, Adolf 19, *28*, 33, 66, 68–70, *68, 69*,
    94, 174, 175, *175*
Hitler Youth 136
Hobsbawm, Eric 42
Hollywood 19–20, 27, 164, 176
Holocaust 158, 183
Home in the Middle (film) 107
Hoover, Herbert 117
How to Keep Well in Wartime
    (booklet) 140
Hungarian Uprising (1956) 35
'Huns', Germans as 82, 158–65
Hutus 183–4

Huxley, Aldous 28
Huxley, Julian 120

I Illingworth, Percy 162–3
Imperial War Graves Commission
    52
Index Librorum Prohibitorum 25
India: first post-independence stamp *46,
    47*; and flag 46, *47*
Information Age 29, 200
Information Research Department
    (IRD) 37–8
information warfare 190
International Information Administration
    (IIA) 40
International Olympic Committee
    (IOC) 63, 64
International Press Exhibition (1928)
    (Cologne) *62*
internet and propaganda 24, 197
IRA (Irish Republican Army) 27, 184,
    185, 186–7
Iraq War (2003) 24, 53, 191–4, *192, 193*,
    195–6, *196*
Italy / Italian propaganda 66, *67*

J Japan / Japanese propaganda 101, *101*;
    anti-Japanese propaganda 174–6, *176,
    177*
Jews: Nazi anti-Semitic propaganda
    180–3, *180, 181*
Johnson, Lyndon B. 108, *110*

K Kealy, E.V. *90*
Kennedy, John F. 74, 108
KGB 23
Khrushchev, Nikita 62
Kim Il-Sung *54–5*, 74
Kitchen Front, The (broadcasts) 123
Kitchener, Lord 81, *81*
Korean War 107, 108
Kosovo War 24, 158, 192
Krauze, Andrzej *2, 3*
Krokodil 57
kulaks 165–8, *166–7*

L Lasswell, Harold 28
leadership, propaganda of 66–76
leaflets 38, 86, *87–8*, 89, *96–8*, 191, *191,
    192, 193*
League of Nations 20, 43
Lee, Joseph *126*
Lenin, V.I. 16, 19, 33, *62*, 70, 72
Lippmann, Walter 28, 154
literacy 12, (Soviet) 131
Little American, The (film) 164
Lloyd George, David 93
London Can Take It (film) 104
Louis XIV, King 9
Louvain (Belgium) 160, 162
Ludendorff, Erich von 39
Lumley, Savile *90*

Picture credits [p. 1] akg-images; **1** Andrzej Krauze; **2** British Museum, London; **3** BL 744.b.19; **4** BL 3906.c.64; **5** British Museum, London; **6** BL E.1052.(2); **7** BL PP.2517.n; **8** Library of Congress, Washington, D.C.; **9** BL 9180.e.6.(30); **10** BL Foster 32; **11** BL 012553.aa.88; **12** Private Collection; **13** akg-images; **14** Goskino/The Kobal Collection; **15** BL Shelley Collection; **16** BL uncatalogued; **17** Bettmann/Corbis; **18** BL Sol.764; **19** Planet News Archive/SSPL/Getty Images; **20a&b** BL BS.51/14; **21** BL UPU Collection; **22** incamera-stock/Alamy; **23** BL Tab.11748.a.; **24** BL Crown Agents Archive; **25a** Private Collection; **25b** BL Philatelic; **26** Library of Congress, Washington, D.C.; **27** NASA; **28** BL Cup.645.a.6; **29** akg-images/De Agostini Pict.Library; **30** Alain Noguès/akg-images; **31** BL PP.4842.cee; **32** Manchester City Art Gallery/Bridgeman Art Library; **33** Roger-Viollet/Topfoto; **34** BL C.132.b.2; **35** Rolls Press/Popperfoto/Getty Images; **36** BL L.45/1458; **37** Lebrecht Picture Library; **38** BL 10711.d.20; **39** Imperial War Museum, London; **40** BL 17075.dd.1; **41** David King; **42** BL OR.5896; **43** James Farley; **44** Anthony d'Offay; **45** BL 16126.d.1; **46** BL 1865.c.2; **47** BL LON LD92A NPL; **48** BL Tab.11748.a.(16); **49** Private Collection; **50** BL WW1.P/5; **51** BL PP Urdu 198; **52** BL Tab.11748.a.; **53** BL Tab.11748.a.; **54** BL Tab.1800.b.9; **55** BL Campbell-Johnston Collection; **56** Anthony d'Offay; **57** BL B.S.14/1004; **58** Private Collection; **59** akg-images; **60** David King; **61** BL Or.15514; **62** Imperial War Museum, London; **63** Anthony d'Offay. Printed by permission of the Norman Rockwell Family Agency © 1943 The Norman Rockwell Family Entities; **64** Imperial War Museum, London; **65** BL VOC/1953/CARR; **66** Keystone-France/Gamma-Keystone/Getty Images; **67** Anthony d'Offay; **68** BL OR.W1986.a.3458; **69** News International; **70** BL 1865.c.20.(36); **71** © Barnardo's; **72** Library of Congress, Washington, D.C.; **73** BL Tab.11748.a; **74** BL 8295.dd.10; **75** BL B.S.51/14; **76a&b** Private Collection; **77** David Welch © Associated News papers Ltd./Solo Syndication; **78** BL AS 863; **79** © Crown copyright; **80** BL PP.7500; **81** RIA Novosti/Lebrecht Picture Library; **82** RIA Novosti/Lebrecht Picture Library; **83** Jan Barker; **84** BL YC.2000.a.2307; **85** BL Cup.900.s.8; **86** BL Cup.648.k.1; **87** BL BS.81/19; **88** BL BS.81/19; **89** Imperial War Museum, London; **90** BL HSSH/1/44/87A © Crown copyright; **91** BL HSSH-1-44-87A © Crown copyright; **92** Bettmann/Corbis; **93** BL 1856.g.8.(15); **94** Copyright Guardian News & Media Ltd 2005; **95** BL G.12101; **96** BL PP.5270.ah; **97** BL 1235.l.28; **98** Private Collection; **99** BL Postcard Collection; **100** Library of Congress, Washington, D.C.; **101** Library of the London School of Economics & Political Science COLL MISC/0660/2/1; **102a** MOSFILM/The Kobal Collection; **102b** MOSFILM/Ronald Grant Archive/MEPL; **103** Private Collection; **104** BL PP/4/6L; **105** BL B.S.14/1004; **106** U.S. War Department/The Kobal Collection; **107** Library of Congress, Washington, D.C.; **108** The U.S. National Archives and Records Administration; **109** Private Collection; **110** akg-images; **111** Imperial War Museum, London; **112** BL LC.37.b.10; **113** BL YD.2006.a.3282; **114** BL uncatalogued; [p. 190] David Furst/AFP/Getty Images; **115** Lee Richards, www.psywar.org; **116** David Welch; **117** Lee Richards, www.psywar.org; **118** Salah Malkawi/Getty Images; **119** Goran Tomasevic/Reuters/Corbis; **120** Peter Macdiarmid/Getty Images; **121** Mohammed Abed/AFP/GettyImages.